TECHNOLOGY IN THE MIDDLE AND SECONDARY SOCIAL STUDIES CLASSROOM

Technology in the Middle and Secondary Social Studies Classroom introduces pre-service teachers to the research underpinning the effective integration of technology into the social studies curriculum. Building off established theoretical frameworks, veteran social studies teacher educator Scott K. Scheuerell shows how the implementation of key technologies in the classroom can help foster higher-level thinking among students. Plentiful user-friendly examples illustrate how specific educational tools—including games, social media, flipped classrooms, and other emerging technologies—spur critical thinking and foster authentic intellectual work. A rigorous study, *Technology in the Middle and Secondary Social Studies Classroom* provides a comprehensive, up-to-date research framework for conceptualizing successful, technology-rich social studies classrooms.

Scott K. Scheuerell is Associate Professor of Education at Loras College in Dubuque, Iowa.

TECHNOLOGY IN THE MIDDLE AND SECONDARY SOCIAL STUDIES CLASSROOM

Scott K. Scheuerell

Routledge
Taylor & Francis Group

NEW YORK AND LONDON

First published 2015
by Routledge
711 Third Avenue, New York, NY 10017

and by Routledge
2 Park Square, Milton Park, Abingdon, Oxon, OX14 4RN

Routledge is an imprint of the Taylor & Francis Group, an informa business

Library of Congress Cataloging-in-Publication Data
Scheuerell, Scott.
   Technology in the middle and secondary social studies classroom /
by Scott Scheuerell.
      pages cm
   Includes bibliographical references and index.
   1. Social sciences—United States—Computer-assisted instruction.   2. Social
sciences—Study and teaching (Middle school)—United States.   3. Social
sciences—Study and teaching (Secondary)—United States.   4. Educational
technology—United States.   5. Education—Effect of technological innovations
on—United States.   I. Title.
   LB1584.7.S35 2015
   300.71'2—dc23   2014036960

ISBN: 978-0-415-74980-0 (hbk)
ISBN: 978-0-415-74981-7 (pbk)
ISBN: 978-1-315-79570-6 (ebk)

Typeset in Bembo
by Apex CoVantage, LLC

Printed and bound in the United States of America by Publishers Graphics,
LLC on sustainably sourced paper.

This book is dedicated to my wife, Anne Marx Scheuerell, whom I love with all of my heart and who has been a pillar of support during this entire project.

CONTENTS

PREFACE

This book is about the integration of educational technology in the middle and secondary social studies classroom. The purpose of the book is twofold: 1) to introduce readers to research-based practices that provide the underpinnings to effective integration of technology in the middle and secondary social studies classroom, and 2) to demonstrate through user-friendly examples to readers how these research-based practices can be integrated with a variety of teaching and learning strategies in a technology-rich classroom. Research-based practices addressed in the book include Mindtools and the Rigor and Relevance Framework, both of which emphasize higher-level thinking with computer-based lessons. The reader will also learn about the Technological, Pedagogical, and Content Knowledge (TPACK) Framework and constructivist learning models to integrate technology. In addition, the book will introduce the reader to the newly proposed College, Career, and Civic Life (C3) Framework for Social Studies State Standards. Once pre-service teachers have an understanding of these research-based practices, they will more easily comprehend how they align with the vision of the C3 Framework and can be incorporated into the various teaching and learning strategies presented later in this textbook, chapter by chapter. These teaching and learning strategies include the following: Authentic Intellectual Work, cooperative learning, problem-based learning, classroom discussion, student historians, authentic assessment, historical images, differentiated instruction, reading strategies, Web 2.0 tools, local history, and emerging technologies.

ACKNOWLEDGMENTS

I would like to thank Loras College for giving me a sabbatical during the spring 2013 semester, which enabled me to conduct the research that is presented in this text. I am also grateful to the social studies teachers and students who participated in the study at three different high schools. The names of these individuals have been altered in the text to protect their identity and respect their confidentiality. Each participant provided rich insights that informed the findings that are presented in the text.

This text would not have been possible without Routledge Publishing. I am grateful that they were willing to give me this wonderful opportunity to share my experiences with technology and the findings from the qualitative case study that I conducted. In particular, I greatly appreciated the assistance from the staff at Routledge, including Catherine Bernard, Trevor Gori, and Madeleine Hamlin. I would also like to thank Joe O'Brien (University of Kansas) and Thomas Hammond (Lehigh University) for their willingness to review the text and provide their insights.

In my career, I have been blessed to have worked with many outstanding educators that have had a profound impact on my teaching philosophy. Some of these individuals include Jim Allan (Loras College), Jeff Johll (Dubuque Community School District), Joe O'Brien (University of Kansas), and Linda Bennett (University of Missouri). I have also learned from many wonderful colleagues during my high school and college teaching experiences. Thank you to these colleagues in the social studies departments at Larned High School (Kansas) and Warrensburg High School (Missouri), and my colleagues at Loras College (Iowa).

During my teaching career, I have also had the opportunity to work with many wonderful high school and college students. Many of them are now teaching social studies in middle and secondary classrooms, and I am very proud of the impact that each of them is already making. In addition, I would like to remember a former student of mine named Thomas Blacklock who died on June 8, 2014. He had a passion for teaching and learning about global perspectives. He touched the lives of countless students who he had the opportunity to work with and is greatly missed.

I am especially grateful to my parents, Kent and Carolyn Scheuerell. They have always been a positive role model to me and supported me with their unconditional love. Since I was a child, they emphasized the importance of working hard, getting an education, and playing by the rules. They consistently live their life as a positive example to me and my siblings.

Finally, I would like to acknowledge my family, Anne and Adam, who give my life purpose and inspire me each day. In summary, I feel very blessed to have both of them in my life.

INTRODUCTION

During my nine years of teaching high school social studies, I saw a great deal of change in regard to technology integration. In fact, there was not even a single computer in my classroom during the first two years of my teaching experience. There were a few computers in the high school library that were available to students, but none of them had Internet access. Yet, I reserved the computers for the students in my World History classes. The only computer software available was some drill-and-practice review exercises on various topics in world history. My students used these occasionally to review for a test. In retrospect, this was not the best way to integrate technology into my social studies instruction. There was a serious lack of higher-level thinking and active engagement with the technology. However, I did not know any better. I was a first-year teacher who had hardly learned anything about technology integration in my teacher preparation program, and I had very little access to technology during my student teaching experience. There were also few professional development opportunities on technology integration during my early years as a high school social studies teacher.

The increasing availability of technology over the years highlighted the need for me to quickly learn how to meaningfully integrate technology into my social studies instruction. For example, during my third and fourth years of teaching, I had a computer in my classroom for the first time. Unfortunately, it did not have any Internet access. I did use the computer to type lecture notes that I turned into transparencies to use with the classroom projector. The computer was also used to type worksheets, tests, and quizzes. It was unfortunate that my students did not have access to computers in my classroom, but they did have access to a much-improved computer lab located in the library. Each of these computers had Internet access. Teachers could reserve the computer lab for their students. Due to their popularity, teachers sometimes had to plan weeks ahead to give their students access to these computers. There were about 1,000 students in the high school and one computer lab. It was an exciting opportunity to integrate technology firsthand with my students. Much of this was through trial and error since I had little exposure to research-based frameworks to guide me. There were also few articles on technology in the social studies journals that I examined. I was searching for ideas and theoretical frameworks that could guide me as I designed lesson plans for my students. Fortunately, the school had recently implemented a block schedule, which enabled us to have the time to incorporate technology more easily in a single lesson. I sincerely felt the students were eager to use the computers and enjoyed seeing the primary sources. In retrospect, I often failed to engage the students in higher-level thinking when they were using the technology. I continued to search for research-based practices and examples of best practices in the literature.

It was in my fifth year of teaching social studies that I finally got a new personal computer in my classroom with Internet access. This enabled me to more easily search for primary sources online and other Internet activities that would enhance the learning experience for my students. My students also had the opportunity to participate in a project called Virtual Warrensburg where they were able to research local history topics and produce Internet webpages on their findings. In my opinion, this helped to move the technology integration in my classroom from passive learning with technology to active learning with technology. The students were actively engaged by examining primary and secondary sources at the local historical society. Due to this experience, they were involved in a great deal of critical thinking and produced Internet webpages that were visible to others beyond the walls of the classroom. I finally felt like we were using technology more effectively. In fact, as I began to read about the use of constructivism with educational technology, I saw that there was a great deal of merit for projects like Virtual Warrensburg. I continued to search for additional opportunities to integrate technology in meaningful ways.

Perhaps the most profound change happened during my last four years of teaching high school. Due to grant money from the Missouri Department of Elementary and Secondary Education, our school was able to purchase wireless laptops for a couple of classrooms. I was eager to participate in this initiative due to my prior experiences with technology in the classroom and from my graduate studies that began to focus more on this growing area. I am grateful that my administrator supported me in this endeavor and my classroom was granted wireless laptops for each of my students. This was an exciting opportunity! During the experience, I began to think about how I could integrate technology each day and saw firsthand the excitement when my students were actively engaged using their computers.

The wireless laptop computers transformed my classroom. Throughout the years, my classroom continued to move in more of a student-centered direction. The students constructed knowledge and often collaborated on projects where

they were able to showcase what they had learned in the social studies curriculum. We continued to examine primary sources as they became increasingly
available to my students online. Most importantly, as I increasingly learned about
research-based frameworks for technology integration, I was more successful at
designing technology-rich lessons that actively engaged the students and fostered
critical thinking in comparison to my earliest experiences with technology integration. Rather than having students simply write down ten things they learned
from a primary source online or complete a fill-in-the-blank worksheet, I began
to have students think more deeply and identify big ideas as they investigated topics online. This moved my technology integration lessons forward. This is what
I hope to share with the reader in the pages that follow. In particular, I hope the
reader will see why it is necessary to use research-based frameworks when social
studies teachers design and implement technology-rich lesson plans. By doing
so, students will more easily be able to learn the objectives in the social studies
curriculum.

1

RESEARCH-BASED PRACTICES FOR TECHNOLOGY INTEGRATION

In the pages that follow, the reader will have the opportunity to learn about research-based frameworks that focus on technology integration. Each of these frameworks can be used by the social studies teacher to help design technology-rich unit plans and daily lesson plans. There will be a heavy emphasis on the Technological Pedagogical and Content Knowledge (TPACK) framework and on using constructivism, where students use technology as a tool for their mind (Mindtool) to guide unit and lesson planning. These two frameworks provide the key underpinnings to facilitate meaningful learning with technology in the middle and secondary social studies classroom. This text will help the reader learn how to accomplish meaningful learning in the social studies classroom by using these frameworks and identifying how they can be easily implemented with middle and secondary students. Examples will be provided chapter by chapter to enable the reader to see how the theory and practice can be meshed to help students learn the objective in the social studies curriculum.

The reader will also be introduced to another set of frameworks that are gaining popularity among practicing middle and secondary teachers in the field of social studies. These include the following: 1) the Rigor/Relevance Framework and 2) the Giving, Prompting, and Making Model. Readers will also learn about the recently adopted C3 (College, Career, and Civil Life) Framework for Social Studies State Standards that have been endorsed by the National Council for the Social Studies (NCSS). In addition, the reader will learn about pivotal decisions that social studies teachers can make with technology based on a qualitative study that I conducted of social studies classrooms with 1:1 laptop programs, which is where each student in the classroom has their own laptop computer. Each of these puts a significant point of emphasis on student-centered learning and higher-level thinking with technology. The reader will also see in the remaining chapters of the book examples of how the frameworks can be used with various teaching and learning strategies in the middle and secondary social studies classroom. Most importantly, once readers have a grasp of the frameworks, they can begin to design lesson plans that integrate technology using student-centered strategies that foster higher-level thinking.

Technological Pedagogical Content Knowledge (TPACK) Framework

Many middle and secondary social studies teachers are looking for the latest technology to more fully engage their students. Some teachers believe technology can be a quick fix or can magically help their students learn in the social studies classroom. There is a growing amount of research that disagrees with this notion. Mishra and Koehler (2006) challenge teachers to rethink technology integration, since they often think solely about the technology itself but fail to consider how it may actually be implemented in the classroom. The TPACK framework gives teachers the necessary structures to deliver meaningful lessons in the social studies classroom. These structures challenge teachers to think about three key components of instruction with technology: content knowledge, pedagogy knowledge, and technology knowledge (Mishra & Koehler, 2006). Each of these structures gives social studies teachers a user-friendly way to think conceptually about the lesson and unit plans that they are delivering every day with technology.

To begin with, content knowledge and pedagogical knowledge have traditionally been perceived as two separate approaches to teaching and learning. Shulman (1986) challenged this assumption and argued that teachers should examine how content knowledge and pedagogical knowledge can be fused together to make a lesson more understandable to their students (as cited in Mishra & Koehler, 2006). For example, some pedagogical strategies will work better than others, depending on the content that the teacher is trying to cover in the lesson. This careful consideration of both the pedagogy and content can increase the likelihood that students will be more engaged with the subject matter rather than if the teacher considers just one of these components. Accordingly, teachers today should also think about how technology can be leveraged in the classroom along with the aforementioned content knowledge and pedagogical knowledge components. This has exciting implications for the middle and secondary social studies teacher.

Mishra and Koehler (2006) argue that technological knowledge, content knowledge, and pedagogical knowledge are critical to good teaching. They make the case that each of these knowledge areas should not be viewed in isolation. The TPACK framework suggests that teachers should examine the interplay among these knowledge areas when designing lessons with technology (see Figure 1.1). As I noted earlier, when I began using technology in my

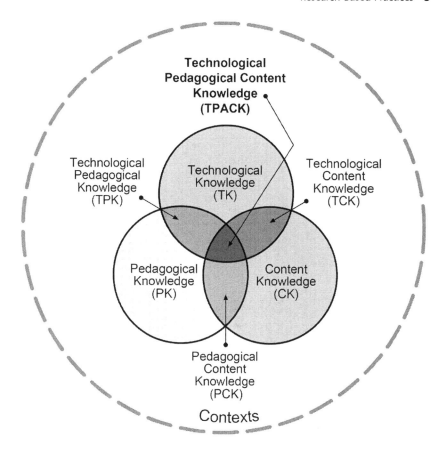

Figure 1.1 Technological Pedagogical Content Knowledge (TPACK)

Source: Reproduced by permission of the publisher, ©2012 by tpack.org.

social studies classroom, I was designing lessons through trial and error. I wish I had been exposed to the TPACK framework much earlier in my social studies teaching career. It would have helped me to think more deeply about designing technology-rich lessons and how each of these areas (technology, content, and pedagogy) intersect to deliver meaningful lessons in the social studies classroom (Daggett, 2014). Many social studies teachers today are struggling with the same issue of how to integrate these three areas.

Sometimes, teachers assume that familiarity with a specific kind of technology will lead to good teaching and learning in the social studies classroom (Mishra & Koehler, 2006). Evidence suggests that teachers who fail to consider the TPACK framework may end up having students learn a great deal about the technology they are using, but not nearly enough about the subject matter in the social studies curriculum (Mishra & Koehler, 2006). The TPACK framework is designed to address this concern by having teachers consider each of these structures.

Mishra and Koehler (2006) suggest that simply using technology itself does not mean that students will automatically learn the subject matter, since the teacher may not know how to teach with the technology. Social studies teachers must have a working knowledge of proven teaching and learning strategies that they can mesh with technology-rich lessons. The TPACK framework can help teachers address this concern so they can think about each of these components when they plan technology-rich lessons in the social studies classroom.

Many readers may wonder what it might look like to implement the TPACK framework when they design daily lessons and construct unit plans. There is much to consider. The goal is to focus on the integration of technology, content, and pedagogy that will best result in students learning the subject matter in the social studies curriculum. For example, if a teacher is developing a lesson on the Alien and Sedition Acts, he or she must consider which type of technology to utilize in the lesson. There are many technologies to pick from. Primary sources located on the Internet can enable students to actually read the text of the acts. Web 2.0 tools, such as Popplet, enable students to construct an interactive graphic organizer where they demonstrate what they have learned about the Alien and Sedition Acts. Students can also use VoiceThread to compose a digital video about the acts or use Audacity to produce an Internet podcast on them. Countless technologies can be implemented. The challenge for the teacher is to find the one technology that will best enable their students to learn the content specified in the lesson.

The next challenge is to identify a teaching and learning strategy that can be utilized with the technology to help students learn the content that they are investigating. It is important to pick the strategy that will help students learn the subject matter with technology. Problem-based learning, cooperative learning, authentic assessment, and Authentic Intellectual Work (AIW) are all examples of teaching and learning strategies that can be utilized with social studies lessons that integrate technology. For example, the teacher can use problem-based learning to have students develop a hypothesis on why the Alien and Sedition Acts were instituted in the United States. In summary, the TPACK framework can, and should, be used by social studies teachers to move technology integration forward in the middle and secondary social studies classroom.

Constructivism: Using Technology as a Mindtool

Constructivism, when paired with technology, places a significant point of emphasis on the process of how students actually construct their own knowledge with technology (Jonassen, 1995). Five building blocks are critically important in helping students construct knowledge when they use technology. These building blocks include teaching and learning experiences with technology that are active, authentic, collaborative, constructivist, and intentional (Howland, Jonassen, & Marra, 2012). These building blocks represent a paradigm shift for many social studies teachers. Some teachers might question the rationale for using these building blocks and wonder how they might actually work. To begin with, teachers can foster in-depth thinking with technology by challenging students to actively construct their own knowledge, rather than simply reciting what their teacher has taught them about the subject matter (Jonassen, 1995). This shifts a constructivist lesson with technology from a teacher-centered classroom, where students are passively learning, to a student-centered classroom, where students are actively engaged with technology. Jonassen (1995) argued that active learning with technology has a great deal of merit since it fosters in-depth thinking about the subject matter which enables students to more fully understand what they are investigating. Evidence also suggests that students enjoy constructing knowledge with technology due to their active participation in their construction of knowledge (Jonassen, 1995).

Constructivism is a research-based framework that encourages students to use technology as a tool for their mind, or Mindtool. Many readers may be somewhat skeptical, wondering if the constructivist theory will work with technology in their classroom. Constructivism encourages teachers to design technology-rich lessons that challenge students to think more deeply about the subject matter rather than participate in drill-and-practice exercises. Social studies students often find themselves in classrooms where they surf the Internet and complete worksheets by regurgitating information covering the lowest levels of Bloom's taxonomy about the subject matter. Unfortunately, this does not actively engage students with technology, nor does it foster in-depth analysis about the subject matter. This makes some teachers nervous since it is contrary to their perception that technology should make learning easier for students. Rather, students should use technology as a tool for their mind (Mindtool) where they have the opportunity to think more deeply about the subject matter in terms of Bloom's taxonomy.

Constructivism and technology together encourage teachers to design teaching and learning activities that foster higher-level thinking. In particular, since technology is exceptionally good at storing a great deal of information, students can analyze the data they find online versus memorizing the information. For example, there are databases online where students can be challenged to provide their own analysis of a particular phenomenon pertaining to the lesson objective. The US Census Report and Gallup Poll are examples of this. As a result, students who have the opportunity to analyze the data from these online databases can identify patterns that may emerge from the sources and organize it to reach conclusions (Jonassen, 1995). This emphasis on students using the computer to enhance their thinking and learning, rather than being controlled by the computer to learn, is a significant idea that moves technology integration forward. Jonassen (1995) described this revolutionary approach to teaching and learning with technology as follows:

> The most pervasive cognitive technology is language. Imagine trying to learn something complex without the use of language. Language amplifies the thinking of the learner. Computers may also function as cognitive technologies for amplifying and reorganizing the way that learners think. (p. 45)

This has significant implications for technology-rich classrooms in middle and secondary schools and challenges students to supply the cognitive load while the computer is used to store information. This is a paradigm shift for many social studies teachers.

David Jonassen (1995), who coined the term Mindtool, argued that technology should not necessarily make learning any easier. According to Jonassen, students should actually be challenged to think harder about the subject matter rather than passively learning when they participate in lessons with technology. Many social studies teachers still design lesson plans where students use technology to listen to podcasts, surf the Web, and view digital videos. This type of teaching and learning with technology does not actively engage students, nor are they thinking deeply about the subject matter in the social studies curriculum. Instead, students can participate in student-centered technology lessons where they are actively involved and challenged to be decision makers on issues pertaining to the social studies curriculum. For example, teachers can have students use the Internet to research the crisis in Ukraine. Students can pretend they are the president of the United States and determine if they would intervene or not in the civil war. Perhaps students can write a blog where they share their analysis and defend their position.

According to Jonassen (1995), there should also be an intellectual partnership between students and technology. This partnership enables students to "learn with technology, not from it" (Jonassen, 1995, p. 41). This is contrary to the popular notion that technology should be used to "teach" middle and secondary students. As Jonassen noted (1995), students should be challenged to use technology as a mind extension tool where they provide the intelligence, not the computer. Many teachers may understandably wonder how this can manifest into an actual lesson plan with technology in the middle and secondary social studies classroom. Jonassen (1995) wrote "when learners use computers as partners, they offload some of the unproductive memorizing tasks to the computer, allowing the learners to think more productively" (p. 45). Some readers may be puzzled by these findings or question Jonassen's assertion. Jonassen (1995) reminds teachers that "our goal should be to allocate to the learners the cognitive responsibility for the processing what they do best while we allocate to the technology the processing that it does best" (p. 45). This makes the intellectual partnership possible.

Students also benefit when they use technology to design their own products rather than viewing what others have designed or produced (Jonassen, Carr, & Yueh, 1998). In particular, students should be given the opportunity to build their own expert systems about the subject matter they are investigating, rather than learning from what others have done on the same subject matter. Digital videos, Internet podcasts, and blogging are examples of expert systems that students can produce to highlight their findings in the social studies classroom. Jonassen (1995) suggested that students build their own expert systems with technology rather than viewing what professional designers or tutors have produced on the same subject matter. By doing this, students are challenged to model the expertise of others when they build their own expert system with technology (Jonassen, 1995). Students can use primary and secondary sources to research local history topics and produce an Internet webpage to share their findings (Scheuerell, 2010). This is similar to what professional historians do. This example will be discussed in greater detail later in the book.

Giving, Prompting, and Making Model for Technology Integration

It is typical to find social studies teachers using technology to transmit information to students. PowerPoint is one example of how teachers use technology to give students lecture information. However, there are other ways that technology can be used in the social studies classroom. In order to address this issue, Hammond and Manfra (2009) developed the Giving, Prompting, and Making Model to use in social studies classrooms with technology (see Figure 1.2). The Giving, Prompting, and Making Model provides a user-friendly way for teachers to think about how they can strategically infuse technology into their unit and lesson plans.

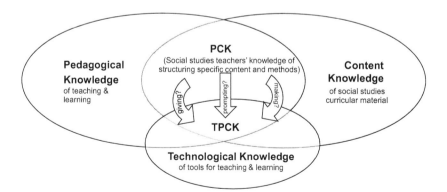

Figure 1.2 Hammond and Manfra (2009). TPCK within social studies with sequencing (PCK before TPCK) and structure (giving, prompting, or making as the intended instructional strategies and requested technological affordances).

Some teachers may feel uncomfortable moving from a teacher-centered to a student-centered approach. In particular, teachers wonder if students will actually learn the lesson's objective when a student-centered approach is utilized and often feel that they are giving up some control of the classroom if they are not delivering the lecture to students. The goal of the Giving, Prompting, and Making Model is to show social studies teachers that there are additional ways to use technology in the classroom.

The Giving, Prompting, and Making Model identifies three major ways that social studies teachers can integrate technology in the classroom (see Figures 1.3 to 1.5). To begin with, Hammond and Manfra (2009) picked the term "giving" to describe when social studies teachers use technology to deliver lecture material to students. Social studies teachers often use the computer to produce PowerPoint presentations for lecture purposes and expect their students to be passive learners, retaining the necessary information for a quiz or test for assessment purposes. Hammond and Manfra (2009) argue that this type of direct instruction fails to provide the necessary evidence that students actually understand the social studies

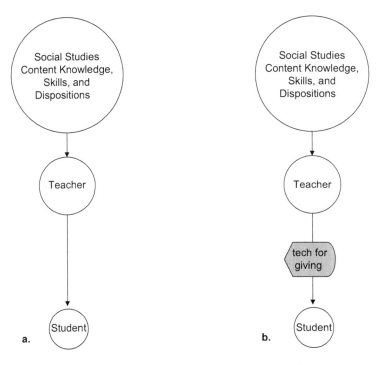

Figure 1.3 Hammond and Manfra (2009). Teaching via *giving*. The student's experience of the content area is completely filtered by the teacher. In version A no technology is used; in version B technology is used to support the teacher's giving of content to the student.

content covered from the lecture. This fits with the research conducted by others. Howland, Jonassen, and Marra (2012) argue that it is impossible for students to construct meaning for themselves when teachers do this for them by transmitting lecture information using technology. Yet, many social studies teachers are still using computers to transmit information. Sheffield (2011) also discovered that most social studies teachers are still using the Internet to locate or gather information for themselves and only a few required their students to gather and analyze information. These teachers rarely had their students participate in higher-level thinking using the Internet (Sheffield, 2011). This is unfortunate, since there already is a great deal of research confirming that a student-centered approach with technology has a great deal of merit.

Teachers can have students view subject matter on the Internet pertaining to issues in the social studies curriculum and have students make their very own inferences based on their investigation. According to Hammond and Manfra (2009), this is known as the Prompting Model of technology integration. Some examples include lesson plans that challenge students to participate in 1) investigations with primary and secondary sources on the Internet to interpret the past, 2) problem-based learning to test their hypotheses, and 3) in-depth discussions on information from online

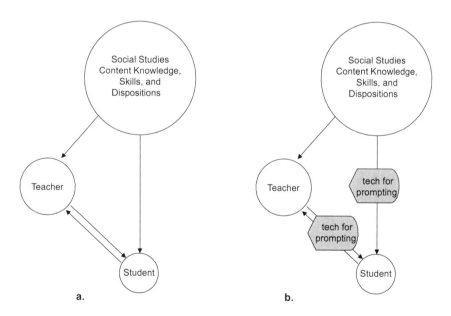

Figure 1.4 Hammond and Manfra (2009). Teaching via *prompting*. The student experiences the content area as part of a dialog with the teacher. In version A no technology is used; in version B technology is used to present the content to the student or to support dialog between teacher and student.

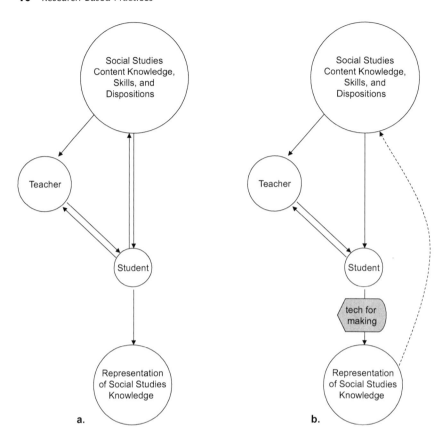

Figure 1.5 Hammond and Manfra (2009). Teaching via *making*. The student learns while creating a representation of the content area. In version A no technology is used; in version B students use technology while making their product. The dashed line represents the possibility that the student product may, in turn, become part of the general body of social studies content (e.g., a local history project).

databases. Each example is a student-centered focus with technology and fosters in-depth thinking about the subject matter. Frequently, the teacher can facilitate the activity by developing a list of questions that involve higher-level thinking.

There are many benefits to using the Prompting Model of technology integration. Friedman and Heafner (2007) conducted a study that documented how students were motivated by an inquiry-based lesson using technology. Hammond and Manfra (2009) have also written extensively on inquiry-based or problem-based learning and how it is quite effective. This type of teaching and learning with technology successfully challenges students to think more deeply, and they are able to make meaning for themselves rather than memorizing names and dates in the social studies curriculum. As a result, evidence suggests that students are able to increase their analytical skills and have a much deeper conceptual knowledge of the subject matter (Hammond & Manfra, 2009). These results are promising for the social studies classroom.

The Making Model of technology integration also has a great deal of promise for the social studies classroom. During a making lesson, students can produce a product using the computer that represents their knowledge of the subject matter in the social studies curriculum (Hammond & Manfra, 2009). Most importantly, Hammond and Manfra (2009) wrote that "the pedagogy should lead the technology, not technology lead the pedagogy" (p. 163). In my opinion, this is a critical point. Social studies teachers need to develop scoring guides for technology projects that require students to demonstrate higher-level thinking about the subject matter. For example, the Making Model may involve students producing products on what they have learned about a specific objective in the social studies curriculum. Students might be asked to produce an Internet podcast, compose a digital video, write a blog, or make an avatar with a Web 2.0 tool. Yet, the key is for students to produce products that involve a great deal of critical thinking about the subject matter. In order to make this happen, social studies teachers will need to be open to the possibility of changing how teaching and learning are taking place in their classroom by thinking philosophically about the role technology will play to ultimately help students learn.

Rigor/Relevance Framework

Increasingly, middle and secondary students are using technology to investigate subjects in the social studies curriculum. Yet, they frequently wonder why it is important to study the subject matter. Many students also desire a student-centered approach where they are challenged to think more deeply. The Rigor/Relevance Framework, created by Dr. Willard R. Daggett, founder and chairman of the International Center for Leadership in Education, provides the building blocks for social studies teachers to design lessons that are focused on real-world application of knowledge and higher-level thinking in technology-rich classrooms. According to research, this approach to teaching and learning can lead to meaningful learning in the classroom because students are able to more fully see the relevancy of the subject matter (Daggett, 2005). In particular, there is a great deal of emphasis on a student-centered classroom instead of the traditional teacher-centered approach. Daggett (2005) noted that in most classroom settings, students spend the vast majority of their day watching their teachers do the work and that "a teacher who relies on lecturing does not provide students with optimal learning opportunities" (p. 2). The Rigor/Relevance Framework addresses this concern by providing social studies teachers with a user-friendly way to move lessons to a student-centered classroom where students are engaged in critical thinking by giving them the opportunity to apply what they are learning.

The Rigor/Relevance Framework includes four different quadrants of learning (see Figure 1.6). Quadrant A, where there is an emphasis on teacher work, includes lesson plans that are teacher centered, where the students are passive learners. It also involves the lowest levels of Bloom's taxonomy, where students are involved in rote memorization of the content that is delivered from the teacher. For example, the teacher may use PowerPoint presentations or examples from an Internet webpage using a liquid crystal display (LCD) projector. Each student may then memorize names and dates from a history lecture for a quiz or test. This fails to engage students in critical thinking and application of knowledge.

Quadrant B, where there is an emphasis on student work, takes place when students have the opportunity to participate in a student-centered lesson using technology. This can involve students producing products where they show what they have learned. Yet, it still involves the lowest levels of Bloom's taxonomy. For

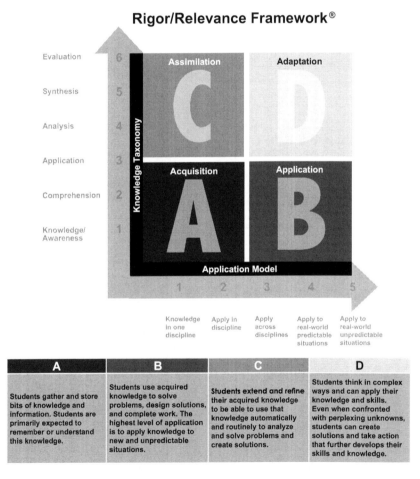

Figure 1.6 Rigor/Relevance Framework, created by Dr. Willard R. Daggett, founder and chairman of the International Center for Leadership in Education.

example, students may produce a Prezi, Internet podcast, or blog to demonstrate what they have learned about a topic in the social studies curriculum. Lessons in Quadrant B are able to engage students more fully by having them involved in active learning with technology. However, they fail to engage students in critical thinking models such as problem solving, creating solutions, and decision making. Quadrants C and D do address this.

In Quadrant C, where there is an emphasis on student thinking, students have the opportunity to be engaged in higher-level thinking with technology. The point of emphasis is on the highest levels of Bloom's taxonomy. Frequently, students have the opportunity to view Internet webpages and Internet databases to access information related to the subject matter in the social studies curriculum. Middle and secondary students can view primary and secondary sources on the Internet where they compare and contrast what they have found. They can use electronic databases to develop a hypothesis or make a recommendation to solve various social issues facing our nation and global issues that our world is confronted with. As a result, students are more fully able to see a real-world connection to the social studies curriculum when they are using technology.

Quadrant D, where there is an emphasis on student thinking and working, includes lessons with technology where there is student-centered instruction and higher-level thinking are taking place. There is a great deal of emphasis on the highest levels of Bloom's taxonomy to foster critical thinking with technology where students are involved in analysis, synthesis, and evaluation. Each student is also engaged when they use technology to provide evidence of what they have learned by teaching others using the product they have produced. For example, they may produce a public service announcement using a digital video documentary, wiki, or Internet webpage that demonstrates their decision making or problem solving about a dilemma facing our country and/or world.

College, Career, and Civic Life (C3) Framework for Social Studies State Standards

In September 2013, the NCSS released the C3 Framework for Social Studies State Standards. These new standards for middle and secondary social studies call for a paradigm shift on teaching and learning content in the subject matter. Significant emphasis is placed on moving instruction from a teacher-centered to a student-centered classroom. Technology is arguably well suited to make this happen and to facilitate the teaching and learning structures outlined in these new standards.

The C3 Framework for Social Studies Standards includes four dimensions that are part of an inquiry arc that emphasizes the need to use questions to facilitate student learning (see Figure 1.7). Dimension #1 of the inquiry arc encourages social studies teachers to develop questions and plan investigations for students

DIMENSION 1: DEVELOPING QUESTIONS AND PLANNING INQUIRIES	DIMENSION 2: APPLYING DISCIPLINARY TOOLS AND CONCEPTS	DIMENSION 3: EVALUATING SOURCES AND USING EVIDENCE	DIMENSION 4: COMMUNICATING CONCLUSION AND TAKING INFORMED ACTION
Developing Questions and Planning Inquiries	Civics	Gathering and Evaluating Sources	Communicating and Critiquing Conclusions
	Economics		
	Geography	Developing Claims and Using Evidence	Taking Informed Action
	History		

Figure 1.7 C3 (College, Career, and Civic Readiness) Framework for Social Studies State Standards.

(NCSS, 2013). Technology provides an excellent vehicle for middle and secondary students to explore answers to questions developed by their teacher or questions that students have identified for themselves pertaining to the subject matter in the social studies curriculum. The Internet includes primary and secondary sources, electronic databases, and countless opportunities for students to explore in-depth data that is relevant or pertinent to their inquiry.

Dimension #2 of the inquiry arc encourages teachers to design lessons where students apply disciplinary-specific concepts and tools. NCSS (2013) states that "each of these disciplines—civics, economics, geography, and history—offers a unique way of thinking and organizing knowledge as well as systems for verifying knowledge" (p. 29). There are many examples from each of these disciplines. The C3 document includes the following example question: "What does liberty look like?" There is an example from Civics that asks, "What is the line between liberty and responsibility?" In addition, there is an example from Geography that asks, "How does liberty change from place to place?" In History, an example asks, "When did Americans gain their independence?" Finally, there is an example from Economics that poses the following question: "Does more liberty mean more prosperity?" (NCSS, 2013, p. 30). Technology provides an ample opportunity for students to explore these types of questions using a multidimensional disciplinary approach where students can see connections between the social studies subject areas.

In Dimension #3, students are asked to investigate questions by gathering, evaluating, and using evidence. The NCSS (2013) states that "students should use various technologies and skills to find information and to express their responses to compelling and supporting questions through well-reasoned explanations and evidence-based arguments" (NCSS, 2013, p. 53). Due to the increasing amount of information found on the Internet, middle and secondary students can more easily access the latest research online pertaining to their inquiry investigation.

Each student can reflect on their findings and evaluate how each source of information can be used to answer the question they are investigating. Most importantly, students can learn how to use evidence to make an argument supporting the position they outline. In summary, technology can be at the center of these investigations where students learn how to gather, evaluate, and use evidence to support these positions. This is a skill needed for college, career, and civic readiness in our democracy.

Finally, Dimension #4 encourages teachers to design lessons where middle and secondary students work collaboratively during inquiry investigations and then communicate their findings or conclusions with others. Students are encouraged to share their findings in public venues. Technology can be harnessed by students to make this happen. Many technology tools can foster critical thinking and be utilized by middle and secondary students to share their findings or conclusions with classmates and with others beyond the walls of the classroom. Increasingly, students have access to these technology tools in their classrooms. Students can share their findings by producing Internet webpages, blogs, podcasts, wikis, digital videos, electronic portfolios and participating in discussion boards. There are also presentation tools such as Prezi and Popplet where students can communicate their findings using an interactive slideshow or outline their conclusions using an online graphic organizer tool. There are many exciting possibilities, and technology is a great tool to showcase student findings from in-depth investigations in the middle and secondary social studies classroom. Most importantly, there is a focus on student-centered learning and higher-order thinking, which is highlighted by the C3 Framework for Social Studies State Standards. Technology-rich classrooms provide the platform to launch these in-depth investigations where students can access information, analyze their findings, and share their conclusions with others in a collaborative classroom setting.

Pivotal Decisions With Technology: Social Studies

The findings from a qualitative study on the integration of technology in social studies will be shared with the reader throughout the remaining chapters of the book. The findings are based on themes that emerged from three high school social studies classrooms that were part of a school-wide 1:1 laptop program. The research examined the following question: "How are social studies teachers designing meaningful teaching and learning lessons that integrate technology?" The purpose of the study was to identify teaching and learning structures with technology that can be used as predictors of success. The findings are based on the field notes, interviews with students and teachers, and artifacts collected from these classrooms. Many of these artifacts included products that the students produced using technology on a wide array of social studies topics. Chapter 2 provides additional information on how the research study was conducted.

The research identified six pivotal decisions with technology that social studies teachers should consider: 1) Should teachers give students background information about a subject before they investigate it on the Internet or should they be given a blank slate? 2) Should teachers have students participate in group work or cooperative learning structures when they participate in collaborative learning with technology? 3) Should teachers use tiered instruction or use the notion that "one size fits all" when students use technology? 4) Should teachers use thick or thin questions when students use technology? 5) Should teachers have students generate a hypothesis prior to Internet investigations or simply have students "dive in" when they use technology? 6) Should teachers encourage students to develop their own intellectual contributions when they use technology or should they regurgitate the teachers' answers? Readers will also see throughout the remaining chapters of the book that there are sections titled "Inside Classrooms" and "Theory and Practice" that highlight examples of how social studies teachers are using technology in their classroom to reinforce these findings.

Summary

Teachers are looking for research-based practices to integrate technology. The frameworks presented in this chapter can be used today in classrooms to help social studies teachers think strategically about technology integration. They are the foundation or infrastructure that can guide technology-rich lessons in the social sciences.

Readers should pick one or two of the frameworks presented here and use them as a guide. In particular, since the frameworks have so many common themes and points of emphasis, teachers should also be encouraged to be risk takers and think outside of the box when they design lessons using technology. It does not mean that the lesson will fail. More often than not, they will discover that the lesson will succeed if they stick to the research-based findings identified in each of these frameworks.

Today, middle and secondary teachers find themselves in classrooms where students are using iPads, iPhones, and countless models of laptop computers. However, this should make little difference in technology integration. No matter what type of technological device the students are using, there is a great deal of commonality in regard to the type of teaching and learning structures that can be used successfully. As mentioned previously, what does matter is the foundation or infrastructure highlighted by these frameworks. These lessons enable students to be actively engaged with technology in a student-centered learning environment where they have the opportunity to think deeply about the subject matter and produce products that provide evidence of their learning.

References

Daggett, W. R. (2005). *Achieving academic excellence through rigor and relevance*. Rexford, NY: International Center for Leadership in Education.

Daggett, W.R. (2014). *Rigor/Relevance Framework. A guide to focusing resources to increase student performance*. Rexford, NY: International Center for Leadership in Education.

Friedman, A.M. & Heafner, T.L. (2007). "You think for me, so I don't have to." The effect of a technology-enhanced, inquiry learning environment on student learning in 11th grade United States history. *Contemporary Issues in Technology and Teacher Education, 7*, 199–216.

Hammond, T.C. & Manfra, M. (2009). Giving, prompting, making: Aligning technology and pedagogy within TPACK for social studies instruction, *Contemporary Issues in Technology and Teacher Education, 9*, 160–185.

Howland, J.L., Jonassen, D.H., & Marra, R.M. (2012). *Meaningful learning with technology* (4th ed.). Indianapolis, IN: Pearson.

Jonassen, D.H. (1995). Computers as cognitive tools: Learning with technology, not from technology. *Journal of Computing in Higher Education, 6*, 40–73.

Jonassen, D.H., Carr, C., & Yueh, H. (1998). Computers as mindtools for engaging learners in critical thinking. *Tech Trends, 43*, 24–32.

Mishra, P. & Koehler, M.J. (2006). Technological pedagogical content knowledge: A framework for teacher knowledge. *Teachers College Record, 108*, 1017–1054.

National Council for the Social Studies. (2013). *The College, Career, and Civic Life (C3) Framework for Social Studies State Standards: Guidance for enhancing the rigor of K–12 civics, economics, geography and history*. Silver Spring, MD: NCSS.

Scheuerell, S.K. (2010). Virtual Warrensburg: Using cooperative learning and the Internet in the social studies classroom. *The Social Studies, 101*, 194–199.

Sheffield, C. C. (2011). Navigating access and maintaining established practice: Social studies teachers' technology integration at three Florida middle schools. *Contemporary Issues in Technology and Teacher Education, 11*(3), 282-312.

Shulman, L. S. (1986). Those who understand: Knowledge growth in teaching. *Educational Researcher, 15*(2), 4–14.

2

AUTHENTIC INTELLECTUAL WORK

Newman, King, and Carmichael (2007) argue that instruction has focused too often on the memorization of facts and dates to comply with test requirements. Increasingly, a greater point of emphasis is being placed on making middle and secondary social studies relevant to the lives of students. Authentic Intellectual Work (AIW) provides middle and secondary teachers the necessary framework to make this happen in the social studies classroom. Many readers may wonder how technology fits into a discussion on AIW. Technology can be leveraged to facilitate AIW by enabling students to see real-world connections between the subject matter they are investigating in social studies and the world around them. This can be quite motivating to students.

Unfortunately, middle and secondary students frequently find themselves in classrooms where they are passive learners and asked to regurgitate lecture information for a quiz or test. Scheurman and Newman (1998) wrote: "Such mastery offers little assurance that students have achieved a deep level of conceptual understanding, or that they will be able to transfer knowledge and skills to situations outside of school" (p. 1).

To make matters worse, Newman, King, and Carmichael (2007) argue that students are given few opportunities to investigate topics in depth and participate in critical thinking where they can develop their own interpretation about the subject matter. In fact, many students are asked to simply identify their social studies teachers' interpretation of history or the social sciences, rather than developing their own conceptual understanding of the past or be challenged to solve issues facing our nation and world. AIW can help students develop the necessary skill sets for citizenship, college, and the workplace.

AIW provides the necessary building blocks to move teaching and learning from lower-level thinking to higher-level thinking instruction centered around real-world connections for students in the middle and secondary social studies classroom. In lesson plans that embrace AIW, students are encouraged to "use their minds to solve important meaningful problems or answer interesting challenging questions" (Newman, King, & Carmichael, 2007, p. 2). There is a growing body of literature on AIW that speaks to the merits of this unique pedagogical approach. Teachers confirm that students find authentic work in the classroom to be more appealing and meaningful than drill-and-practice methods of instruction (Newman, King, & Carmichael, 2007). There is also research that has discovered that students who are exposed to authentic work tend to understand what they are learning much more deeply due to the in-depth focus and real-world connections they are able to make with the subject matter they are investigating (Newman, King, & Carmichael, 2007). In addition, studies have found that students are willing to put forth greater effort in their school work since they are more likely to be interested in the subject matter (Newman, King, & Carmichael, 2007). These are noteworthy findings on why it is important to move instruction from a teacher-centered to a student-centered classroom where students are able to see the necessary connections between the subject matter in the social studies curriculum and the world around them.

Criteria for Authentic Intellectual Work

Construction of knowledge, disciplined inquiry, and value beyond school are the hallmark characteristics of AIW (see Figure 2.1). Middle and secondary social studies teachers can use each of these criteria to design and implement technology-rich lessons that have a great deal of authenticity and connectedness to the real world. The user-friendly criteria also enable teachers, who are confronted with increased workloads, to quickly design meaningful lessons to help their middle and secondary students learn the objectives in the social studies curriculum.

Newman, King, and Carmichael (2007) argue that AIW begins with student construction of knowledge. In order to make this happen, it is necessary for students to be involved in a great deal of critical thinking or higher-order thinking (HOT) and to see how their prior knowledge about the subject matter connects to the new information they are presented with. There is also a need for students to problem-solve by "organizing, interpreting, evaluating, or synthesizing" (p. 4) what they have previously learned and applying it to create solutions to real-world problems (Newman, King, & Carmichael, 2007). By using this approach, teachers can design lesson plans that foster student construction of knowledge. Examples will be provided for the reader later in this chapter.

Technology enables students to construct their own knowledge where they can develop their own intellectual contributions on a subject or issue in the social studies curriculum. For example, students can produce products using technology

Criteria for Authentic Intellectual Work	Instruction (Lessons Taught)	Tasks (Assignments)	Student Work (Student Performance)
Construction of Knowledge	Higher Order Thinking	Construction of Knowledge	Construction of Knowledge
Disciplined Inquiry	Deep Knowledge and Student Understanding		Conceptual Understanding
	Substantive Conversation	Elaborated Communication	Elaborated Communication
Value Beyond School	Value Beyond School	Value Beyond School	Note: Students don't have control over the audience. Directions come from the task.

Figure 2.1 Framework for Authentic Intellectual Work

Source: Newmann, F.M., Carmichael, D.L., & King, M.B. (in press). *Authentic intellectual work: Improving teaching for rigorous learning,* Thousand Oaks, CA: Corwin. http://centerforaiw.com/aiw-framework-and-research.

where they share their own intellectual contributions with others by producing Internet podcasts, composing a digital video, or writing a wiki. Howland, Jonassen, and Marra (2012) discussed the rationale for teachers to use technology in these transformative ways, writing:

> We believe that the students' task should not be to understand the world as the teacher does. Rather, students should construct their own meaning for the world. If they do, then the teachers' roles shift from dispensing knowledge to helping learners construct more viable conceptions to the world. (p. xiii)

Readers can use these findings to design their very own AIW experiences for students.

Lesson plans that use AIW begin with the notion of a student-centered classroom and student construction of knowledge, rather than the teacher being at the center of teaching and learning and the notion that the teacher has all of the answers. Many social studies teachers may still wonder how they can make this happen. Middle and secondary students today have access to an increasing amount of technology, which enables them to more easily investigate topics and solve problems for themselves with the teacher being the guide on the side, as outlined by AIW, rather than relying on the teacher to provide all of the subject matter via lecture.

Disciplined inquiry is a necessity in lessons that exhibit the characteristics of AIW. Yet, many teachers try to cover too much material in a single lesson. Lesson plans that utilize disciplined inquiry put a point of emphasis on teaching and learning that feature the pedagogical philosophies of "less is more" and "depth versus breadth" in terms of knowledge acquisition in the classroom. This enables each student to have the opportunity to focus on an in-depth investigation to understand more fully the subject matter in the social studies curriculum and apply what they have previously learned about the subject matter. As a result, each student can more fully understand the complexity of an issue in greater detail and become a problem solver.

Focus questions are another key characteristic of AIW. They challenge students to think critically about the subject matter in an in-depth investigation. Each focus question takes time to develop. The goal is to create a question that will foster higher-level thinking about the subject matter under investigation. Focus questions, sometimes known as essential questions, can help to narrow the focus of a lesson to feature in-depth investigations and keep the goal of the lesson on big ideas. Most unit plans will feature a few focus questions. Frequently, teachers post these questions on the whiteboard or liquid crystal display (LCD) projector so each student in the classroom is clear on the big ideas that they are exploring in the social studies lesson. Each objective identified in the individual lesson plans should be aligned to help students answer the focus questions. Examples of focus questions will be featured later in this chapter and throughout the text.

AIW argues that students should have a prior knowledge base on a topic or issue in social studies before they investigate it in greater depth. Newman, King, and Carmichael (2007) wrote that "students must acquire a knowledge base of facts, vocabularies, concepts, theories, and algorithms, and other conventions necessary to conduct rigorous inquiry" (p. 4). Teachers can help students build a prior knowledge base about the subject matter by delivering brief lectures and assigning student readings prior to the in-depth investigations that take place in the social studies classroom. Anticipatory set activities at the beginning of a lesson plan can also be used to activate prior knowledge or build the necessary background knowledge before a more in-depth investigation with technology. For example, a very brief video on the subject matter can give students a great deal of introductory information in five to ten minutes before they investigate the topic further in the remainder of the lesson. By doing these types of activities, students are then more easily able to investigate problems or issues since they are able to connect their prior knowledge to new information, which helps them make sense out of what they are learning (Newman, King, & Carmichael, 2007). As noted earlier, a prior knowledge base can help students make the necessary connections between what they have learned from a lecture, reading, or video to something they encounter on the Internet about the same subject. This is vitally important when students are then challenged to develop their own intellectual contributions about the subject matter and share what they have learned with others.

Elaborate communication about the subject matter is a vitally important characteristic of AIW. Students should be challenged to communicate their intellectual contribution to others. This may involve an essay or research paper (Newman, King, & Carmichael, 2007). Students can also participate in a class discussion on what they have found from primary sources or databases found online. This elaborated communication helps students reflect on what they have learned and on how it can be applied to the world around them by making decisions or solving problems related to the subject matter that they investigated. Technology is one way that students can communicate their findings to their classmates, community, or even globally by posting their work on the Internet. For example, students can produce an Internet podcast or digital video to share their intellectual contributions. Blogs, discussion boards, and Internet webpages are other possible ways for students to disseminate their intellectual contributions about the subject matter in the social studies curriculum.

AIW is also characterized by moving away from traditional forms of assessment such as tests and quizzes. Alternative or authentic assessment is frequently used instead so students can provide evidence of what they have learned in a real-world context. This is accomplished by having students perform, create, or produce products that demonstrate what they have learned about the subject matter. Newman, King, and Carmichael (2007) argue that this is critically important to enable students to see the relevancy of the subject matter they are learning and that the social studies curriculum has value beyond school. They wrote that "particular intellectual challenges that when successfully met would have meaning to students beyond complying with teachers' requirements" (Newman, King, & Carmichael, 2007, p. 5). Yet, students are unable to see the connectedness to the real world since they are rarely given intellectual challenges in the classroom. This is a distinctive element of AIW. It is necessary for students to be engaged in intellectual challenges in the middle and secondary classroom since the future workplace they will find themselves in will have many challenges that demand a great deal of analysis and problem-solving skills (Newman, King, & Carmichael, 2007). Technology can be used to encourage this type of teaching and learning.

AIW, used in conjunction with technology, can enable students to more easily see that the subject matter does have value beyond the walls of the classroom. Newman, King, and Carmichael (2007) wrote that "intellectual challenges raised in the world beyond the walls of the classroom are often more meaningful to students than those contrived only for the purpose of teaching students in the school" (p. 5). As noted earlier, it is very important for social studies teachers to consider moving instruction from a teacher-centered approach to a more student-centered approach to facilitate this type of learning experience in their classroom. By doing so, students can participate in the type of teaching and learning experience identified by AIW and experience its benefits firsthand. This can also work hand in hand with a classroom equipped with technology. Scheurman and Newman (1998) wrote that "authentic intellectual achievement has aesthetic, utilitarian, or personal value beyond merely documenting the competence of a learner" (p. 3). In particular, AIW is much more appealing to middle and secondary students than objective test questions, which simply assess knowledge (Scheurman & Newman, 1998). This enables students to investigate the subject matter in great depth and see more deeply the complexities of an issue and to then express their understanding or findings to others (Scheurman & Newman, 1998).

Pivotal Decisions With Technology: Should Students Develop Their Own Intellectual Contributions or Regurgitate the Teachers' Answers?

As discussed previously, the findings from a qualitative research study on the integration of technology in social studies is shared periodically throughout this book. The findings identified pivotal decisions that were made by social studies teachers that could make or break a lesson. The names of the social studies teachers and their schools have been altered to protect their confidentiality. Findings from the study are based on thirty-five hours that the author spent observing three social studies classrooms with 1:1 computers taking field notes, interviewing students and teachers, and collecting artifacts. The limitation of the study was that it only involved rural high schools in the upper Midwest.

Mr. Jones, a social studies teacher at River High School, designed a lesson where students read about slavery on the class Edmodo Internet site. Each student was challenged to consider diverse perspectives on the slavery issue prior to the Civil War. He had students consider the perspective of an abolitionist in the North and a plantation owner in the South. Each student had to cite either the Declaration of Independence or the United States Constitution to justify their position. About one-third of the students wrote from the perspective of the Southern plantation owner and two-thirds from the perspective of a Northern abolitionist. As a result, the students developed their own intellectual contributions on the subject matter rather than simply reproducing what their teacher had shared with them about the subject or what they had read elsewhere. This helped the lesson to succeed and served as an excellent example of AIW using technology.

Mr. Smith, a world geography teacher at Bluff High School, had his students use Google Maps to compare and contrast different regions of the world. This enabled his students to participate in critical thinking since they had to construct their own knowledge about certain regions of the country and the world. Students were able to identify similarities and differences between different regions of the world, which challenged them to think deeply about the geography of our world. Google Maps also enabled his students to study the topography of various regions and enabled them to become more familiar with latitude and longitude. Most importantly, the students had the opportunity to develop their own intellectual contributions on big ideas pertaining to geographic concepts, rather than memorizing information from these maps through drill-and-practice exercises. It also served as an example of AIW.

Mr. Brown, an American history teacher at Bridge High School, taught his students about the battles in France and England during his World War II unit. The lesson began with a map of Europe on the whiteboard for students to view, and he posed a question: "What do you think was Germany's strategy?" His students also read an article on their iPads that Mr. Brown had sent them that provided in-depth information on the German strategy. Each student had to answer questions about the reading on their iPads and send the answers directly to Mr. Brown. The students were able to write their answers for the worksheet using their fingertips on the iPad. The students seemed to enjoy this feature. Most importantly, the students were using technology to construct their knowledge of the subject matter, rather than simply reproducing what their teacher had told them about it.

As mentioned previously, focus questions can help students identify the main idea that they are supposed to investigate during a social studies lesson. Focus questions, which are associated with AIW, encourage students to develop their own intellectual contributions rather than regurgitating the teachers' answers. They enable students to more easily identify the key concepts or powerful ideas (Harris & Yocum, 2000). Middle and secondary teachers can use focus questions to enable students to identify big ideas when they use technology to research information pertaining to the social studies curriculum. Focus questions are also characterized by questions that elicit higher-level thinking, in-depth knowledge, conversation about the subject matter, and connection to the real world (Harris & Yocum, 2000).

The focus questions used by Mr. Jones greatly helped to keep the focus of the lessons and unit on big ideas. He used them on a daily basis, and there were focus questions that were part of a year-long focus. These questions included "Who is included and excluded from We the People?" He also featured another focus question that read "What is the American Identity?" In this question, he expected students to identify examples of unique individuals and examples of freedom and conflict. These questions proved to be most helpful in fostering higher-level thinking with the students in his high school social studies classroom. Focus questions were not used as frequently in the other classrooms that I had the opportunity to observe during the research study. It was more difficult for these students to make connections about the subject matter they were learning when the focus question tended to be on the simple recall of information or a lower-level thinking question, rather than on big ideas or answering thick questions. These findings suggest it is critically important that technology-rich lessons in middle and secondary social studies 1) use focus questions, and 2) the focus questions should foster critical thinking about the subject matter in the social studies curriculum. This can enable middle and secondary students to more easily develop their own intellectual contributions about the subject matter when they use technology.

Mr. Brown used some focus questions. During a lesson on World War II, he posed a question at the beginning of class that asked "How did Hitler gain power in Germany?" The entire focus of the lesson involved this key issue. He presented a lecture that gave students some background information on Hitler's rise to power. Mr. Brown used Near Pad, an app that specializes in interactive lectures. The app enabled his students to follow along with his lecture on their personal iPads. He was also able to control when the students could view each slide on their iPads so they could stay at the same pace as his lecture. Mr. Brown used the app to pause and ask students questions during his lecture on Hitler's rise to power and to check for their understanding of the subject matter. He also assessed students on significant details from his lecture, including Hitler's childhood, his experience as a soldier during World War I, and *Mein Kampf*. The students then used the Near Pad app to produce a graphic organizer where they identified the key events that were turning points in Hitler's rise to power. In summary, the key to Mr. Brown's lesson was the focus question that aligned the entire lesson around the big idea of Hitler's rise to power. This example speaks to the value of using focus questions in technology-rich lessons in the middle and secondary social studies classroom.

Theory and Practice: Firsthand Experience Using Technology and Authentic Intellectual Work in World Geography

Mr. Curt Deutsch, a teacher at Dubuque Hempstead High School (Iowa), has his students use AIW in a World Geography course. There is one unit that focuses on the Human Development Index (HDI). According to the United Nations, HDI is a way to statistically measure the quality of life in each country around the world. HDI takes into consideration three different dimensions. These include health, education, and living standards. The four indicators that serve as measurements for these dimensions include the following: life expectancy at birth, mean years of schooling, expected years of schooling, and gross national income per capita (United Nations, 2013). Each student in the course learns about these important dimensions and indicators that can improve the quality of life for those who are less fortunate around the world. The students then have an opportunity to focus in depth on how the quality of life, or HDI, could be improved for a specific country that they investigate.

Each student was placed in a group of three to four students for this project, and they worked with a teacher candidate from Loras College. The students were given a list of countries to pick from. It is important to point out that the list included countries that have a very poor standard of living. In fact, they are some of the very lowest in the world, according to their HDI. Some of the countries that the students picked from included Sierra Leone, Burkina Faso, Guinea-Bissau, Niger, Mali, Mozambique, Chad, Ethiopia, Congo, and Burundi. The goal was for the students to determine a strategy to help the country raise its HDI over the next five to ten years.

The students learned about four major strategies that can be used to raise HDI. These strategies included the following proposals: 1) poverty reduction, 2) trade not aid, 3) good governance, and 4) sustainable development. The students had to identify which strategy would be best suited for the country that they were investigating. Interestingly, the students learned that there was a nonprofit agency willing to award a grant for $50,000,000 to one nation that developed a project using one of these strategies. The students needed to develop a plan that they could present to the agency's directors to persuade them that the agency's money would be well spent in the country that they were investigating. This took a great deal of research about the country in order to develop an appropriate plan.

Mr. Deutsch's students spent two entire class periods in the computer lab conducting research using the Internet. Each group member spent a great deal of time researching the country that they were assigned to. The students were eager to learn more about the factors that contributed to the country's low HDI ranking. Most of the students used the World CIA Factbook Internet website to learn more about the country that they were working with. They also had to learn about the four strategies that could be used to potentially raise the country's HDI ranking. Much of this information could be found on Internet webpages sponsored by the United Nations. Due to their extensive research online, the students discovered that there was plenty of information on the Internet to help shape their proposal.

The students learned about the specific project details from a rubric that Mr. Deutsch had developed. AIW was at the heart of the project design. The students learned that they were required to present their proposal to the nonprofit agency using a Prezi, which is a user-friendly online Web 2.0 interactive tool. The most important part of the grade for the project was the proposal that they had put together to potentially improve the HDI ranking for the country that they had investigated. The rubric identified the need for students to convey a strong argument on why their project proposal should be funded in the amount of $50,000,000. In addition, the students needed to address in their proposal the key problems that plagued their nation. Otherwise, it would be difficult for the nonprofit agency to award their nation the grant money. This was no easy task for the students. They had to work collaboratively to develop a detailed plan that could solve some of the nation's problems.

According to the project rubric, each group had to develop an actual budget on how they would spend the $50,000,000 grant money if their proposal was funded by the nonprofit agency. This motivated the students to learn a great deal of information about the country they were investigating and about the four major strategies that could be used to improve the lives of the citizens. There was a great deal of critical thinking among the students as they worked collaboratively on this authentic issue. Students had to solve problems together and create solutions that could potentially work. Most importantly, the students had to know enough about the country, its problems, and the possible solution in order to convince the nonprofit agency to award their proposal.

The students also learned from the rubric that there were clear, step-by-step expectations on what they had to include in each of the Prezi presentation slides. For example, the students were required to include an overview of their nation and the general problems facing it in slides one and two. In particular, students were asked to describe the political, economic, and social challenges facing the nation. This set the stage for the rest of the presentation to the nonprofit agency. In slides three and four, the students were required to introduce the strategy that they proposed for their nation to raise the HDI for its citizens. This had to include one of the four strategies (poverty reduction, trade not aid, good governance, and sustainable development). The students were asked to identify the potential positives and negatives of the strategy that they had devised to address the ills of their nation. In addition, the students needed to present a detailed outline on how all of the $50,000,000 would be spent. Mr. Deutsch also reminded the students to take into consideration how much things cost in their country. Finally, in slides five and six, the students needed to identify how the project would be measured in terms of success or failure to improve the nation's HDI. In slide seven, the final slide, the students were asked to explain how the project will develop the country and increase its score on the HDI. As a result, the students needed to consider all of the in-depth research they had conducted about their nation and the analysis they had conducted on ways to potentially solve the issues facing it.

As a result of the project, the students in this World Geography course had the opportunity to problem-solve an issue that had a great deal of value beyond school. The students were involved in a lot of decision making and had an opportunity to present their findings to others. They developed their own intellectual contributions about the subject matter, which is one of the underpinnings behind AIW. Technology enabled the students to participate in a great deal of research and to provide a medium to share their proposal with others. Prezi is an example of how students can produce products using technology in the middle and secondary social studies classroom to provide evidence of what they have learned. The students in Mr. Deutsch's class enjoyed the technology-rich experience, and AIW provided the framework for students to think deeply about HDI. Readers will hopefully find that this example can help them shape their own lessons using AIW with technology. There are many possibilities for AIW in the middle and secondary social studies classroom equipped with technology.

Inside Classrooms: Using Technology and Authentic Intellectual Work in American History

Ms. Brenda Foust teaches American History at Hempstead High School in Dubuque, Iowa. She also serves on a technology committee for the Dubuque Community School District. During the past few years, she initiated a local history project where her students researched how World War I had an impact on the citizens of Dubuque. The students then shared their historical findings by producing an Internet podcast using Audacity. AIW is evident in the projects produced by her students. Each student works in a small group of two to three students where they develop their own intellectual contributions based on their historical research.

Each group researched in depth one subtopic on Dubuque and World War I. Some of the topics included 1) people who dodged the draft; 2) citizens who violated the Sedition Act by allegedly being pro-German sympathizers; 3) businesses in Dubuque that changed their name because they sounded too German; 4) citizens who supported the war effort by conserving fuel, purchasing liberty loans, and growing war gardens; 5) how women contributed to the war effort by serving in the Red Cross; 6) the veterans from Dubuque who served in World War I; and 7) how Armistice Day was celebrated in Dubuque. Each student in the group had the opportunity to spend three class periods on the campus of Loras College and was assisted by Mr. Michael Gibson, the director of the Center for Dubuque History. The students had the opportunity to use the microfilm machine to research newspaper articles from 1917 and 1918 newspapers. These primary sources provided firsthand accounts on the profound impact that the war had on the lives of people in Dubuque during this era. It is important to note that these were topics that were discussed in their textbook, but the opportunity to see examples from their own community made this distant war seem much more relevant to their lives.

During the project, each student examined at least two different primary sources. They had the opportunity to compare and contrast the insights from the sources they examined with those of their fellow group members. Many of these were historical findings that had been long forgotten in the city of Dubuque. This presented an exciting opportunity for these high school students. Ms. Foust asked each group to share their findings with others in their community by producing an Internet podcast that was two to three minutes in length. The students used Audacity to record the podcast and save it as an MP3 file. Most importantly, the students shared their own intellectual contributions with others beyond the walls of the classroom. This made the project an excellent example of AIW. As noted earlier, AIW does not involve students simply memorizing information from a teacher's lecture or regurgitating information from a textbook. AIW challenges students to think deeply about the subject matter by participating in a great deal of analysis around an essential question or focus question from a disciplinary inquiry. Ms. Foust's essential question for this unit included the following: Evaluate the impact of World War I on American history. Did it have a positive or negative impact on America at home and the American image abroad?

The students answered Question Answer Relationship (QAR) questions about each of the primary sources that they investigated. Due to this reading strategy, each student was more easily able to identify the necessary details from each newspaper article that they had the opportunity to view firsthand. Students identified pertinent information related to the subtopic that they were assigned and challenged to think deeply about some of the main ideas presented in the newspaper article. For example, some of the QAR questions required students to connect several different details found in the newspaper article to comprehend the main idea related to their subtopic on Dubuque during World War I. Yet, other questions simply asked students to identify something that was found exactly within the text itself. Most importantly, the students were learning from primary sources from their very own community. Often, the newspaper articles captivated students because they provided insights that were much more interesting than any from the traditional textbook they were using.

Students were also challenged to participate in Summarizing, Contextualizing, Inferring, Monitoring, and Corroborating (SCIM-C) questions where they had to compare and contrast all of the primary sources that each group member had investigated. This enabled each student within the group to more easily see connections between the primary sources and identify the major themes that were emerging from their research. Due to the QAR and SCIM-C questions, students were ready to share their historical findings by writing and producing their own Internet podcast using their own intellectual contributions on this unique subject matter.

The students were presented with a rubric or scoring guide that outlined the expectations of the project. Historical information was the biggest point of emphasis for the project grade. The students needed to include at least five historical findings from the newspapers in their podcast script. Each of these historical findings needed to relate to the World War I subtopic that their group was responsible for investigating while at the Dubuque Center for History. The rubric also required students to write a script before they began to record their Internet podcast. It was important that the script not have any historical or grammatical errors, and each group needed to cite their sources at the end of their podcast.

Area	Met (2 points)	Emerging (1 point)	Not Met (0 points)
Historical Information	The students used what they had learned in the podcast. The podcast shows evidence of their interpretation by using at least five examples from their newspaper articles. The focus of the podcast is their Dubuque during World War I topic.	The students generally used what they had learned in the podcast. The podcast shows evidence of their interpretation, but only used three to four findings from their newspaper articles. The focus of the podcast is their Dubuque during World War I topic.	The students failed to use what they had learned in the podcast. The podcast shows little evidence of their interpretation, with fewer than three examples from their newspaper articles. The focus of the podcast is their Dubuque during World War I topic.
Historical Accuracy	The students included all relevant information that pertains to their topic in a way that is comprehensive and thorough. There are no historical errors, and the sources are cited at the end of the podcast.	The students provided some information that is helpful for their podcast, but could have added a few supporting details. There are one to three historical errors. The sources are cited at the end of the podcast.	The students failed to include the necessary relevant/accurate information. There are more than three historical errors and/or the sources are not cited at the end of the podcast.
Podcast Length	The students created a podcast that was two to three minutes in length.	The students created a podcast that was one to two minutes in length.	The students created a podcast that was less than one minute in length.
Podcast Format	The students used one of the following formats for the podcast: radio commercial, radio show, newscast, public service announcement, or talk show with interviews. The students incorporated music and spoke clearly to make the podcast appealing to listeners.	The students used one of the proper formats for the podcast. The students used music and generally spoke clearly to make the podcast appealing to listeners.	The students failed to use one of the proper formats and/or did not use music or speak clearly during the podcast.
Written Script	The script includes two or fewer spelling and grammar errors. The script used the proper written podcast script format.	The script includes three to five spelling and grammar errors. The script generally used the proper written podcast script format.	The script has more than five spelling and grammar errors. The script failed to follow the proper written podcast script format.

Figure 2.2 Internet Podcast Project: Dubuque and World War I.

Source: Brenda Foust and Scott K. Scheuerell.

As mentioned, the rubric identified that each podcast be two to three minutes in length, and students could use a variety of formats to deliver it (see Figure 2.2). Some of these included the following formats: radio commercial, newscast, public service announcement, or talk show with interviews.

Podcast: Armistice Day in Dubuque

One group of students spent the entire project researching how Armistice Day was recognized in Dubuque. The students were able to discover several newspaper accounts of how citizens celebrated this event in diverse ways. They quickly realized that it was a memorable day in the lives of Dubuque residents. The students decided to present their historical findings by using a radio talk show format. They titled their program *The Dubuque Daily Show*. This enabled the students to present to listeners how the citizens of Dubuque celebrated Armistice Day in very diverse ways.

The podcast begins with an interview of a resident who witnessed a downtown business in Dubuque being vandalized on Armistice Day. According to the eyewitness, the front door of the business was painted yellow and the store was vandalized. The eyewitness suggested that the business owner was targeted because he had allegedly said pro-German remarks earlier during the war.

Later in the podcast, there was another eyewitness who reported that he had seen wild celebrations taking place around the city of Dubuque on Armistice Day. He suggested that these celebrations lasted well into the night and included a great deal of excitement. During the interview, he conveyed that he had seen many people shouting and holding banners to celebrate the Allied win in Europe. He also conveyed that he heard people singing the National Anthem and he witnessed a dummy of the German kaiser. Yet, he conveyed that other residents of Dubuque celebrated Armistice Day by going to church services throughout the city.

The students finished their podcast by including an eyewitness account of the wild scene that took place across the Mississippi River in East Dubuque, Illinois. The eyewitness suggested that there was a great deal of drinking taking place and many people were very excited to learn that the war had ended. However, one man in the crowd was accused of being a German sympathizer and a huge fight broke out. Due to these vivid accounts, the students had successfully featured the varied ways that Armistice Day was celebrated in their own community. The students were able to describe these accounts in great detail due to the historical research they had conducted from the Dubuque newspapers in 1918. As a result, the students were well positioned to share their own intellectual contributions on this memorable day in the history of Dubuque, Iowa. The project also serves as an excellent example of AIW in a technology-rich classroom.

Podcast: The Home Front in Dubuque

During the project, there was a group that specifically focused their historical research on how the citizens of Dubuque rallied to support the troops overseas. They found many articles from the Dubuque newspapers that discussed how the residents of the city grew war gardens, purchased liberty bonds, and conserved energy. These were topics that were discussed somewhat in their textbook, but this project enabled the students to see how this actually took place on a grand scale in their own community. The students presented these findings using a radio talk show format.

The podcast began by stating their radio talk show was taking place on January 1, 1918. They featured an interview with the chairperson of the war bond sales in Dubuque. The chairperson conveyed that these war bonds, or liberty bonds, were used to purchase supplies and weapons for the American troops in the battlefields of Europe. He also encouraged Dubuque residents to grow their own garden in their backyards, since this enabled the government to more easily feed the troops overseas. The students also included an interview with someone from the food council. She pointed out that it would be helpful for Dubuque citizens to turn in any excess flour and sugar that they had. This would also be used for the troops in the war effort. Finally, the students included a great deal of information about the "lightless nights." They detailed how the lights in Dubuque would be turned off after 7:00 p.m. every Tuesday, Wednesday, and Thursday evening. This would enable the government to conserve energy during the war.

Podcast: Draft Dodgers in Dubuque

There was another group who focused their historical research on the alleged draft dodgers that were identified in Dubuque during World War I. In Dubuque, they were sometimes known as slackers. Many students were surprised to learn that many people in their own community had taken a stance to avoid the draft. The students featured their findings in a talk show format where they identified many of these individuals. One of the individuals that they identified was a thirty-three-year-old Dubuque resident who lied about his age so he wouldn't have to serve in the United States Army. The students also featured a school teacher from the Dubuque area who had lied about his age to avoid being drafted. His father paid a $1,000 bond to bail him out of jail. In the podcast, the students pointed out that he served as a poor example to his students. The students also shared the story of an individual who refused to serve in the Red Cross, which was supporting the troops. Later, the students pointed out that the Dubuque city council had cracked down on those who had avoided the draft or allegedly made any pro-German remarks during the war.

Summary

Technology, when used in conjunction with AIW, challenges students to think much more deeply about the subject matter in the middle and secondary social studies curriculum. It can be leveraged to make teaching and learning more relevant to students. AIW provides teachers with the foundation for how this can happen by facilitating active learning with technology. Each student can then realize how the subject matter in the social studies curriculum can have value beyond school. Most importantly, each student can develop their own intellectual contributions about the subject matter. In the past, students memorized information from a teacher's lecture or details from the textbook. AIW provides teachers with a user-friendly framework to implement this in their own classroom. The examples in this chapter show that this is possible in the middle and secondary social studies classroom using technology.

Student construction of knowledge, disciplined inquiry, and value beyond school were the key ingredients featured in these examples. Each student also had to connect their prior knowledge to the new information that they were learning from their investigations. In addition, each example involved an in-depth examination of the subject matter in the social studies curriculum. This allowed the students to understand the complexity of the issue they were investigating much more deeply and develop their own intellectual contributions on the subject matter, where they could use technology to communicate their findings with others beyond the walls of the classroom. In fact, many of the podcasts and HDI Prezis were the first of their kind produced on these topics to be posted to the Internet.

References

Harris, D.H. & Yocum, M. (2000). *PASS. Powerful and authentic social studies. A professional development program for teachers.* Washington, D.C.: National Council for the Social Studies.

Howland, J.L., Jonassen, D.H., & Marra, R. M. (2012). *Meaningful learning with technology* (4th ed.). Indianapolis, IN: Pearson.

Newman, F.M., King, B.M., & Carmichael, D.L. (2007). *Authentic instruction and assessment.* Des Moines, IA: Iowa Department of Education.

Scheurman, G. & Newman, F.M. (1998). Authentic intellectual work in social studies: Putting, performance before pedagogy. *Social Education, 1,* 23–25.

United Nations. (2013). *Human development reports.* Human development index. Retrieved from http://hdr.undp.org/en/statistics/hdi. Accessed 11/15/13.

3

COOPERATIVE LEARNING

Currently, many social studies teachers are using cooperative learning. In addition, more classrooms are equipped with technology where students have access to the Internet. Therefore, it only makes sense to explore how cooperative learning and technology can be leveraged together in the social studies classroom. There will be a discussion in this chapter on the argument for using cooperative learning with technology and the structures that are needed to implement it successfully in the social studies classroom.

In the past, many teachers have perceived the use of the Internet in the classroom to be an individual activity, where students work silently by themselves viewing an Internet webpage. The opportunity for students to collaborate face to face with their peers on topics they investigated online offers a great deal of promise. Cooperative learning strategies like Think-Pair-Share and Jigsaw can guide Internet investigations in the social studies classroom. Cooperative learning solves the dilemma of having students in the classroom working alone and with no opportunity to develop the collaborative skills needed for citizenship in our democracy. Examples of cooperative learning structures using graphic organizers, Think-Pair-Share, and Jigsaw will be shared in this chapter to give readers insights on how to get started utilizing this approach. These examples can be easily replicated with other objectives in the social studies curriculum.

Argument for Cooperative Learning Structures

The introduction of the 1:1 laptop program in my classroom gave me the opportunity to see how cooperative learning structures can easily mesh with lessons using technology. Each of the students benefited by developing skills needed for citizenship in our democracy and simultaneously learned the content in the social studies curriculum. Borich (2014) wrote that "most of our attitudes and values are formed by discussing what we know or think with others" (p. 354). In social studies, there are many opportunities for students to discuss what they have learned with their peers and share their opinion on a wide array of issues. This can involve students talking about what they have learned from primary sources that they have viewed on the Internet or debating a controversial issue after researching it in depth on the Internet. Due to experiences such as these, students benefit by encountering perspectives that may be different from their own (Borich, 2014). The social studies classroom equipped with technology is well suited to foster this type of teaching and learning.

Borich (2014) argues that cooperative learning works because it forces students to interact with their classmates and they are challenged to think deeply about the subject matter by working collaboratively. Cooperative learning fosters higher-order thinking since students are involved in a great deal of discourse where they are challenged to participate in "analyzing, synthesizing, and decision making" (Borich, 2014, p. 355). As discussed earlier in the book, students can certainly learn from a teacher's lecture or readings from the textbook, but these teaching and learning activities rarely challenge students to think critically and problem-solve (Borich, 2014). Cooperative learning can be used to leverage these types of skill sets in social studies since it challenges students to participate in higher-level thinking and problem solving.

Cooperative Learning Structures

Cooperative learning involves positive interdependence (P), individual accountability (I), equal participation (E), and simultaneous interaction (S), also known as P.I.E.S. (Kagan, 1999). Positive interdependence (P) involves students who are assigned a job or role within a group. In order for the group to complete the larger task assigned to them, everyone in the group must complete their job or role. Individual accountability (I) is when activities in class are structured so students within the group may get a different grade, especially if someone is not completing their assigned job or role. As a result, there is much more accountability for students in a group structure. This is critically important since there are frequently students who do not pull their weight in collaborative structures.

Equal participation (E) takes place when students perceive that their job or role is roughly the same work load as their peers in the group. As a result, there are no hard feelings amongst the group members as to who is pulling a more significant part of the workload. Finally, simultaneous interaction (S) is the goal of a cooperative learning structure. Ideally, everyone in the group is actively involved with their job or role during the entirety of the cooperative learning activity (Kagan, 1999). In this type of teaching and learning structure, each student has something to do, rather than having students waiting around for partners to finish their assigned task. Consequently, everyone is actively engaged as students collaboratively construct their knowledge, and the likelihood of on-task behaviors increases greatly. These cooperative learning structures, or P.I.E.S, can help any social studies teacher more easily put into place a user-friendly framework to help their students succeed when they design lessons using technology.

Borich (2014) emphasizes that cooperative learning has a great deal of merit due to the amount of task specialization. Each student has a specific task to complete, which plays a part in producing the final product for the group. Due to the specialization of roles within the group, students learn to work together to produce a final product. For example, students can be researchers, recorders, or summarizers (Borich, 2014). Students quickly discover that much can be accomplished when they share and collaborate with one another (Borich, 2014).

It is also important that teachers communicate their expectations for cooperative learning (Borich, 2014). Frequently, this is where cooperative learning breaks down into a more chaotic classroom situation where students are not working toward the objective in the social studies curriculum. Borich (2014) warns that this can happen if teachers fail to communicate their expectations, resulting in a lesson where "cooperative learning will quickly degenerate into undisciplined discussion, in which there may be numerous uninvolved and passive participants" (p. 357). In order to prevent this from happening, it is vitally important for teachers to communicate their expectations before students begin working collaboratively.

Teachers can make it a point to emphasize collaborative skills when students work in groups. Some of these collaborative skills include an emphasis on how to communicate your ideas and feelings to others and to respect the opinions of your peers (Johnson & Johnson, 2005, as cited in Borich, 2014). Students can learn how to paraphrase the viewpoints of others in their group and recognize how to negotiate meanings within their group (Johnson & Johnson, 2005, as cited in Borich, 2014). Each of these skills is critically important to develop participatory citizens in our democracy and to work toward the greater good. They can also be a point of emphasis in technology-rich lessons in middle and secondary social studies classrooms where students are working collaboratively. The role of the teacher during cooperative learning is to intervene briefly with each group to keep students on task and to make sure they are identifying the necessary connections with the subject matter in the social studies curriculum.

Pivotal Decisions With Technology: Group Work or Cooperative Learning?

Collaborative learning was an integral part of technology integration in each of the social studies classrooms that participated in the qualitative research study. Students were placed in groups almost daily. These groups ranged in size from two students to as many as five or six students. However, the students rarely had any jobs or roles assigned to them during their group work. These were pivotal decisions, specifically the size of each group and whether to assign jobs or roles for each group member. Frequently, it should be noted, these decisions would arguably make or break each lesson.

In Mr. Jones' class at River High School, for example, he had students work in pairs and each student was assigned a job or role to investigate landmark Supreme Court decisions related to the Civil Rights movement. This provided the necessary structure as the students investigated the following Supreme Court cases: *Dred Scott v. Sanford, Plessy v. Ferguson*, and *Loving v. Virginia*. Each student viewed one of the Supreme Court decisions and shared what they learned about it with their partners. The students then answered questions posed by Mr. Jones. Some of these questions included the following: 1) What was the issue presented to the Supreme Court? 2) What factors involving the case were presented to the Supreme Court? 3) What was the decision of the Supreme Court? 4) What was the rationale for it? 5) What was the effect of the Supreme Court decision? At the end of the lesson, the students had to answer how these Supreme Court cases fit into their thoughts and opinions on the essential question for the unit. They had to share whether they felt the average person or the federal government won the Civil Rights movement. During the lesson, group members came together to share their thoughts on each of the questions presented, and a great deal of meaningful dialogue took place in the classroom. Each student recognized that they had a job or role to play. This resulted in a great deal of student engagement. The increased on-task behaviors resulted in students making the necessary connections between the subject matter they investigated and the larger essential question for their unit on the Civil Rights movement. The lesson in Mr. Jones' class succeeded due to the cooperative learning roles or jobs that each of the students had during the activity with technology.

In the World Geography class at Bluff High School, Mr. Smith had his students work in groups where they were assigned a country in Europe to investigate online and consider what role the European Union should have in determining health care in Europe. Mr. Smith added that each group would have to present their ideas to the classroom at a later date. Each student had the opportunity to participate in a simulation where they had to represent the views of the nation they were assigned to. Mr. Smith placed them in groups of three to four students, and most of them used an Internet webpage on their topic from NPR (National Public Radio). While the students researched the topic online, Mr. Smith walked around the classroom to check on each group and see how they were doing.

In most instances, it appeared that these groups were too big to keep everyone busy or on task during the project. No jobs or roles were assigned to each group member. In retrospect, it may have helped greatly if the groups were much smaller—perhaps two students per group—and for students to have a job or role assigned to them, much like you would find in a cooperative learning structure.

It may have enhanced the likelihood of productivity and learning for everyone involved in the group structure. The students may have also benefited from additional structures such as a teaching and learning strategy affiliated with cooperative learning. For example, Jigsaw or Think-Pair-Share would have arguably enhanced this collaborative lesson by focusing each student much more on their specific task for their group and to help them identify more easily the main ideas that surfaced from their investigations using the Internet.

In Mr. Brown's Modern United States History class at Bridge High School, he had his students work in teams of three to five to investigate a topic related to his lesson on President Franklin D. Roosevelt's New Deal. He asked the groups to investigate online the following questions regarding Social Security: 1) What are Social Security benefits? 2) Is Social Security a Ponzi scheme? 3) What are the pros and cons of Social Security? He emphasized to the students the need to write four to five sentences per answer. During the lesson, Mr. Brown moved from group to group to check and see if his students understood the material and clarified any misunderstandings they may have had about the subject matter. This seemed to work well for Mr. Brown since he was making sure that the students were on task and he challenged them to think independently for themselves.

His students took notes as they conducted research online by using different apps that were featured on their iPad computer. They used two apps called Pages and Notability to take notes on the information that they found on the Internet. The students found a great deal of information on the New Deal and Social Security. Mr. Brown spent part of the class period showing me how easy it was for him to e-mail his students the worksheet questions via his personal iPad and how the students could easily e-mail him the answers to these questions using their personal iPad computer.

The students enjoyed working collaboratively. Mr. Brown developed some excellent higher-order thinking questions for their investigation. The only flaw of the lesson was that the students were placed in groups that were way too big to keep each student actively engaged in the subject matter and the students did not have a specific job or role. Due to the structure of the activity, some students naturally did a great deal more than other students, as there were no clear expectations on who was responsible for building the final product.

As mentioned previously, group work was a common theme in each of the three classrooms. Sometimes this included jobs or roles, but in many cases it did not. Frequently, students were placed in groups and then determined on their own which group member was responsible for doing each task to complete their project or assignment rather than using the notion of equal participation from the P.I.E.S. cooperative learning structure (equal participation). Sometimes this worked and sometimes it did not. According to Spencer Kagan (1999), an expert on collaborative learning, cooperative learning structures are a way to move group work forward and help everyone involved become much more productive with their class time. Students can become easily frustrated when they are left with most of the work. This is when cooperative learning is sometimes given a bad reputation.

In summary, social studies teachers who find themselves in classrooms using technology are faced with a pivotal decision on how to structure collaborative learning in their lessons. It is a vital part of their decision making to consider the size of the group; in most instances, I would suggest two students per group, rather than a group that is too big without enough jobs or roles to keep everyone in the group on task. The actual jobs or roles designed and assigned by the social studies teacher are critically important. Students are often upset about the inconsistency among group members related to their perceived workload in these technology-rich lessons. In group work, students are not given assigned jobs or roles. Cooperative learning, with jobs or roles, is critically important when students are working collaboratively with technology in the middle and secondary social studies classroom.

Theory and Practice: Firsthand Experience Using Technology and Cooperative Learning in American History

Cooperative learning structures guided each of the examples in the pages that follow. Students were assigned jobs or roles as they used technology to investigate topics in the social studies classroom. There was some built-in accountability for each student to complete their assigned job or role and share what they had learned with their peers. Each of the examples is from an American History class in a high school classroom where each student had a laptop computer. The students were familiar with the cooperative learning structures since they participated in them frequently throughout the school year. This helped classroom transitions since there was a great deal of familiarity with the expectations for the cooperative learning structure. The classroom also featured a liquid crystal display (LCD) projector, which enabled students to easily follow along step by step on the Internet. This also enabled students to see the graphic organizers that were used to identify the main ideas from the online investigations. Each student was familiar with the expectations for the cooperative learning activity since they were frequently posted on the board and spoken aloud before the activity began.

Manifest Destiny: Using a Graphic Organizer With a Cooperative Learning Activity

In 1845, President Polk gave his inaugural address to his fellow citizens in the midst of an historical era labeled "Manifest Destiny" by historians. During the period, many Americans, including President Polk, believed God intended the United States to expand from the Atlantic to the Pacific Ocean—specifically, to spread free enterprise, civil liberty, and democracy to all citizens (Woods & Gatewood, 1998). President Polk's inaugural address gives students an opportunity to see how the president outlined his thoughts related to Manifest Destiny. The online source can be found at the following Internet link: http://avalon.law.yale.edu/19th__ century/polk.asp.

The webpage is sponsored by Yale University Law School. The students can be assigned to pairs for a cooperative learning activity. Partner "A" can be assigned the researcher job and partner "B" assigned the secretarial job. Each group can be asked to create a bubble organizer, much like an outline, where they find details from the inaugural address that serve as examples of the Manifest Destiny mind-set in 1845.

Partner "B" can begin by writing "Manifest Destiny" in the middle of their page and wait for partner "A" to find additional details. Students will find evidence of the president's goal to spread American interests westward. For example, in his inaugural address, President Polk conveyed his goal by stating "our domain extends from ocean to ocean" (Yale University Law School, 2009). Interestingly, the debate on expansion was a key issue in the election of 1844 and helped Polk win the presidency (Woods & Gatewood, 1998). Students can write the concept of expansion down as one of the main ideas in a smaller circle, which can branch out from the main circle in the middle of their page. Partner "A" will discover additional details that supported the president's rationale for expansion. He stated the nation had grown from thirteen to twenty-eight states and the population had grown from three to twenty million (Yale University Law School, 2009).

Later in the inaugural address, partner "A" will find more details to support the concept of expansion. President Polk said, "The Republic of Texas has made known her desire to come into our Union, to form a part of our Confederacy and enjoy with us the blessings of liberty secured and guaranteed by our Constitution" (Yale University Law School, 2009). Texas was interested in being annexed by the United States for a variety of reasons. The young republic suffered from serious financial debt and was involved in a conflict with Mexico. Meanwhile, the United States feared Great Britain would make claim to Mexico. President Polk also saw the financial benefits of adding Texas. He felt expansion was necessary to fulfill a vision of a young American nation where there was enough land for farmers to spread out across the west (Woods & Gatewood, 1998).

The Oregon Territory was another feature of Polk's inaugural address that supported Manifest Destiny's goal of expansion. In his speech, the president stated his belief that it is "the right of the United States to that portion of our territory which lies beyond the Rocky Mountains" (Yale University Law School, 2009). Partner "A" can share this information with partner "B" and include it in the bubble organizer. President Polk also gave some historical context to support his desire to spread American values westward. He reminded his fellow citizens that "eighty years ago our population was confined on the west by the ridge of the Alleghenies" and later "filled the eastern valley of the Mississippi, adventurously ascended the Missouri to its headsprings, and are already engaged in establishing the blessings of self-government in valleys of which the rivers flow to the Pacific" (Yale University Law School, 2009).

In the third paragraph of the inaugural address, partner "A" will discover evidence to support President Polk's and other pro-expansionists' belief that God was on their side. In the address, President Polk tells the American people, "In assuming responsibilities so vast I fervently invoke the aid of that Almighty Ruler of the Universe in whose hands are the destinies of nations and of men to guard this Heaven-favored land" (Yale University Law School, 2009). Partner "A" can inform partner "B" to write down the notion of divine intervention, and it can became another circle that branches out from the main circle on their page. President Polk had his critics. Many Americans believed Manifest Destiny was simply an excuse for greedy businessmen to make a great deal of money. Land speculators, railroad builders, and other businessmen gained substantially from President Polk's desire for westward expansion (Woods & Gatewood, 1998).

Great Depression: Using a Think-Pair-Share Cooperative Learning Activity

President Roosevelt took office in March 1933, in the midst of the Great Depression. Nearly thirteen million Americans were unemployed, and nine million had lost their savings accounts due to bank closures. Farm prices had fallen, and many small businesses closed throughout the country (Cayton, Perry, Reed, & Winkler, 2000). Students can learn more about the serious issues facing the nation by reading President Roosevelt's 1933 inaugural address. The speech can be found online at the Avalon Project Internet webpage using the following link: http://avalon. law.yale.edu/20th_century/froos1.asp.

The Think-Pair-Share cooperative learning activity is an effective method of getting students to discuss face to face information related to their social studies investigation online. The activity begins by partnering two students up so they can have the opportunity to discuss issues related to the online reading. During the "Think" portion of the activity, the teacher can pose questions to the students and have them individually write down their thoughts. Students will generally need about two minutes to reflect on the Internet source and put their thoughts into words. Next, during the "Pair" segment of the activity, students can discuss with their partner what they wrote down in regard to the question posed by the teacher. Students will likely need about two minutes to share what they had written with their partner. However, teachers can certainly give students more time if they seem to need it. During this portion of the lesson, the teacher can walk around the classroom and listen to the students discuss what they had written down on paper about the subject matter. Finally, in the "Share" phase of the activity, the teacher can facilitate a class-wide discussion on the topic. As a result, the students will learn a lot from each other. The teacher can write their thoughts down on the whiteboard and ask follow-up questions as needed.

The Think-Pair-Share activity takes a great deal of lesson planning. Many themes emerge from President Roosevelt's 1933 inaugural address. For example, students should be able to describe some of the problems facing the nation that were outlined by the president. The students will read online how President Roosevelt was concerned because "farmers find no markets for their produce" and "the savings of many years in thousands of families are gone" (Yale University Law School, 2009). During the class discussion, students can also share how the value of American products had decreased and taxes had risen (Yale University Law School, 2009).

Students will discover many additional lessons that President Roosevelt emphasized to the American people in his inaugural address, and they can share these with their partner. President Roosevelt warned the American people about the perception that material wealth was needed to be considered successful. He also spoke out against those involved in banking and business who were greedy. Moreover, he reminded his fellow citizens to help those in need by being a "loyal army willing to sacrifice for the good of the common discipline" (Yale University Law School, 2009).

Teachers may also want to ask students to compare and contrast the Great Depression with the troubling economy our nation is faced with today. Students will find some interesting similarities. For example, in 1933, President Roosevelt discussed the foreclosures of homes and the need for the federal government to provide relief. The president also discussed the need for tighter regulations on business. He stated, "There must be a strict supervision of all banking and credits and investments; there must be an end to speculation with other people's money" (Yale University Law School, 2009). Most students will recognize a similarity to the issues facing President Obama and the American people today.

Causes of the American Revolution: Using a Jigsaw Cooperative Learning Activity

In 1764, the British government had recently defeated her enemies in the French and Indian War. However, the victory came at a devastating expense. The British faced a war debt of 137 million pounds and an annual interest on the debt of 5 million pounds. Consequently, the government needed to raise revenue to pay off its debt (Woods & Gatewood, 1998). The British government decided to levy a series of taxes on the colonists. In their opinion, the tax was justified. They had waged an expensive war to protect the colonists from the French and Native Americans. Thus, the British government believed it was only fair for the colonists to pay their fair share of the war burden (Woods & Gatewood, 1998).

Students can work in pairs and participate in a Jigsaw cooperative learning activity to analyze themes that emerge from the Stamp Act and the Sugar Act. Partner "A" can read the Sugar Act and partner "B" can read the Stamp Act. Each student can take notes on the primary source they were assigned and later teach what they learned from the source to their partner. Each student will need to think deeply about what was important from the source that they read online and how to teach what they learned to their partner. In particular, they need to convey the information in an understandable manner. This is where most of the learning will likely occur since students will need to consider what details to keep and what details to leave out.

Partner "A" will need to think deeply about the details found in the Sugar Act of 1764. The legislation was felt by colonists throughout British North America. Students will quickly find the government's justification for the tax. The measure stated, "It is expedient that new provisions and regulations should be established for improving the revenue of this kingdom, and for extending and securing the navigation and commerce between Great Britain and your Majesty's dominions in America" (Yale University Law School, 2009).

By outlining the rationale for the taxation to the colonists, the legislation then proceeded to list new taxes, item by item. Students will soon discover most of the taxes had nothing to do with sugar. There were taxes levied on foreign cloth, coffee, wine, and many other items (Yale University Law School, 2009). In addition, the document lists how much of a tax or duty existed for each item. Plus, there were lengthy plans on how to raise the revenue if someone refused to pay the necessary money. For example, students can read about the specified consequences to those who refused to pay an import duty on wine. The document stated the "wine shall be sold to the best bidder" and the revenue will go to the government (Yale University Law School, 2009). The Sugar Act can be found on the Avalon Project website at the following link: http://avalon.law.yale.edu/18th_century/sugar_act_1764.asp.

The Stamp Act of 1765 also has many interesting details. Immediately, partner "B" will discover the rationale for levying the tax. The document stated the tax was necessary to help defray "the expenses of defending, protecting, and securing the said British colonies and plantations in America" (Yale University Law School, 2009). Moreover, students will discover how many people were affected by the tax in the colonies. A stamp or tax was needed for countless items purchased by colonists. Some of the items included newspapers, legal documents, pamphlets, liquor licenses, playing cards, and dice (Yale University Law School, 2009). Interestingly, the tax greatly affected newspaper editors and tavern owners, two of the main groups who shaped public opinion in the colonies (Woods & Gatewood,

1998). Students can combine their findings and produce a cause-and-effect chart that highlights what they discovered from the documents related to the causes of the American Revolution. The Stamp Act can be found at the Avalon Project Internet site at the following link: http://avalon.law.yale.edu/18th_century/stamp_act_1765.asp.

Inside Classrooms: Using Technology and Cooperative Learning in World History

Mr. Joel Allen is a World History teacher at Wahlert High School in Dubuque, Iowa. Each of the students in his classroom has a Lenovo ThinkPad computer. He has the students download the Audacity software to their computer. Audacity is free software that enables students to record audio and produce an MP3. The students are also instructed to legally download a karaoke version of a song that they can use with Audacity to produce a song on a topic found in Chapter 8 of their World History textbook. This chapter covered the Age of Enlightenment and the revolution during the 1700s.

The students are placed in groups of three to four. Mr. Allen instructs each of the groups to identify the job or role for each student that is a part of the group. The students can pick from the following list of jobs: secretary, lead researcher, song lyric supervisor, and project editor. Each student must complete their job or task in order to complete the song lyrics on a world history topic. The groups are allowed to pick a modern-day song, but they must develop their own lyrics based on the historical topic that they have chosen. There were several topics that the groups could pick from. Some of the topics included the Enlightenment, Adam Smith, French Revolution, neoclassical art, Horatio Nelson, the Haitian Revolution, Simon Bolivar, and Catherine the Great.

Mr. Allen developed an outline of steps to provide some structure for the groups to complete the projects. The steps he outlined included the following: 1) select a song, 2) select the content of the unit, 3) develop lyrics to go along with the song, 4) type out the actual lyrics to the song, 5) sing the song using Audacity, 6) save the song to a flash drive, and 7) turn in the finished project to Mr. Allen. Each of these steps enabled the students to more easily manage a significant project that took more than one class period to complete.

The rubric that Mr. Allen developed outlined some clear expectations for each of the students in his World History class. Four major categories were identified in the project that totaled 100 points. Historical content was worth 40 points. In order to get 40 points, the groups needed to cover all of the content for their topics that was emphasized in their class textbook. In addition, the students needed to include in their lyrics at least three additional facts about their topic that were not included in their textbook. This clearly challenged the students to conduct some additional research. The paperwork for the project was worth 20 points. In this category of the rubric, each student could not have any spelling or grammar errors in their musical lyrics to earn full credit, and their research had to be cited appropriately.

Mr. Allen also included another category that addressed the length of the project. This category was worth 20 points. Each student needed to have a three-minute musical lyric in order to earn the 20 points identified in the category. The last category of the rubric was worth 20 points and specified to the groups that the project needed to show some evidence of creativity and rhythm for the finished product. In particular, the rubric outlined that students needed to develop clever lyrics with some musical rhythm that demonstrated a clear understanding of the historical topic that they had investigated. Mr. Allen's scoring guide helped students recognize the expectations for their group technology project before they even began to research their world history topics, compose musical lyrics, and produce their videos.

Example From Mr. Allen's Class: Transcontinental Railroad

One group in Mr. Allen's class decided to focus their research on the transcontinental railroad and called their musical group "Cho Cho Chainz." The group did a great deal of research and analysis on the impact of the transcontinental railroad on the western half of the United States in the late 1800s. This enabled the group to produce a musical rap that highlighted the findings from their historical research. These findings included significant insights into the profound impact that the transcontinental railroad had on the lives of many people and how it transformed the nation.

The group worked collaboratively to produce lyrics for the rap, and each student performed a specific portion of the song that they videotaped. It was evident from the musical video that the students were able to capture how the transcontinental railroad was a transformative event in the history of our nation. The song identified how Chinese immigrants were employed to build the railroad tracks that connected America from coast to coast. Yet, the group was also able to convey in their project how these immigrants had to endure hazardous working conditions as they tunneled the tracks through the mountains.

Much of the song focused on diverse perspectives related to the transcontinental railroad. The group highlighted how Native Americans were forced to move west as the railroad expanded on the western plains and into the Rocky Mountains. In fact, the group pointed out that these Native Americans were sometimes labeled "savages" by the railroad workers who they came into contact with. The group pointed out in their musical lyrics that many Civil War veterans and Irish immigrants also worked on the transcontinental railroad. The group shared with viewers that in 1869, the golden spike symbolized the completion of the transcontinental railroad, which was itself a symbol of the Industrial Revolution in the United States.

The group performed their musical video on the railroad tracks and near the flood wall located on the banks of the Mississippi River in Dubuque, Iowa. The video is about five minutes in length. The students are dressed like rappers, and it is evident that they enjoyed the opportunity to collaboratively produce a musical video for their history class using technology. It is important to note that the cooperative learning jobs or roles helped the students produce a musical video that captured the subject matter in the social studies curriculum. Most importantly, it was evident that the students learned a great deal about the transcontinental railroad using technology.

Example From Mr. Allen's Class: Napoleon's Invasion of Russia

Another group in Mr. Allen's class decided to research and produce a musical video about Napoleon's invasion of Russia. The students worked collaboratively to conduct their historical research about this pivotal event in European history. As a result, the group was able to write musical lyrics that identified the significant findings from the research that they had conducted. The musical video that they produced is titled "When I Was Your Man" and is about 3:30 minutes in length.

The musical lyrics included many insights into Napoleon's invasion of Russia. In particular, the musical lyrics emphasized repeatedly how Napoleon's troops were unprepared for the long Russian winter. In fact, the students made it a point of emphasis in their song to share that Napoleon thought it would be a quick and easy victory. The students included a verse in the song that stated they "never thought it would take this much time." According to the group, there were several examples of how the French were unprepared. They did not have the clothing needed for the Russian winter. The group pointed out that the French soldiers sometimes had to march ten to twenty miles per day. The students included a verse in the song that stated "I should have brought a coat." The song also emphasized how there was a serious lack of food and water for Napoleon's troops. These were underlying circumstances for Napoleon's loss in Russia.

This resulted in a humiliating defeat for the French in Russia. The students sang about the enormous loss of life for the French, the loss of their horses due to the brutal weather they experienced, and the soldiers who were captured by their enemy. Interestingly, the students highlighted this point by singing, "Our troops on the battlefield are digging their own graves." The students shared in their historical analysis that Napoleon was at fault. This was underscored in their lyrics when they sang that Napoleon "should have made a plan" and that he "failed his command." They also included a verse that stated, "My pride, my ego, my selfish ways caused my army to lose their lives."

It was evident that the group enjoyed the opportunity to work collaboratively with technology and perform their musical video. Their research enabled them to write musical lyrics that conveyed a deep conceptual understanding of Napoleon's invasion of Russia in the early 1800s. The cooperative learning jobs or roles used in conjunction with technology provided the necessary structure for the students to collaboratively produce a musical video and share it with others.

Summary

Cooperative learning, when used in conjunction with technology, can make for a meaningful learning opportunity in the middle and secondary social studies classroom. Students enjoy the experience of using technology and engaging with one another as they mutually construct knowledge about the subject matter in the social studies curriculum. Most importantly, students are learning the content in the social studies curriculum and simultaneously developing important skills needed for readiness in college, careers, and citizenship. Technology can make this happen by providing small groups of students access to information and the tools to produce products that demonstrate what they have learned in the social studies curriculum.

The examples provided in this chapter enable the reader to think about how technology can be leveraged with cooperative learning to provide students with the necessary access to information and build products with technology. Readers can use these examples and the cooperative learning building blocks from P.I.E.S. to design their very own projects for students. Yet, it is important to remember that there is a distinction between group work and cooperative learning. Evidence suggests that one pivotal decision for middle and secondary social studies teachers is to use jobs or roles to structure the groups to help them become much more productive in the classroom. This can increase the likelihood of on-task behaviors as the students collaborate with one another and ultimately help students collaboratively learn the lesson's objective when they are using technology in the social studies classroom. In addition, cooperative learning can help middle and secondary social studies students develop twenty-first-century skills needed for the workplace and higher education. These are great benefits of cooperative learning that would be difficult to attain in teacher-centered classrooms where the teacher simply used technology to give students information through lecture using PowerPoint or Prezi.

References

Borich, G.D. (2014). *Effective teaching methods: Research-based practices.* Boston, MA: Pearson.

Cayton, A., Perry, E., Reed, L., & Winkler, A. (2000). *America. Pathways to the present.* Upper Saddle River, NJ: Prentice Hall.

Johnson, D. & Johnson, R. (2005). Learning groups. In S. Weelan (Ed.), *The handbook of group research and practice* (pp. 441–461). Thousand Oaks, CA: Sage.

Kagan, S. (1999). Positive interdependence. *Kagan Online Magazine.* Retrieved from www. kaganonline.com/free_articles/dr_spencer_kagan/286/Positive-Interdependence. Accessed 9/2/14.

Woods, R.B. & Gatewood, W.B. (1998). *America interpreted. A concise history with readings.* New York: Harcourt Brace College Publishers.

Yale University Law School. (2009). *The Avalon project at Yale University Law School. Documents in law, history, and diplomacy.* Retrieved from http://avalon.law.yale.edu/. Accessed 5/26/09.

4

PROBLEM-BASED LEARNING

Students need to develop a wide variety of skills for college, career, and civic life. The College, Career, and Civic Life (C3) Framework for Social Studies State Standards was developed by ten to fifteen social studies–related organizations to help students attain these goals (NCSS, 2013). In addition, middle and secondary social studies classrooms equipped with technology are well positioned to help students reach these goals. Problem-based learning is one student-centered instructional strategy that can be used with technology to encourage the type of teaching and learning associated with this new framework.

Problem-based learning represents a paradigm shift in the middle and secondary social studies classroom. In problem-based learning, students are encouraged to participate in active learning instead of passively listening to lecture, as in the traditional classroom. Students who find themselves in technology-rich social studies classrooms are able to quickly access information. This enables students to participate in the type of student-centered learning associated with problem-based learning that is featured in the C3 Framework for Social Studies State Standards. As a result, students benefit by learning the content in the social studies curriculum and simultaneously develop the skills needed for college, careers, and participation in our democracy.

Problem-Based Learning: A Step-by-Step Guide

The problem-based learning lesson plan begins with a question or problem. It is important that the question or problem pertain to an objective in the social studies curriculum. The question or problem needs to be carefully crafted. Students may quickly lose interest in the subject matter if the question is deemed too easy or too difficult. There needs to be a happy medium where students feel like it is an appropriate challenge so they will be eager to explore the question or problem for the remainder of the class period. The question or problem should also have multiple answers. The lesson will likely lose a great deal of momentum if the question or problem has one answer. Frequently, the question or problem may address real-life scenarios (Arends, 2009). There are countless real-world problems facing our nation and world that students can explore.

In the next portion of problem-based learning, students develop a hypothesis for the question or problem that they have been presented with. Teachers should encourage students to develop a list of items for their hypothesis. Arends (2009) suggests that students should be encouraged to make predictions on what they may find when they test their hypothesis. For example, a lesson on the Great Migration could involve students developing a hypothesis on the following question: "Why do you think 1,000,000 African-Americans migrated from the South to the North from 1916 to 1930?" (Scheuerell, 2008). As soon as students make predictions on what they might find, they can be encouraged to share aloud their hypothesis with their peers, and the teacher can list these on the whiteboard.

As soon as the students have shared their hypotheses aloud, they are encouraged to test them by going to the Internet. Teachers can do this in a couple of ways. I often found it was helpful to simply give the students a list of Internet websites that directly related to their problem or question. This is helpful when time is limited during the class period and especially when students have difficulty locating a credible Internet site directly related to their inquiry. It is sometimes useful for students to identify these Internet sites on their own when time permits since they need to learn how to locate credible sites. During this phase of the problem-based learning lesson, students are determining whether their hypothesis was correct or not. I frequently found it helpful for students to use a graphic organizer to help them more easily see the themes that were emerging from their online research. As soon as the students have completed their Internet research, it is important for them to spend some time analyzing the big ideas that emerged from their investigation.

Students can also share with their peers what they learned from their Internet investigation in small groups and aloud in the large group discussion facilitated by the social studies teacher. This is where a great deal of learning takes place as the students compare and contrast their findings. Students will frequently find that many of the items they listed in their hypothesis were correct, and this adds to their prior knowledge. According to John Dewey, problem-based learning is how people naturally construct knowledge about the world around them, and this creates a great deal of curiosity about the subject matter (as cited in Arends, 2009).

Problem-based learning can also involve students sharing their findings by producing products on what they have learned (Arends, 2009). Middle and secondary students can easily use technology to produce products where they share with others what they have learned beyond the walls of their classroom. Internet podcasts, Prezi presentations, and digital videos are just a few examples of how students can share their problem-based learning findings with others.

Pivotal Decisions With Technology: Make Predictions or "Dive In"?

In the classrooms that participated in the qualitative case study, there were countless examples of students pursuing answers to questions posed by their social studies teacher. However, it was rare for the teacher to give students the opportunity to develop a hypothesis before they began their investigation using the Internet. This would have allowed these students to participate in a great deal of higher-level thinking about the subject matter and add to the level of curiosity about the subject matter in the social studies curriculum. Exposure to problem-based learning would have provided these teachers with user-friendly building blocks to make this happen. There will be examples in the pages to follow that point to these findings.

The students at Bluff High School were given a project on European history where they were asked to produce a product that could be used as a visual aid for a presentation to their peers. Many of the students produced a Keynote presentation with their Apple Notebook computer where they shared their findings from their research on a variety of European history topics. Some of these topics included the Reformation, the Enlightenment, and the Industrial Revolution. However, the technology projects that the students produced displayed little evidence of critical thinking about the subject matter. Most of the information that the students shared involved lower levels of Bloom's taxonomy, including names and dates. Problem-based learning arguably would have moved this lesson forward by encouraging students to think more deeply about the subject matter by encouraging them to develop a hypothesis before they investigated these topics online.

European history is filled with potential questions for students to investigate using the problem-based learning structure. Mr. Smith could have asked questions such as 1) Why do you think it was known as a Reformation? 2) Why do you think it was known as the Enlightenment? and 3) Why do you think the Industrial Revolution was labeled a revolution? Any of these questions would have encouraged the students to think more deeply about the subject matter and motivated them to see if their hypothesis was correct or not. There is a great deal of information on the Internet about these subjects, and the students could have tested their hypothesis by researching them online. The students would have been involved in a great deal of analysis if they had been given the opportunity to compare and contrast their findings about the subject matter. This would have enabled the students to identify major themes that emerged and determined which parts of their hypothesis aligned to their findings. Many students find this to be much more appealing than listening to their teacher lecture again.

The students who researched the Industrial Revolution in Mr. Smith's class decided to divide their topic up into issues involving this turning point in European history. Child labor, women's contributions, benefits of the Industrial Revolution, and the effects of the Industrial Revolution were some of the subtopics. These were missed opportunities by the teacher to move this lesson from lower-level thinking to higher-order thinking. The teacher could have posed questions related to these issues—for example, "How do you think children and women were affected by the Industrial Revolution?" or "What do you think were some of the benefits and consequences of the Industrial Revolution?" These questions would have let students participate in inquiry or problem-based learning where they would have been challenged to think more deeply about the subject matter using technology. In some instances, it appeared students were simply copying and pasting the information they viewed from the Internet into their Keynote presentation instead of thinking analytically about the findings from the research that they had conducted in class.

Problem-based learning would have also been helpful in Mr. Smith's lesson on the Berlin Wall. The students researched the Berlin Wall and its construction by East Germany. They read about the citizens who tried to move from East Germany to West Germany when the wall was constructed. There was a missed opportunity to move this lesson forward by engaging students in critical thinking. The students could have been asked to develop their own hypothesis on why so many residents tried to move from East Germany to West Germany when the wall was constructed. This was a complex issue, but many students would have been able to develop their own hypothesis and then test it using the Internet. It is likely that the students would have also remembered a great deal more about the subject matter due to the higher levels of analysis involved in a problem-based learning structure rather than traditional teaching and learning structures. The students would have arguably felt much more ownership in the lesson too, since they would have been given the opportunity to begin the lesson with their opinions to see if they could figure out the answer for themselves before they investigated the topic on the Internet.

Mr. Smith's World Geography class also used traditional teaching and learning structures when they investigated the European Union. He had his students complete a fill-in-the-blank worksheet about the European Union based on their Internet research. This was another missed opportunity to move the lesson from lower-level thinking questions to higher-level thinking questions. The students examined the purpose of the European Union. Perhaps the students could have been asked questions such as 1) Why do you think the European Union was formed? and 2) What do you think are some of the strengths and weaknesses of the European Union? This would have enabled the students to make predictions about what they might find, and the students would have quickly realized that these are complex issues that involve more than one answer.

In Mr. Smith's lesson, they also had to examine the national health care system found throughout most of the countries in Europe. He asked some great questions—for example, he asked the students to think about the pros and cons of the national health care systems. This lesson could have involved a deeper level of analysis if the students had been able to participate in a think-aloud where they shared their hypotheses about the subject instead. The anticipatory set portion of the lesson may have been a great opportunity for the students to do this. This was a pivotal decision during the lesson that was arguably missed by the teacher. Of course, time is frequently a factor and may have limited what Mr. Smith could have done in this lesson.

Mr. Brown had his students involved in some higher-level thinking questions at Bridge High School. However, there were several missed opportunities for his students to participate in problem-based learning, which would have enabled his students to think more deeply about the subject matter. In one lesson, he used the Near Pad app with his Apple iPad to enable his students to follow along slide by slide on their very own iPads as he lectured about Hitler. During the middle of the lecture, he paused and asked the students a question about Hitler's motivation for blaming the Reichstag fire on the Communists. This was an excellent higher-level thinking question. His lesson was mainly focused on the students passively listening to his lecture. However, the lesson could have been a rich opportunity for problem-based learning by asking students to develop their own hypothesis on why Hitler blamed the Communists for the fire. By using the Internet, the students could have tested their hypotheses by examining different sources available online.

These are pivotal decisions with technology. For example, in another lesson, Mr. Brown taught the students about Social Security. He asked his students questions such as "What are the pros and cons of Social Security?" This could have led to a problem-based learning lesson where students used the C3 Framework to investigate the subject matter in greater depth by beginning with their hypotheses. There were similar scenarios in Mr. Jones' social studies classroom. He taught a major unit on the Civil Rights movement in his American History class. During the unit, he posed a question that read "Who won the Civil Rights movement, the average person or the federal government?" The question enabled students to think very deeply about this monumental event in the history of our nation. However, the lesson arguably would have been enhanced even more if Mr. Jones had encouraged his students to develop their own hypothesis about the subject matter based on their prior knowledge and preconceived ideas about the Civil Rights movement. This would have allowed students to then connect their prior knowledge and preconceived ideas to the new information that they discovered from their research using the Internet and other technology-related sources.

Theory and Practice: Firsthand Experience Using Technology and Problem-Based Learning in American History

The C3 Framework for Social Studies State Standards includes four dimensions that can be utilized through problem-based learning and the Internet in the social studies classroom. These dimensions include the following: 1) developing questions and planning investigations, 2) applying disciplinary concepts and tools, 3) evaluating sources and using evidence, and 4) communicating conclusions and taking informed action. These are teaching and learning structures that can be easily replicated across the social sciences in the middle and secondary social studies classroom (NCSS, 2013).

The PBS webpage can be a valuable resource in the social studies classroom. The site has several history links with a rich collection of sources. There are primary sources, including letters, diaries, and newspaper articles. In addition, there are political cartoons, photographs, and maps, which provide an interesting opportunity for students to dig deeper into historical topics while meeting the outcomes identified in the new C3 Social Studies Framework. The PBS Internet links featured in this chapter include Woodrow Wilson, America in 1900, President Truman, and Marcus Garvey. Each of these Internet links can be easily viewed at the following: www.pbs.org/history/history_united.html.

The PBS webpage is a user-friendly way for middle and secondary social studies teachers to have their students participate in problem-based learning with technology. There is a rich collection of primary sources already organized around historical questions. This saves teachers a great deal of time when they are planning lessons and enables the classroom to move from a teacher-centered to a student-centered instructional approach where students are involved in a great deal of decision making about the subject matter. Rather than using technology to memorize names and dates, the reader will discover from these examples that students are actively engaged with technology to reach their own conclusions.

C3 Dimension #1: Developing Questions and Planning Investigations: Woodrow Wilson Webpage

In August 1914, President Wilson issued a "Declaration of Neutrality" in regard to the conflict in Europe. My students read the declaration by viewing the "Woodrow Wilson" Internet link on the PBS historical webpage. In the introductory paragraph, President Wilson stated, "Every man who really loves America will act and speak in the true spirit of neutrality." Yet, the issue of American neutrality was very complex, and it is an excellent investigation for students. Readers can find the primary sources on President Wilson at the following Internet link: www.pbs.org/wgbh/amex/wilson/filmmore/ps.html.

Problem-based learning is a powerful method of getting students to investigate an issue using higher-level thinking skills. As noted earlier, the approach begins by posing an interesting question or problem to students. The most important thing is to ask a question that students will perceive to be a "happy medium" in terms of level of difficulty. Otherwise, some students may not be interested if the question doesn't challenge them enough or is too hard for them to even get started. In addition, it is important to pick a problem or question that will have multiple answers. In this case, the teacher can ask, "Why do you think President Wilson publicly encouraged the nation to remain neutral in World War I?" Next, the teacher can ask students to develop a hypothesis. It is helpful to remind students that their hypothesis should be an educated guess or hunch (Maxim, 2006). As soon as the students are finished with their hypothesis, they can actually test it by investigating the topic. Finally, each student can share their findings with their classmates. It is extremely important to point out in this example that the students made predictions before their Internet investigation rather than diving in and reading the primary source or listening to their teacher list all of the reasons for American neutrality at the beginning of World War I. This challenges students to think more deeply about the subject matter rather than becoming a passive learner with technology.

The students will find many interesting answers from their problem-based learning investigation. In President Wilson's opinion, American neutrality was needed for a variety of reasons. During his "Declaration of Neutrality" speech, he stated, "The people of the United States are drawn from many nations and chiefly from the nations now at war" (PBS, 2009). Interestingly, there were eight million German Americans who sometimes had sympathies toward the Central Powers at the beginning of the war. In addition, there were five million Irish Americans who opposed the British government, primarily due to the issue of Irish nationalism. Therefore, many of them supported the Central Powers on the eve of World War I (Woods & Gatewood, 1998).

Yet, the Allied Powers had many supporters as well. In 1914, when the war began, they inherited a great deal of domestic support due to cultural and economic ties to Great Britain (Woods & Gatewood, 1998). During the war itself, Americans usually got their news from a pro-British perspective, since information from the battlefront came from transatlantic cables controlled by the Allies. The pro-British perspective was amplified even more as events unfolded during the war. British supporters in the United States were outraged when Germany invaded Belgium, a neutral country during the war (Woods & Gatewood, 1998).

Eventually, due to the changing tide in public opinion, the United States became involved militarily in the conflict. The change in public opinion was due to a culmination of events and can serve as an excellent problem-based learning question for students. The teacher can ask students the following question: Why do you think the United States ended her neutrality and aligned herself with the

Allies? Again, students can develop a hypothesis and test it by doing an investigation. During their online research, students will find many reasons, including the significant economic ties of the United States to the Allies. In fact, the war was seriously hurting the American economy due to German submarine warfare cutting off international trade between the United States and Europe. In addition, American businessmen such as J. P. Morgan had loaned about $500 million to the French during the war effort. Overall, American bankers and investors had loaned $2 billion to the Allied war effort. There were high economic stakes for the country. A German victory in the war would have caused American investors to have significant financial losses (Woods & Gatewood, 1998). Consequently, there were powerful interest groups and stakeholders in the country who sided with the Allies.

American Allied support involved much more than economics. In 1915, the Germans sank the *Lusitania*, which outraged many Americans. The sinking of the British passenger vessel killed 1,198 passengers, including 128 Americans (Woods & Gatewood, 1998). This was just the beginning of a conflict on the high seas. Later in January 1917, the German government notified the US State Department that they would use submarine warfare to cut off any supplies going to Great Britain and France for the war effort.

American public opinion worsened even more toward Germany when a telegram sent by its foreign minister, Alfred Zimmerman, to the German Embassy in Mexico was intercepted and printed in American newspapers. The telegram encouraged the German ambassador to Mexico to approach Mexican government officials to possibly form an alliance in the war against the United States. Furthermore, the telegram offered Mexico territory they lost in their 1848 war with the United States, including Texas, New Mexico, and Arizona (Woods & Gatewood, 1998). In summary, students will discover there was a culmination of reasons that contributed to the end of American neutrality in World War I, and it is important to note that students can use the Internet to investigate the question in depth using a problem-based learning approach where they have to make predictions and test them using online sources. As a result, students will participate in a great deal of critical thinking about the subject matter.

C3 Dimension #2: Applying Disciplinary Tools and Concepts: President Truman Webpage

Today, students can easily access primary sources on the Internet. *Digital history* is a term used to describe the collection of primary sources located on the Internet, which can be used in the social studies classroom (Bass & Rosenzweig, 1999). Students can examine primary and secondary sources, consider multiple perspectives, conduct analysis, and develop an interpretation (Bass & Rosenzweig, 1999). These are the disciplinary tools used by historians.

The PBS webpage features several collections of primary sources, including documents related to President Truman's decision to drop the atomic bomb. Each document enables students to be student-historians involved in much critical thinking. In this lesson, students can view the primary sources online and determine if they would have used the atomic bomb if they were President Truman. In 1939, Albert Einstein wrote a letter to President Franklin Roosevelt describing the scientific potential of creating a nuclear bomb by writing that it is possible "to set up a nuclear chain reaction in a large mass of uranium" (PBS, 2009). Furthermore, the same letter informed President Roosevelt that "this new phenomenon would also lead to the construction of bombs, and it is conceivable—though much less certain—that extremely powerful bombs of a new type may thus be constructed" (PBS, 2000). Later in the same letter he suggested to the president that it may be "desirable to have some permanent contact maintained between the Administration and the group of physicists working on chain reactions in America" (PBS, 2009). The correspondence from Einstein had a profound impact on President Roosevelt. Afterward, the president decided to authorize the Manhattan Project, a top-secret $2 billion project, to develop the atomic bomb for the war effort (Woods & Gatewood, 1998). The program financed nuclear research initiatives throughout the nation, including laboratories in Oak Ridge, Tennessee; Hartford, Washington; and Los Alamos, New Mexico (Woods & Gatewood, 1998). The primary sources on President Truman can be found at the following Internet link: www.pbs.org/wgbh/americanexperience/films/truman/player/.

Although President Truman was vice president of the United States, he knew nothing about the Manhattan Project when President Roosevelt died in 1945. The PBS webpage has a letter from Secretary of War Henry Stimson to President Truman about the Manhattan Project. In the letter, Stimson informed Truman about the urgent need for the two to talk about the Manhattan Project, stating, "I think it is very important that I should have a talk with you as soon as possible on a highly secret matter" (PBS, 2009). Stimson wrote in the next paragraph that the subject "has such a bearing on our present foreign relations and has such an important effect upon all my thinking in this field that I think you ought to know about it without much further delay" (PBS, 2009). Meanwhile, the Manhattan Project moved on, and testing would eventually take place to see if the atomic bomb was feasible to use in war.

By 1945, nuclear physicists increasingly became fearful of the consequences of using an atomic bomb. As mentioned, Albert Einstein corresponded with President Roosevelt and brought to his attention the potentially serious implications to the world. Einstein indicated that Dr. Leo Szilard, a nuclear physicist, wanted to inform President Roosevelt about these issues. Einstein wrote, "He was greatly disturbed by the potentialities involved and anxious that the United States Government be advised of them as soon as possible" (PBS, 2000). Students can read the letter on the PBS webpage and see firsthand the degree to which Einstein encouraged President Roosevelt to meet with Dr. Szilard. Einstein ended his letter by writing, "I understand that he now is greatly concerned about the lack of adequate contact between scientists who are doing this work and members of your Cabinet who are responsible for formulating policy" (PBS, 2000). In summary, the physicists saw the long-term environmental and political implications of using the bomb and wanted to alert the president. Students can also read firsthand the urgency of this matter since they have access to these primary sources online and are able to make their own inferences, just like professional historians do.

By July 1945, the war in Europe had ended and the United States was extremely interested in bringing the war in the Pacific to a halt. The United States had suffered significant casualties fighting the Japanese. During the Battle of Iwo Jima, 4,000 Americans were killed. Later in the Battle of Okinawa, 80,000 Americans were killed or wounded. Meanwhile, the US military planned for a possible invasion of Japan. Planners estimated one million Americans could possibly die in an invasion (Conlin, 1997). During the same period, President Truman traveled to Germany to attend the Potsdam Conference. The PBS webpage included a series of diary entries from President Truman during his trip. Each provided significant insights for my students.

President Truman wrote in his diary about his experiences at the Potsdam Conference. On July 17, 1945, he described his meeting with Stalin, writing, "Just spent a couple of hours with Stalin" (Conlin, 1997). Later, he wrote, "I can deal with Stalin. He is honest, but smart as hell" (Conlin, 1997). Truman also indicated that Stalin had agreed to enter the war against the Japanese on August 15 (Conlin, 1997). Some have speculated that part of Truman's motivation to use the atomic bomb was to intimidate the Soviets since the United States had become increasingly concerned about the post-war settlements (Woods & Gatewood, 1998).

The last primary source in the PBS collection included a memorandum from General Leslie Groves describing the first nuclear test in the New Mexico desert on an evening in July 1945. There was a very detailed and vivid account of the absolute destruction left by the atomic bomb at the test site. The general wrote, "For a brief period there was a lightning effect within a radius of 20 miles equal to several suns in midday" (PBS, 2009). He also described the destruction, writing there was "a crater from which all vegetation had vanished, with a diameter of 1,200 feet" (PBS, 2009). Accounts like this can help to inform students of the overwhelming force inflicted by the atomic bomb. The various sources also enable them to see all of the things President Truman had to take into consideration when he made the decision to use the atomic bomb. Due to this unique learning experience, students can apply the disciplinary concepts and tools used by historians. They can also think critically about the subject matter, rather than memorize a bunch of facts, such as names and dates. In particular, students can be asked to consider whether they would have dropped the atomic bomb if they were President Truman, based on all of the primary sources that they have on the PBS webpage related to this topic. A graphic organizer can help students organize their materials for this investigation.

C3 Dimension #3: Evaluating Sources and Using Evidence: America in 1900 Webpage

In 1900, the United States was victorious in the Spanish-American War and was involved in a war to annex the Philippines. During the insurrection, there was much debate about American foreign policy. Specifically, should the United States become an imperialistic country?

The PBS webpage has several primary sources related to the Spanish-American War and the annexation of the Philippines. In particular, the 1898 Treaty of Paris and several political cartoons featuring American imperialism. The political cartoons can be found on the Ohio State University eHistory site (http://ehistory. osu.edu) and are attributed to *The Verdict*. Cooperative learning, used in conjunction with the "America 1900" webpage, can help students develop the appropriate collaborative learning skills and give them the opportunity to evaluate the sources associated with the investigation. Think-Pair-Share is one cooperative learning activity that can be used when students investigate topics online. The structure works extremely well when students view primary sources on the Internet. During the "Think" phase of the activity, students can be asked a question about the sources and each student can write down an answer after a significant amount of reflection. Next, during the "Pair" portion of the activity, students can discuss what they had written with their partner. Finally, during the "Share" segment of the activity, students can discuss aloud with the rest of their classmates what they had discussed with their partner.

Several primary sources on the PBS webpage can be used for the Think-Pair-Share activity. In particular, the Treaty of Paris document is well suited for the activity. Several questions can be used to stimulate discussion. For example, students can be asked to identify the territories spoken about in the treaty. They will discover that Spain was forced to evacuate the island of Cuba and cede Puerto Rico and the Philippines to the United States. The document also indicated the United States and Spain had to turn over their prisoners of war to each other (PBS, 2009).

Many students may wonder why the United States was interested in expansion, which can serve as another Think-Pair-Share question. At the turn of the century, several groups of Americans were interested in having the United States spread its influence around the world. Business leaders sought for the United States to exert more influence in the Pacific to establish a market for their goods. In particular, they wanted to use the Philippines as a base in the Pacific to launch an effort to sell goods in the growing Chinese market. Naval leaders also wanted to use the Philippines as a base to refuel ships in the Pacific region. Protestant leaders also hoped to civilize the Filipinos and believed it was America's calling as a democracy to do so (Woods & Gatewood, 1998). Yet, many members of Congress viewed the American occupation of the Philippines as undemocratic and attempted to block these efforts. Their effort to block the annexation of the Philippines was unsuccessful, failing by one vote in Congress (Woods & Gatewood, 1998). The vast number of sources found on this webpage gives students an opportunity to weigh both sides of the issue confronting the nation during this pivotal time.

The political cartoons featured on the "America 1900" webpage are also well suited for cooperative learning. In particular, the Jigsaw activity can be used. Each student can examine one of the political cartoons and then share what the political cartoon was about. In essence, each student can become an "expert" on the topic and teach a partner what she or he has learned.

There is a political cartoon labeled "The Imperialism 'Stunt'" that can serve as an interesting source to students (see Figure 4.1). There is an image of an

Figure 4.1 "The Imperialism 'Stunt.'"

Source: The Verdict (New York), 1898–1902 (ehistory.osu.edu).

American dressed in red, white, and blue with a long sword on a high wire over the Pacific Ocean, trying to stay balanced between the United States and the Philippines. The Philippines are surrounded by American vessels, and Uncle Sam is observing this from the western shore of the United States (PBS, 2009). The political cartoon can show students how difficult it was for America to be an imperialist. In summary, the cost of imperialism and becoming a world power was immense.

The PBS webpage has another political cartoon titled "McKinley and the Philippines" that has an image of President McKinley with his arms crossed and stepping on a small Filipino on a tiny island (see Figure 4.2). It is interesting to note that the native is made to look like an animal. Meanwhile, in the background of the image are silhouettes of Napoleon and Julius Caesar, trying to portray President McKinley as a conqueror with little regard for the Filipinos (PBS, 2009).

IS HE TO BE A DESPOT?

Figure 4.2 "Is He to Be a Despot?"

Source: The Verdict (New York), 1898–1902 (ehistory.osu.edu).

A GAME THAT LOSES MUCH TO WIN LITTLE.

Figure 4.3 "A Game That Loses Much to Win Little."

Source: The Verdict (New York), 1898–1902 (ehistory.osu.edu).

President McKinley found himself involved in an insurrection in which the native Filipinos turned on the Americans occupying the archipelago island nation. The conflict involved guerrilla warfare and lasted for two years (Woods & Gatewood, 1998).

Another political cartoon featured on the site is titled "Aguinaldo" (see Figure 4.3). Emilio Aguinaldo was the leader of the Filipino insurrection against the United States. The political cartoon shows an image of Uncle Sam looking off in the distance, where he sees a tent labeled "Aguinaldo" with his image on it. In front of the tent are many dead American soldiers. Underneath the image is a caption that reads "A Game That Loses Much to Win Little." The title was very appropriate since 5,000 Americans died in the conflict, including many who were decapitated by their Filipino captives. Many Americans also died from the intense tropical heat, insects, and diseases (Conlin, 1997).

In summary, the webpage gives students the opportunity to view these primary sources firsthand and evaluate them for themselves and use evidence to support their position on the broader issue of American imperialism at the turn of the century, in particular, the pros and cons of the United States becoming an imperialistic global power at the turn of the century.

C3 Dimension #4: Communicating Conclusions and Taking Informed Action: Marcus Garvey Webpage

Marcus Garvey was a significant African-American leader in the early 1900s, and there is an Internet link featuring him on the PBS webpage. In order for African-Americans to fulfill their dreams, Garvey believed in the need to economically uplift the race. He encouraged African-Americans to end their economic dependence and move the race from consumer to producer (Levine, 1982). He developed a number of economic initiatives, including the Negro Factories Corporation (NFC) and Black Star Line. During its existence, the NFC employed about 1,000 African-Americans in the United States (Levine, 1982). The corporation began in 1919 and developed many small businesses throughout the country, including grocery stores, restaurants, laundries, tailor shops, and publishing companies (Lewis, 1998). Levine (1982) points out the significance of the NFC, stating, "Here was a step toward Garvey's dream of a self-contained world of Negro producers, distributors, and consumers who could deal with or be independent of the rest of the world as necessity and circumstances dictated" (p. 127). Each of the primary sources on Marcus Garvey can be found at the following Internet link: www.pbs.org/wgbh/amex/garvey/index.html.

The PBS webpage featured a newspaper advertisement selling NFC shares in Image #2 of the "Gallery" segment of the webpage. This primary source offers students many interesting insights into Garvey's business ventures. The advertisement tried to recruit African-American investors by posing the following question to its readers: "Mr. Black Man, what are you doing to insure a brighter future for the race? Are you investing your money wisely as to turn over profits for you and your children and posterity?" (PBS, 2000). The same advertisement informed readers of its future business plan to employ thousands of African-Americans by building factories, owned by African-Americans, in their neighborhoods (PBS, 2000). Finally, the advertisement can provide students with further insights into the day-to-day functions of the business, stating, "The factories will manufacture goods of all kinds, to be sold in American markets, and shipped by the Black Star Line Steamship to foreign countries" (PBS, 2000).

As soon as the students finish this type of investigation, they can design a technology project where they share their findings from the webpage with others. For example, they can use a graphic organizer to compare and contrast Garvey's views with other African-American leaders such as Booker T. Washington, W. E. B. Dubois, Martin Luther King Jr., and Malcolm X. Perhaps the students can share their analysis using digital videos, podcasts, and/or a blog.

Summary

Many teachers have seen firsthand how technology can motivate students. Marzano (2007) believes "teachers who have brought technology into their classrooms are aware that it provides an opportunity to differentiate instruction and change their classrooms into dynamic learning environments" (p. 2). Problem-based learning is a proven instructional strategy to help student achievement using technology.

Problem-based learning can also be used with technology to help middle and secondary students develop the skill sets needed for the twenty-first-century workforce. Students in social studies can learn the content in the curriculum and simultaneously develop skills such as problem solving and critical thinking.

The PBS webpage is one way to incorporate technology into the social studies classroom. Most importantly, when used appropriately, the webpage can enable students to be involved in the types of teaching and learning structures associated with the inquiry arc of the C3 Social Studies Framework.

In the past, students have frequently been passive learners using the Internet in the classroom. However, there is no reason why students can't use the Internet in conjunction with the teaching and learning strategies presented in the C3 Framework to develop the necessary skill sets to prepare them for college, careers, and citizenship in our nation.

References

Arends, R. I. (2009). *Learning to teach*. Dubuque, IA: McGraw-Hill.

Bass, R. & Rosenzweig, R. (1999). Rewiring the history and social studies classroom: Needs, frameworks, dangers, and proposals. *Journal of Education, 3*, 41–61.

Conlin, J. R. (1997). *The American past. A survey of American history*. Fort Worth, TX: Harcourt Brace.

Levine, L. W. (1982). Marcus Garvey and the politics of revitilization. In J. H. Franklin & A. Meier (Eds.), *Black leaders of the twentieth century*. Champaign, IL: University of Illinois Press.

Lewis, R. (1988). *Marcus Garvey. Anti-colonial champion*. Trenton, NJ: Africa World Press, Inc.

Marzano, R. J. (2007). *Using technology with classroom instruction that works*. Denver, CO: ASCD.

Maxim, G. W. (2006). *Dynamic social studies for constructivist classrooms. Inspiring tomorrow's social scientists* (8th ed.). Columbus, OH: Prentice Hall.

National Council for the Social Studies (NCSS). (2013). *The College, Career, and Civic Life (C3) Framework for Social Studies State Standards: Guidance for enhancing the rigor of K–12 civics, economics, geography, and history.* Silver Spring, MD: NCSS.

PBS. (2009). *American experience. 1900.* Retrieved from www.pbs.org/wgbh/amex/1900/. Accessed 5/10/14.

PBS. (2000). *American experience. Marcus Garvey. Look for me in the whirlwind.* Retrieved from www.pbs.org/wgbh/amex/garvey/. Accessed 5/10/14.

Scheuerell, S. (2008). The Great Migration: Using a problem-based learning approach and the Internet. *Social Studies Research and Practice, 1,* 68–79.

Woods, R.B. & Gatewood, W.B. (1998). *America interpreted. A concise history with readings.* New York: Harcourt Brace College Publishers.

5

FACILITATING DISCUSSION

Unfortunately, twelfth graders have a limited understanding of the basic functions of Congress. In fact, only 27 percent of twelfth graders are "proficient" in their understanding of civics (Lutkus & Weiss, 2007). For example, just 18 percent are able to identify how Congress provides checks and balances. In addition, only 42 percent are able to explain the concept of federalism. Consequently, many social studies teachers are exploring alternative teaching methods, such as the Internet, to increase their students' understanding of Congress.

Increasingly, students have access to the Internet in social studies classrooms. Nearly 100 percent of public schools in the United States have access to the Internet, and the student-to-computer ratio is 4.4 to 1 (Parsad & Jones, 2005). Currently, there are many schools with one-to-one laptop computer initiatives. For example, Pennsylvania has a plan to give every high school student a laptop computer with Internet access. A study in Pennsylvania found that in high schools with one-to-one laptop computers, students were more likely to be involved in "real-world" tasks and spent less time "off task" (District Administration, 2008).

Theory and Practice: Firsthand Experience Using Technology and Facilitating Discussion in American Government

Several Internet webpages can help students apply what they have learned from a prior lecture or reading. In particular, the US House of Representatives webpage can help students learn about the legislative branch (www.house.gov/). The webpage has a number of interactive features that help students think critically about the House of Representatives. The Mindtools framework can serve as a guide to develop a lesson that fosters critical thinking about Congress by posing higher-level thinking questions. If possible, a liquid crystal display (LCD) projector can enable students to follow along step by step using the webpage and stopping for discussion questions. Mindtools, the Rigor/Relevance Framework, and a decision-making model that prompts discussion are the underpinnings that guide the lesson that will be discussed in the pages that follow.

Rigor/Relevance: A Framework With Implications for Technology Integration in Civics

Teachers are frequently trying to identify ways to integrate technology into the classroom. The Rigor/Relevance Framework can provide the necessary structure to encourage higher-level thinking and application with technology. Daggett (2005) argues it is critical for students to apply what they have learned from rigorous thinking to real-world settings. Instead, students are frequently taught isolated bits of content-specific information and are rarely given the opportunity to see how the information can be used in a real-world setting (Daggett, 2005). The Rigor/Relevance Framework can be used to address this problem. Yet, many social studies teachers have not considered using the framework for a technology-rich lesson about Congress.

The Rigor/Relevance Framework has combined both the Knowledge and Application Models to form four different learning quadrants. These are described as Quadrant A, Quadrant B, Quadrant C, and Quadrant D (Daggett, 2014). In Quadrant A (Acquisition), students are simply expected to remember the information they have acquired from a lesson. For example, students might be asked to memorize how many members are in the House of Representatives, or, according to the Constitution, the minimum age to be a member of Congress. In Quadrant B (Application), students are challenged in the lesson to apply what they have learned to new and unpredictable situations. This may involve students producing a project that demonstrates how they would have handled a situation as a member of Congress. For example, they could put forth a piece of legislation dealing with climate change and develop an Internet podcast to share with their constituents their rationale for the bill.

In Quadrant C (Assimilation), students are involved in more rigorous work by analyzing and solving problems. For example, students could be involved in a class discussion on how they would deter gun violence in the United States and what type of legislation they would sponsor if they were a member of Congress. Finally, in Quadrant D (Adaptation), teachers ask students to create solutions to unique problems (Daggett, 2005). In addition, in Quadrant D, students typically produce projects where they share their solutions. In this case, students can think about how they would handle the threat of Iran attaining nuclear weapons. For example, they can pretend that they are a member of Congress and give a speech in the legislature, using digital video, where they can describe how they would deal with the dilemma facing America.

It is important to note that each of these quadrants can guide social studies teachers as they plan technology-rich lessons. In particular, the quadrants can help teachers develop a lesson that involves a greater amount of rigor and relevance, instead of having students memorize information from an Internet webpage and being tested on this lower-level recall information. For example, students sometimes find themselves in classrooms where they are asked to fill out a worksheet or simply list what they have learned about Congress from a webpage. Unfortunately, this fails to engage students in critical thinking about the subject matter.

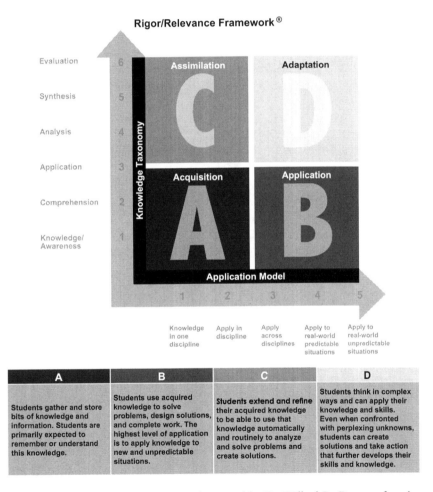

Figure 5.1 Rigor/Relevance Framework, created by Dr. Willard R. Daggett, founder and chairman of the International Center for Leadership in Education.

Rigor/Relevance: A Framework to Foster Student Thinking in Civics Using the Internet

Jonassen, Howland, Marra, and Crismond (2008) recommend five types of questions that challenge students to think critically and more deeply when they are using technology. These recommendations can help teachers develop critical thinking questions when they use the House of Representatives Internet webpage in their classroom. Their framework to foster critical thinking includes the following types of questions: 1) cause-effect, 2) compare-contrast, 3) problem solving, 4) reflection, and 5) experiential. It is important to note that each of these types of critical thinking questions will be used as a framework in the rest of the chapter. Specific examples, which can be easily replicated, will be provided. Examples may vary depending on the congressional district a classroom is located in and any day-to-day issues that arise on the floor of the House of Representatives.

The Rigor/Relevance Framework can be adapted to more easily show teachers how they can integrate technology that fuses both higher-order thinking and relevancy for students (see Figure 5.1). In Quadrant A, the focus is solely on the teacher using technology in the social studies classroom. Since it is in Quadrant A, the information shared with students focuses on lower-level thinking, such as facts, including examples such as names and dates. Most likely, the teacher is using technology such as a PowerPoint presentation to deliver a lecture, showing their students a YouTube video, or, in this instance, showing the House of Representatives webpage on the LCD projector and using it to highlight something during the lecture. However, this fails to elicit higher-level thinking with technology, which is vitally important in technology integration. In Quadrant B, students are developing products using their computers. It is important to note that Quadrant B still involves lower-level thinking, so the products the students produce will likely involve rote memorization of information, such as identifying or describing concepts about Congress. Some examples of the technology products they may produce about the House of Representatives include Internet podcasts, digital videos, PowerPoint presentations, and an Internet webpage.

In Quadrant C, the teacher is moving to a greater degree of rigor, or higher-level thinking, where students have an opportunity to discuss more deeply what they are learning from the Internet. This may include information from an Internet webpage, Internet database, or significant details from a primary source found online. The key point in Quadrant C is that the teacher is facilitating a higher-level thinking discussion, using Bloom's taxonomy as a guide to ask critical thinking questions. It is important to note that Quadrant C can involve higher-level thinking that is the impetus of a lesson in this quadrant framework. Finally, Quadrant D can involve lessons where students are challenged to participate in upper levels of Bloom's taxonomy and produce products using technology that demonstrate their conclusions. For example, they could write a blog describing how they might solve the nation's economy if they were a member of Congress. By having the opportunity to do this, students will be able to share their findings with others beyond the walls of the classroom, which certainly adds to the relevancy of their lesson about Congress.

In fact, Thomas Friedman (2005), in his book *The World Is Flat*, wrote about the increasing power of the Internet, where anyone can publish or contribute something online. In particular, he shared how the Internet can give anyone around the world, including middle and high school students, the opportunity to share their intellectual contributions with others. He described this as a global "flattener," Friedman wrote:

> It was long assumed that producing any product of substance or complexity takes some kind of hierarchical organization or institution. The assumption was that you needed top-down vertical integration to get such things done and out into the world. But thanks to our newfound ability to upload—which came about as a direct result of the flat-world platform—you can now produce really complex things, as an individual or as part of a community, with so much less hierarchy and so much less money than ever before. (p. 96)

Due to the increasing popularity of and access to the Internet, Quadrant D of the Rigor/Relevance Framework, meshed with Friedman's notion of "flatteners," has exciting implications for social studies teachers. The lesson that follows captures this synergy and is just one example of how this can be done in the social studies classroom. It is also important to note that the notion of having students use the computer as a tool for the mind, or Mindtool, serves as a significant underpinning of the transformation of classrooms today from a teacher-centered model to a student-centered model, where students are engaged in a great deal of higher-level thinking as they use their laptop computers, iPads, or other electronic devices to explore the World Wide Web.

The Mindtools Framework: A Rationale for Using the Internet to Teach About Congress

The full potential of computers in the social studies classroom has not been fully harnessed. Frequently, students are asked to memorize details from the Internet or produce PowerPoint presentations that involve lower-level thinking. The Mindtools framework challenges this notion. Instead, the focus is on moving from lower-level thinking with technology to higher-level thinking. Jonassen (1995) wrote, "Learners should be responsible for recognizing and judging patterns of information and then organizing it, while the computer should perform calculations, store, and retrieve information" (p. 46). This has important implications for the social studies classroom. There are many opportunities for students to analyze information that they find online. The House of Representatives Internet webpage is an excellent example of this. It is important to note that this is the paradigm that should be used with computers in the social studies classroom. In fact, experts who have researched educational technology suggest that "computer systems should be used as thinking tools for the mind to promote discussions, reflection, and problem solving" (Jonassen, Carr, & Yueh, 1998). Jonassen (1995) added, "Rather than using the power of computer technologies to disseminate information, computers should be used in all subject domains as tools for engaging learners in reflective, critical thinking about the ideas they are studying" (p. 66). How does this theory fit the lesson described in the pages to follow? Electronic databases, like those found on the House of Representatives Internet webpage, are excellent at storing information, or "memorizing information." Thus, there is no need to have students regurgitate this information for the next exam. Students can find this information in a matter of seconds online. Instead, students should be asked to do what they can do better than any computer or electronic database found online. In particular, students should be challenged to analyze the data, make inferences, and reach conclusions. As a result, students will be using the computer as a Mindtool. This is a paradigm shift for some teachers.

Interestingly, it has frequently been a misconception that you can put a student in front of a computer and he or she will magically learn from it. Instead, students should "learn with, not from technology" (Jonassen, 1995, p. 41). It is important to point out that educators must strategically think about how they are using computers in their social studies lessons. Please note this does not necessarily mean that learning is going to be any easier when students learn with computers in the social studies classroom. In fact, the Mindtools framework "often requires learners to think harder about the subject matter domain being studied, while generating thoughts that would be otherwise impossible without the tool" (Jonassen, 1995, p. 43). The Mindtools framework that has been identified here has profound implications for the lesson to follow on the US House of Representatives.

Decision-Making Model: Using the Internet to Facilitate Discussion About Congress

The US House of Representatives Internet webpage is fertile ground for teachers to prompt student dialogue on a plethora of issues facing our country and world. This is a critical part of citizenship. Ochoa-Becker (1999) wrote:

> Controversial issues are and should be at the center of democratic citizenship education. If citizens are to govern themselves intelligently in a free society, they must know something not only about the issues they face, but also about the several points of view that shape public debate. Just as important, they must know how to analyze those issues, examine all sides, identify relevant values, and justify their decisions . . . the validity of democracy is at stake . . . unless young people develop those abilities, they will not be able to contribute qualitatively to the fiber of this democracy. (p. 339)

Many other experts have also advocated for the use of inquiry at the heart of the social studies classroom. Engle (2003 [1960]) wrote, "A good citizen has many facts at his command, but more, he has arrived at some tenable conclusions about public and social affairs" (p. 302). In the same article, Engle added, "If the quality of decision making is to be the primary concern of social studies instruction, we must take steps to upgrade the quality of intellectual activity in the social studies classroom" (p. 305). Engle's position is supported by other teachers who believe it is critical to expose students to decision making in the classroom. For instance, Evans, Newman, and Saxe (1996) argue that the "purpose of issues-centered instruction is not just to raise the questions and expose students to them, but to teach students to offer defensible and intellectually well-grounded answers to these questions" (p. 2). This quote summarizes the rationale to move this lesson about Congress from rote memorization of facts to a more meaningful dialogue about the kinds of issues that members of Congress tackle each day.

There are many bills that members of Congress are debating, which can be easily viewed online by students in a social studies classroom. Therefore, it only makes sense to give students the opportunity to voice their opinion about these bills as they move through committees and to the floor of the House of Representatives. This can help prepare students for citizenship. Parker (1997) writes:

> When aimed at democratic ends, interaction in schools can help children develop the habits of behavior and character necessary for public life: the courtesies, manners, tolerance, respect, sense of justice, and knack for forging public policy with others, whether one likes them or not. (p. 18)

It is important to note that there is evidence that students can improve their discussion skills when teachers make discourse a point of emphasis in the classroom. In particular, evidence suggests that students enjoy discussion in the social studies classroom, and their ability to discuss improves when a teacher integrates it frequently in the classroom (Hess & Posselt, 2002). As a result, the US House of Representatives Internet webpage has a great deal of potential, since it can help to foster meaningful dialogue among students on issues ranging from health care to the war in Afghanistan. However, the Internet is not always used to foster dialogue in the social studies classroom. In fact, the Internet is sometimes used to simply show or give students information, such as names and dates, rather than prompting students to think critically about the subject matter.

The Giving, Prompting, and Making Model: Technology Integration Structures in Social Studies

Technology integration in the social studies classroom sometimes focuses on the teacher using PowerPoint and lecturing about the substance of an Internet webpage. However, many experts believe technology integration can also involve student-centered instructional models in the social studies classroom. Hammond and Manfra (2009) describe a technology integration model that involves both teacher-centered and student-centered instructional approaches when technology is used in the social studies classroom. They describe their framework as the "Giving, Prompting, and Making Model" (see Figure 5.2). In the Giving Model, teachers lecture using technology-related artifacts, such as the Internet or PowerPoint. In the Prompting Model, teachers use questions to encourage their students to analyze what they are viewing on the Internet. Finally, in the Making Model, students are asked to use technology to produce products that actually show what they have learned (Hammond & Manfra, 2009). In the lesson described in this article, the focus is on using the Prompting Model, where students are asked to be involved in higher-level thinking about Congress.

How can teachers use the Prompting Model to have their students solve problems and create solutions? Many issues can be explored online. Current events provide us with many relevant examples. In regard to domestic affairs, a teacher can ask, "Should the US Congress pass additional gun control legislation?" Another potential question is "How would you propose to reduce the federal deficit?" In regard to foreign affairs, a teacher may ask, "How would you solve the current standoff with North Korea?" Yet another question may be "How would you handle the civil war in Syria?" Of course, the key is for the teacher to identify the objective in the social studies curriculum and the type of prompting questions that will fit the Internet investigation. Most importantly, the key is that the use of the Internet is focused on higher-level thinking by prompting students through a series of questions, rather than giving students a great deal of lower-level information, such as facts and dates to memorize. In summary, the US House of Representatives Internet webpage gives students the unique opportunity to participate

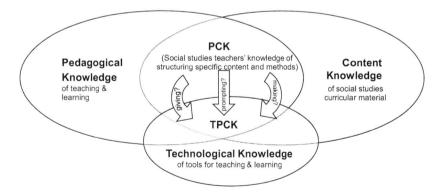

Figure 5.2 Hammond, T.C. & McGlinn Manfra, M. (2009). Giving, prompting, making: Aligning technology and pedagogy within TPACK for social studies instruction. *Contemporary Issues in Technology and Teacher Education, 9,* 160–185.

in critical thinking by taking part in a great deal of decision making on matters pertaining to legislation facing our nation.

House of Representatives: Decision Making on Issues in Your Congressional District

The House of Representatives webpage has a link that enables students to find out who their representative is by typing in their local zip code. This feature is found in the upper-left corner of the webpage. Students can view legislation recently voted on by their representative and committees on which they serve. For example, Bruce Braley (D-IA) voted in favor of the Stem Cell Research Enhancement Act, which "would expand the federal funding of embryonic stem cell research by lifting the restrictions on the embryonic stem cell lines that can be used for federally-funded research" (US House, 2008). Representative Braley also serves on the Small Business and Transportation Committees. This feature of the webpage can be used to pose the following questions: Pretend you are Representative Braley. He voted in favor of lifting the restrictions on the embryonic stem cell lines that can be used for federally funded research. Determine how you would have voted on the issue of stem cell research (experiential question). Of course, opinions will vary greatly on this issue and most issues facing members of Congress. Most importantly, students will have the opportunity to think deeply about these challenging issues.

It is important to note that Congressman Braley serves on the Transportation Committee, which can lead to some interesting issues for discussion. For instance, explain some of the difficult decisions Representative Braley faces as a member of the Transportation Committee (reflective question). There are many difficult decisions to pick from. Perhaps the biggest challenge is weighing the costs and benefits of transportation projects. The burden to taxpayers is great, yet the bridge collapse on the Mississippi River in Minnesota a few years ago highlights the need to maintain a solid infrastructure.

Representative Braley's congressional district is in northeast Iowa bordering the Mississippi River. As a result, the geographic region that a member of Congress comes from can lead to a line of questions. For example, describe how the transportation needs of Iowans may be different from other parts of the nation (compare-contrast question). Of course, there are competing interests among different regions of the country for various transportation projects. In particular, the urban areas of the northeast may be more interested in urban transit projects than are rural areas of the Midwest.

Members of the House of Representatives will run for election every two years. This can lead to another interesting line of questions. For example, summarize how an upcoming election might affect how Representative Braley votes on issues (cause-effect question). Politicians will frequently take into consideration the public opinion of their constituents. Ultimately, the constituents will determine whether they want their representative to serve them again for another two years. To make things even more interesting, Representative Braley is running for the US Senate this year. Therefore, the students can be asked how this may have an impact on his decision making in Congress. For instance, a statewide campaign as a US Senator can be different from a congressional campaign, since the politician may need to appeal to a wider spectrum of voters statewide. It is also important to note that questions can involve foreign policy or domestic issues facing the nation. For example, the United States is currently facing a troubling economy and paralyzing national debt. As a result, students can investigate alternative solutions to the crisis and make suggestions to alleviate the problem, pretending they are a member of Congress (problem-solving question).

Congressional Committees: Engaging Students in Higher-Level Thinking About Congress

Currently, there are twenty-four committees in the House of Representatives. Each committee focuses its time and energy on an issue facing our nation. For example, there is a committee that deals with foreign affairs and another is focused on natural resources (US House, 2008). House members typically serve on two to three committees, which enables them to become experts on a few issues. By clicking the "Committees" link on the left side of the Internet webpage, students can view a list of the committees found in the House of Representatives. There is a link for each of the committees. Teachers may want to explore some of the committee webpages with the students. For example, by clicking the "Agriculture" committee link, students will find another link that features the names of committee members. Students will find there are more Republicans than Democrats on the Agriculture Committee. This is a teachable moment. Many students may wonder why this is the case. The majority party in the House of Representatives controls the committee chairmanships and is awarded the greater number of seats on the committee (Sanford & Green, 1983). Teachers can replicate this point by clicking the links for the other committees found on the House of Representatives webpage.

The committees feature of the webpage can be used to ask some additional questions. For example, pretend you are a member of the House of Representatives. Explain which committee you would like to serve on (experiential question). Most students will likely find that there is at least one committee that deals with issues they are passionate about. It is also important to note there are several committees labeled "Select Committees." The teacher may want to explain to students that these committees deal with new issues when they arise and they tend to last less than a year (Sanford & Green, 1983). Currently, there is a select committee dealing with the issues of energy interdependence and global warming. Teachers can have students identify an issue that needs immediate attention and describe why they believe a select committee should exist to tackle the problem (reflection question).

Current events also shape what takes place in the chambers of Congress each day. For example, Americans today are paying much more for gasoline than they were fifteen years ago. Therefore, a teacher can ask students to pretend that they are members of the Energy Committee. Students can be asked to examine various alternatives to solve our nation's energy crisis and summarize how they would resolve the dilemma if they were a member of Congress (problem-solving question). For instance, the Education and Labor Committee is confronted with a debate on the merits of No Child Left Behind (NCLB). Students can investigate the causes of the achievement gap and determine whether NCLB is having a positive impact on educational achievement (cause-effect question). Finally, students can be asked to problem-solve various issues facing the country and the world. The Energy and Commerce Committee has been investigating the issue of climate change. As a result, students can compare and contrast what European countries are doing to limit greenhouse gases versus what our nation has been doing to minimize them (compare-contrast question). There are countless potential questions that can foster critical thinking using the committees segment of the webpage. Many of these questions will depend on the issues that arise each day in the House of Representatives.

The day-to-day functions of committees can be easily tracked on the House of Representatives webpage. The webpage has a segment titled "Currently on the House Floor" with a link labeled "Committee Hearings," which will give students daily up-to-date information on the issues being debated by the various committees. For example, in June 2008 the Foreign Affairs Committee held a hearing on the role of the FBI at Guantanamo Bay, and the Judiciary Committee held a hearing on problems with immigration detainees' medical care. The issues debated each day by the committees will vary greatly. However, the feature gives students an insider look at the workings of a committee. Most importantly, it provides immediate information that would be impossible for a textbook or lecture to cover. As a result, the Internet webpage greatly enhances students' ability to comprehend how their Congress works.

Debating and Voting on Bills: Critical Thinking to Foster Skills Needed for Citizenship

The House of Representatives webpage allows students to view bills that have been recently debated and voted on in Congress. The segment titled "Find Vote Information" has a link called "Roll Call Votes," which students can click to see detailed information related to these bills. Once students have clicked the link, the webpage will give them the option of picking a congressional session to examine. The most recent congressional session is the 113th Congress – 1st Session (2013). Once students have clicked a congressional session, they will see a long list of legislation that has appeared before Congress in a given year. Students can click

"Roll" to see how members of the House of Representatives have voted on a specific bill. The webpage also clearly identifies how Democrats and Republicans have voted on each piece of legislation.

There are many bills to pick from that will foster critical thinking and decision making. For example, the HR 6 bill in the 110th Congress caused large numbers of Democrats and Republicans to vote differently. The bill states the desire "to reduce our nation's dependency on foreign oil by investing in clean, renewable, and alternative energy resources, promoting emerging technologies, developing greater efficiency, and creating a strategic energy efficiency and renewable reserve to invest in alternative energy, and for other purposes" (US House, 2008). Students will find the specific language of the bill calls for an end to subsidies for big oil companies. In this instance, Democrats voted overwhelmingly in favor of this bill, while more than half of the Republicans opposed it. Students can examine what caused the parties to vote differently on an issue like this (cause-effect question). As a result, students can learn about the influences of interest groups, such as the oil companies that generally support Republicans, and environmental groups that tend to support Democrats.

Students can also view the actual text of any bill by clicking "Issue." Many of the bills have evolved over time, due to compromises among members of the House, since they are willing to adjust a bill to increase the chances of its passage. For example, the HR 6 bill dealing with energy had twenty other related bills that preceded it in the House and Senate. Students can view the other similar bills by clicking the "Related Bills" feature. I then had my students view the different variations of the bill to see how it evolved over time (compare-contrast question). This point would be very difficult to emphasize without the House of Representatives webpage. The feature can also give teachers the opportunity to challenge students to consider how they might revise a specific bill if they were a member of the House of Representatives (reflection question). Most importantly, the question can spark interest in the legislative process.

Building on the interest sparked by this feature of the webpage, the teacher can ask students to explain how they would have voted on a particular issue if they were a member of Congress (experiential question)—for example, bill HR 6 dealing with energy interdependence. Finally, students can investigate why the bill was able to muster enough support to pass through the House of Representatives. Some teachers may even want their students to develop a hypothesis on why a bill did or did not pass before they investigate the topic further online (problem-solving question). In the case of the HR 6 bill, there may be many factors that students must take into consideration. For example, politicians must frequently consider public opinion. Yet, public opinion sometimes contradicts what the politician feels is the right thing to do. Therefore, members of Congress sometimes face extremely difficult decisions, which is another teachable moment for students.

Rigor/Relevance: Investigating Congressional Bills Using an Electronic Database

Members of Congress tackle countless domestic and foreign policy issues each day. Most students can find at least one issue that interests them that has been debated on the floor of the House. The House of Representatives Internet web-page has an electronic database, sponsored by the Library of Congress, that enables students to more closely investigate an issue that appeals to them. There is a seg-ment titled "Bills & Reports" under the "Legislative Activity" tab where students can search for bills using a key word or phrase. This feature of the webpage began in 1995 to allow the public to more easily see legislation as it proceeds through Congress (US House, 2008). By utilizing this link, students can access an interac-tive database where they can type in a phrase to find information related to a bill on an issue they are curious about. It is important to scroll down and click the "Search Bill Text" tab.

There are countless issues for students to explore. For example, entering the phrase "guns" uncovered twenty-four different bills related to this topic that had been proposed during the 110th session of Congress in 2007–2008. Students can then click the bill number to see a summary and status of the bill. There is also a PDF version of the bill if viewers prefer to see the text using that feature. In addition, by clicking the link titled "Summary and Status," students can then find another link titled "Text of Legislation" to see word for word the bill they are seeking. For example, the search on guns unveiled bill HR 3766 titled "To assist local governments in conducting gun buyback programs" sponsored by Repre-sentative Eleanor Holmes Norton (D-DC).

The webpage will also allow students to view the text from debates on the floor of the House and Senate. The "Congressional Record" link featured under the "Find a Bill, Amendment, or Debate" segment will take students to this interesting feature of the webpage. Again, the link will take students to an interactive database where they can enter a phrase to examine a particular issue. For example, typing in the phrase "No Child Left Behind" found 366 speeches that were delivered on the House or Senate floor in 2007–2008. For instance, Representative Walberg (R-MI) gave a speech on March 14, 2007, where he argued for state and local control of education. There are countless issues debated in Congress, and this feature allows students to see in greater detail how members of Congress are working to tackle the problems facing our country.

Summary

The Internet gives high school social studies students the opportunity to access information that would have been very difficult to attain in the past. In this case, students are able to view up-to-date information. As a result, students can apply what they have learned from a lecture or textbook by seeing current examples on the Internet. A great deal of critical thinking occurs as students take into consideration their prior knowledge and apply it to what they are viewing on the Internet, especially if teachers foster critical thinking using the formats previously discussed. When the Internet is used with this type of framework, the computer enhances the students' thinking and learning instead of students being controlled by the computer itself (Jonassen, Carr, & Yueh, 1998).

In summary, when students have the opportunity to use computers as a tool for their mind, they can be involved in a great deal of decision making. As noted earlier, this allows students to interact with the data and reflect on what they have learned to make sense out of the information (Jonassen, Carr, & Yueh, 1998). The databases found online can move learning from a teacher-centered to a student-centered classroom. In conclusion, the increasing availability of the Internet in high school classrooms and student interest in using technology provides a promising alternative to traditional approaches used to teach students about Congress.

References

Daggett, W. R. (2008). *Achieving academic excellence through rigor and relevance*. International Center for Leadership in Education. Retrieved from www.leadered.com/leadershipIn stitute.html. Accessed 4/10/14.

Daggett, W.R. (2014). *Rigor/Relevance Framework. A guide to focusing resources to increase student performance*. Rexford, NY: International Center for Leadership in Education.

District Administration. The Magazine of School District Management. (2008). *Study: Pennsylvania's laptop program works, but cost favors affluent schools*. Retrieved from www.districtadministration.com/newssummary.aspx?news=yes&postid=48884. Accessed 6/15/08.

Engle, S.G. (2003 [1960]). Decision making: The heart of social studies instruction. *The Social Studies, 1,* 7–10.

Evans, R. W., Newman, F.M., & Saxe, D.W. (1996). *Handbook on teaching social issues. NCSS Bulletin 93* (pp. 2–4). Washington, D.C.: National Council for the Social Studies.

Friedman, T.L. (2005). *The world is flat*. New York: Picador.

Hammond, T.C. & McGlinn Manfra, M. (2009). Giving, prompting, making: Aligning technology and pedagogy within TPACK for social studies instruction. *Contemporary Issues in Technology and Teacher Education, 9,* 160–185.

Hess, D.E. & Posselt, J.R. (2002). How high school students experience and learn from the discussion of controversial issues. *Journal of Curriculum and Supervision, 4,* 283–314.

Jonassen, D.H. (1995). Computers as cognitive tools: Learning with technology, not from technology. *Journal of Computing in Higher Education, 6*(2), 40–73.

Jonassen, D.H., Carr, C., & Yueh, H. (1998). Computers as mindtools for engaging learners in critical thinking. *Tech Trends, 43,* 24–32.

Jonassen, D.H., Howland, J., Marra, R.M., & Crismond, D. (2008). *Meaningful learning with technology* (3rd ed.). Columbus, OH: Prentice Hall.

Lutkus, A. & Weiss, A. (2007). The nation's report card. *NAEP: Civics 2006*. Washington, D.C.: National Center for Education Statistics.

Ochoa-Becker, A.S. (1999). Decision-making in middle school social studies: An imperative for youth democracy. *The Clearing House, 6*, 337–340.

Parker, W. C. (1997). The art of deliberation. *Educational Leadership, 54*(5), 18–21.

Parsad, B. & Jones, J. (2005). *Internet access in US public schools and classrooms: 1994–2003.* Washington, D.C.: National Center for Education Statistics. Retrieved from http:// nces.ed.gov/pubs2005/2005015.pdf. Accessed 9/4/14.

Sanford, W.R. & Green, C.R. (1983). *Basic principles of American government.* New York, NY: AMSCO School Publications, Inc.

US House. (2008). *United States House of Representatives.* Retrieved from www.house.gov/. Accessed 6/10/08.

6

STUDENT HISTORIANS

Frequently, middle and secondary students in social studies classrooms find themselves listening to lecture and memorizing information for an exam. This fails to provide students the opportunity to think deeply about the subject matter and analyze for themselves an historical event or issue. How can middle and secondary social studies teachers make this happen? Fortunately, students today have increased access to the Internet where there are many primary and secondary sources pertaining to an array of historical issues. This enables students to do what professional historians have done for many years. Middle and secondary students can use the Internet to examine these primary and secondary sources, analyze them, and develop their own historical interpretation. Rather than relying on the social studies teacher to tell them what happened and why it happened, students can move from being a passive learner to an active learner, constructing their own historical interpretation based on the evidence from the primary and secondary sources they have examined on the Internet. In summary, technology enables middle and secondary students to have access to the same sources that professional historians have had in the past. The technology, used in conjunction with a change in pedagogy, enables the learners to be student historians where they can read like historians.

Rationale for Developing Student Historians

Bolick (2006) wrote that "digital archives have democratized historical research" (p. 122). In the past, middle and secondary social studies students relied on their classroom textbook and lectures from their teacher to learn about the history of our nation and world. Unfortunately, this limited the breadth of history covered in middle and secondary classrooms. Frequently, students were not exposed to the varied experiences of women and minorities throughout the history of our nation (Bolick, 2006). Technology has changed this. Middle and secondary students can more easily access primary sources that include the voices of women and minorities. This involves "the inclusion of all histories" (Bolick, 2006, p. 123). Today, students can access these diverse perspectives online without having to leave the classroom (Bolick, 2006).

Aldridge (2006) argued that high school teachers rely on the textbook too much and that they should infuse primary sources more frequently in their lesson plans. There is concern that the reliance on textbooks only gives one perspective on the historical issue that the students are investigating in the social studies curriculum. According to Aldridge (2006), unfortunately, "the result is that students often are exposed to simplistic, one-dimensional, and truncated portraits that deny them a realistic and multifaceted picture of American history" (p. 663). The literature describes this as a master narrative since social studies students are exposed to a single perspective of history from their classroom textbook where "the dominance of master narratives in textbooks denies students a complicated, complex, and nuanced portrait of American history" (Aldridge, 2006, p. 663). Aldridge (2006) uses the example of how Martin Luther King, Jr. is covered in middle and secondary social studies textbooks to make his point. He writes that "textbooks present prescribed, oversimplified, and uncontroversial narratives of King that obscure important elements in King's life and thought" (Aldridge, 2006, p. 662). As a result, students are often unaware of the complexity of the Civil Rights movement and the African-American experience.

History can arguably be much more interesting to middle and secondary social studies students when they have access to more than one perspective from primary sources rather than a singular perspective from the textbook and teacher. Aldridge (2006) writes that "when master narratives dominate history textbooks, students find history boring, predictable, or irrelevant" (p. 663). Primary sources can give middle and secondary students the ability to access firsthand diverse perspectives in history. *Digital history* is the term that is frequently associated with primary sources found on the Internet. By using digital history, social studies teachers can facilitate lesson plans that challenge students to participate in historical inquiry. In fact, "digital history archives enable teachers to engage in historical inquiry in a way that was not possible in the past" (Bolick, 2006, p. 128). Bolick (2006) also found that digital history shifted the classroom from a teacher-centered to a student-centered instructional approach and that students were able to access diverse historical accounts that were not found in the classroom textbook. Fortunately, the increased access to diverse perspectives can be motivating and more rigorous for students. Aldridge (2006) argued that access to these diverse perspectives can give students "insight into the dilemmas, challenges, and realities of living in a democratic society such as the United States" (p. 663). These are issues and perspectives that students would often fail to be exposed to in the traditional textbook found in the social studies classroom.

Middle and secondary social studies teachers can expose students to the complexity of our nation's history by giving them the opportunity to participate in historical inquiry lessons where they examine primary and secondary sources using technology. Historical inquiry enables students to do what historians do. They can view primary and secondary sources firsthand, analyze them, and develop their own conclusions. This is possible in today's classroom due to the increasing amount of technology available to students and is frequently known as the "student historian approach." Some prefer to call this teaching and learning pedagogy "reading like a historian." Both phrases describe the same student-centered, inquiry-based approach using historical documents.

Student Historians: How It Works in the Classroom

Today, middle and secondary social studies students can more easily do what historians have done in the past due to the increased access to technology in the classroom. There are many databases where students can view primary and secondary sources online. This enables students to access many of the same resources that professional historians have used for years. Historians view primary and secondary sources, analyze these sources, and develop their own historical interpretation. This involves a great deal of critical thinking about the subject matter. Frequently, the term *historical thinking* is associated with the type of in-depth analysis that is involved when historians view these sources and develop an interpretation from their research. Middle and secondary students can easily do the same when they have an opportunity to analyze the sources that they find online using technology in the social studies classroom.

Drake and Nelson (2009) identified how students can be historians in the middle and secondary social studies classroom. They suggest that students begin by using a technique that is known as sourcing heuristic. The term is used to describe the work that should be done by students before they actually read the sources. During this part of the lesson, the teacher instructs students to ask questions "about the author's credentials, motivations, and participation in the events at the time the document was written" (Drake & Nelson, 2009, p. 58). Students are also encouraged to consider the audience that the source was intended for (Drake & Nelson, 2009). This level of analysis enables students to then begin the process of actually reading the primary sources.

Corroboration heuristic is the term used to describe the next step involved in a lesson using the student historian approach. In this part of the lesson, students are asked to compare the information that they have learned from each of the sources that they examine to reach a conclusion or historical interpretation (Drake & Nelson, 2009). This can be a very time-consuming feature of this instructional approach, but it is a vitally important part of the lesson. Students can then develop their own historical interpretation of the historical event or period that they are investigating. It is also suggested that the teacher encourage students to participate in contextualization during this segment of the lesson. This is a term used to describe the portion of the lesson when students should consider the "time frame and conditions both locally and nationally" (Drake & Nelson, 2009, p. 60). Knowledge of the conditions of the time under study may have an impact on the interpretation that the student develops. Contextualization may give the student greater background information and prior knowledge to help them make sense of what they are reading in the primary source that they are investigating on the Internet. For example, students reading primary sources about a single event in the Civil Rights movement, such as the Montgomery Bus Boycott, should recognize that the event was one part of a wider struggle for equality throughout the nation at the time.

The student historian approach also encourages students to participate in comparative thinking about the time period they are investigating. There is an emphasis on learning about the conditions globally during the time period of the historical investigation (Drake & Nelson, 2009). This enables students to have a greater understanding of the historical situation around the world. Students are more likely to understand what they read in the primary source due to the prior knowledge and background information that they have been exposed to. For example, students reading primary sources on the struggles of Americans during the Great Depression would also benefit by knowing that there was a global depression taking place at the same time.

In summary, a great deal of historical thinking takes place as students examine the primary and secondary sources on the Internet and develop their own interpretation. This transforms the classroom from a teacher-centered to a student-centered instructional environment. The students are also challenged to think deeply about the subject matter rather than memorizing names and dates for a test or quiz. This aligns with the decision-making model of social studies instruction where teachers facilitate higher-level thinking and students are challenged to defend the positions that they develop. Middle and secondary social studies classrooms that are equipped with technology can more easily make this happen by enabling students to access primary sources online.

SCIM-C: A Step-by-Step Guide to Lessons Using the Student Historian Approach

Doolittle, Hicks, and Ewing (2005) designed an Internet webpage to introduce middle and secondary social studies teachers to the Summarizing, Contextualizing, Inferring, Monitoring, and Corroborating (SCIM-C) strategy for interpreting history. The webpage can be found at the following Internet link: www.historicalinquiry.com/scim/. The SCIM-C strategy is designed to enable students "to develop the knowledge and skills necessary to interpret primary sources and reconcile various historical accounts, in order to investigate meaningful historical questions" (Doolittle, Hicks, & Ewing, 2005). As discussed earlier, there are many digital sources that middle and secondary students can find with technology. The SCIM-C strategy is one more tool that gives students the necessary skills, or building blocks, to help them develop their own historical interpretation by viewing primary and secondary sources firsthand on the Internet.

Middle and secondary social studies teachers can view a multimedia presentation on the Internet site that explains more deeply the SCIM-C strategy. The link to the multimedia presentation is featured in the upper-right corner of the Internet webpage and is labeled "SCIM-C Explanation." There is also a description of each of the SCIM-C steps listed on the introductory portion of the webpage. In addition, viewers will find a list of sample questions that teachers can use to help their students do what historians do. The questions are user friendly and an easy way for students to capture the main ideas from the sources that they view with technology in the classroom. Most importantly, the SCIM-C strategy helps students to become student historians and think more deeply about the subject matter in the social studies curriculum rather than passively learning with technology.

Scaffolding is a significant underpinning to the SCIM-C strategy. The title of the SCIM-C Internet webpage is "Historical Inquiry. Scaffolding Wise Practices in the History Classroom" (Doolittle, Hicks, & Ewing 2005). The SCIM-C strategy uses a series of four analyzing questions per each of the five phases. Doolittle, Hicks, and Ewing (2005) explain that the analyzing questions featured on the webpage "serve to scaffold a concerted level of engagement with each source in order to allow students time to linger and learn from each source in light of the historical question being asked."

In summary, each spiraling question is purposely designed to enable students to become more fully engaged when they view each source and to eventually become self-regulated learners as they investigate historical questions in the middle and secondary social studies classroom (Doolittle, Hicks, & Ewing, 2005).

The SCIM-C Internet webpage has a few additional features that middle and secondary social studies teachers should be aware of. The tab on the webpage labeled "Links" includes several useful collections of primary sources. These collections can help students learn many of the objectives in the social studies curriculum. For example, there is a link to the "Digital History Reader" Internet site where there is an outstanding collection of lesson plans with digital sources on a wide array of American and European history topics. Each lesson includes an already prepared historical question. The Internet webpage can be found at the following link: www.historicalinquiry.com/scim/.

Theory and Practice: Firsthand Experience Using Technology and the Student Historian Approach in American History

Middle and secondary social studies teachers have a limited amount of time to identify primary sources online that can be used with each lesson's objective. It is important for teachers to be able to quickly identify primary sources that can be used in the classroom. The Avalon Project Internet site has an excellent collection of primary sources on a wide range of American and world history topics and is sponsored by the Yale University Law School (Yale University Law School, 2008). There are many documents organized by time periods and whether the document is from American or world history. Teachers can utilize these online sources by having students participate in historical inquiry using the student historian approach. This can arguably transform a classroom from a teacher-centered to a student-centered instructional model where the students can use technology to develop their own historical interpretation or conclusion. The Avalon Project's collection of primary sources can be found at the following Internet address: http://avalon.law.yale.edu/.

Students can examine many primary sources from the online collection. Some of them include the Alien and Sedition Acts (1798), George Washington's Proclamation about the Whiskey Rebellion (1794), George Washington's Farewell Address (1796), Woodrow Wilson's Fourteen Points (1918), and the Truman Doctrine (1947). Teachers may want to use an anticipatory set activity before students have the opportunity to read these sources online. Anticipatory set activities may include a brief video highlighting the main ideas of the historical event that potentially will grab the students' attention before they learn more in-depth information about the historical event. Following the anticipatory set activity, teachers may want to lecture for fifteen to twenty minutes about the historical event to give students more background information so they can have some prior knowledge before they view the primary source online. This background information can help students make sense out of the primary sources they will examine on the Avalon Project Internet site.

If possible, a liquid crystal display (LCD) projector can help students follow the teacher along online step by step and enable the teacher to point things out about the primary source using this visual aid. The students can examine primary sources related to the lesson's objective and use some type of graphic organizer to capture many of the big ideas from the source. In some instances, students can use graphic organizers that focus on cause-effect, compare-contrast, or problem-solution questions (Scheuerell, 2009). This portion of the lesson is vitally important to help students organize their findings from the primary sources by capturing the main ideas as they examine the source online.

If time permits, the teacher can have a large group discussion about the students' findings. In some instances, the LCD projector can be used to feature the primary source on the whiteboard and the teacher can ask students to come to the board to circle or underline some of the key points from the source. This also enables students to share their interpretation or conclusions about the historical event from their inquiry online. This debriefing is critically important to make sure students were able to capture the main ideas from each of the digital sources that they examined on the Internet. At the end of the lesson, students can also be involved in some type of formative assessment using a closure activity. This can involve exit slips or students writing text messages, billboard slogans, bumper sticker slogans, or newspaper headlines to share the big ideas that they learned from the lesson.

Digital History Webpage: A User-Friendly Way to Identify Primary Sources on the Internet

The Digital History Internet webpage, hosted by the University of Houston, has a significant collection of primary and secondary sources covering American history topics that are readily available to middle and secondary classrooms. Several user-friendly historical categories featured on the site enable viewers to quickly identify sources that students can use during a lesson. Some of the categories include eras, topics, primary sources, voices, multimedia, and exhibitions (Digital History, 2013).

The "eras" feature of the Internet site contains a great deal of historical information. Middle and secondary students can find an electronic textbook when they click each historical era that is featured. For example, slavery is one of the historical eras featured on the Internet site. Viewers can then click the "Documents" tab and find many primary sources about slavery located there. Students can read "Excerpts from the Texas Slave Narratives" by Andy Anderson or an Internet link with a primary source that described how slaves were captured titled "How Slaves Were Acquired" by John Barbot dated 1732. The Internet site also features an account of a slave rebellion titled "A Description of an Uprising Aboard a Slave Ship" by John Barbot dated 1732 and a 1788 firsthand account of the journey across the Atlantic Ocean titled "An Account of the Middle Passage" by Alexander Falconbridge. There are also several firsthand accounts by slaves where they detail for readers what life was like day by day. In one example featured on the site, a slave named Moses Roper wrote about his experiences when he tried to escape a slave plantation and is titled "How He Was Punished After Trying to Run Away" dated 1837.

Middle and secondary students can also find music from many of the historical eras featured on the interactive website. These are valuable primary sources. For example, the site has a vast collection of music from World War I that can be accessed by clicking the historical era tab. There also is a specific link titled "Music," which students can easily find. Some of the songs featured on the site that are accessible to teachers include "Over There" and "L–I–B–E–R–T–Y." Most students will enjoy listening to the music, and it is helpful to give students a hard copy of the song's lyrics so they can more easily see the main themes that were a point of emphasis in the music. Many lyrics can be easily found on the Internet by using a simple Google search. Historical music from the Internet can also be used as an anticipatory set for a lesson.

The Digital History webpage also has many interesting historical images for students to analyze. For example, there are some interesting pictures about the

Civil War. Some of these images include pictures of soldiers and slaves. These images can be used as an anticipatory set activity or Think–Pair–Share activity where students analyze the images. Most importantly, the images are another type of primary source that enables students to be historians in the classroom using technology.

Middle and secondary students can also find Internet links to political cartoons featured under the "Do History Topics" and diverse perspectives from a wide variety of Americans found under the "Voices" section. Students can find firsthand accounts from women, children, Native Americans, and African-Americans. These are the perspectives that are frequently not featured in depth in the traditional classroom textbook in the middle and secondary social studies classroom. The Digital History site can provide these perspectives to students and is located at the following Internet link: www.digitalhistory.uh.edu/index.cfm.

Reading Like a Historian: Ready-to-Go Lessons That Incorporate Digital History on the Web

The Stanford History Education group hosts an Internet webpage that is gaining a great deal of popularity in middle and secondary social studies classrooms. Teachers will find that the site contains many lessons that are already packaged for American and world history. Each lesson includes an essential question and primary sources pertaining to the historical issue under investigation. Middle and secondary students will find the primary sources easy to access using technology. Most importantly, students will learn to read like a historian. The Internet webpage can be found at the following link: http://sheg.stanford.edu/rlh.

Middle and secondary social studies teachers will find that the lesson plans are well organized and feature a wide array of topics in American and world history. The "U.S. History Lessons" link features lessons ranging from the Colonial Era to the Cold War. Some of the world history lesson plans include topics such as Ancient Egypt, the Middle Ages, and China's Cultural Revolution. Each lesson that is featured on the website follows a three-step process. The lessons generally begin by identifying the essential question that will be tackled and provide students with some background knowledge about the historical event or issue. This enables students to make sense out of the primary sources that they later will be reading online during the lesson. The lessons sometimes include a PowerPoint presentation, mini-lecture, or short digital video about the subject matter to build up some background knowledge before the students begin to read the actual primary sources featured in the specified online collection (Stanford History Education Group, 2014). As noted on the website, this is a critically important part of the lesson because "establishing background knowledge is the first step in the inquiry process" (Stanford History Education Group, 2014).

The second step in any lesson featured on the webpage is to have students read the digital sources identified in the appropriate lesson plan collection. In each lesson, students are challenged to think about the essential question and how it pertains to the historical documents they are investigating. The students are then challenged to think deeply about the subject matter by evaluating the evidence presented in the documents and to construct their own argument related to the essential question (Stanford History Education Group, 2014). There are some ways that teachers can vary this step. For example, teachers can have students take opposing viewpoints and then debate each other. However, the key is for students to participate in a student-centered lesson plan where they are reading like a historian and making decisions about the subject matter in the social studies curriculum.

Middle and secondary social studies teachers are strongly encouraged by the Stanford History Education Group to finish the lesson by having the students participate in a class discussion about the essential question and the documents they read pertaining to it. According to the website, this is the part of the lesson where "students see that history is open to multiple interpretations and that the same piece of evidence can support conflicting claims" (Stanford History Education Group, 2014). There is a great deal of higher-order thinking about the subject matter when students participate in this type of engagement about the subject matter using technology. The Reading Like a Historian program is a user-friendly way for middle and secondary students to participate in historical inquiry by reading digital sources on the Internet, analyzing these sources, and developing their own historical interpretation.

Historical Scene Investigations: Prepackaged Lessons Using Digital History

Kathleen Owens Swan and Mark Hofer developed the H.S.I. (Historical Scene Investigations) Internet webpage where students can examine primary sources and reach their own historical interpretations based on their findings. The webpage features primary sources that are already packaged for middle and secondary students to use with technology. Students can examine documents, diaries, historical images, newspapers, and journals that are organized on the Internet site around specific historical issues. The historical issues are featured on a tab on the webpage labeled "Open Cases." The Internet site can be found at the following link: http://web.wm.edu/hsi/.

The H.S.I. model featured on the Internet site includes four critically important steps for middle and secondary students to follow as they investigate each of the historical cases featured on this site. Each investigation begins with the "Becoming a Detective" step where students first learn about the case that they are about to be engaged in. The students are given background information about the investigation and presented with an engaging focus question. They are also assigned a task to complete (Swan & Hofer, 2014). The next step is labeled "Investigating the Evidence" where students are encouraged to crack the case by viewing the primary sources that are already organized for them on the site (Swan & Hofer, 2014). Students are then led to the "Searching for Clues" portion of the case where they view a series of questions step by step to analyze each of the primary sources for the historical investigation. "Cracking the Case" is labeled the "Detective's Log" on the site (Swan & Hofer, 2014). The last stage of the investigation is called "Cracking the Case" where students are encouraged to present their answer and share the evidence that they have to support their historical interpretation (Swan & Hofer, 2014).

For example, there is a historical investigation on the events of Lexington and Concord that features a focus question that reads: "Who fired the first shot at Lexington and Concord?" Students will find eight different primary sources online that they can use to solve the investigation. These sources include diary entries and newspaper accounts from both the British and American colonial perspectives.

Each of the historical investigations also features tabs called "Student View" and "Teacher View." The "Teacher View" gives middle and secondary teachers additional background information pertaining to each historical investigation. For example, the Historical Scene Investigation titled "The Atomic Bomb: The Year of Decisions" features some pertinent notes for the social studies teacher who is planning to facilitate this investigation in the classroom. The focus question for the investigation reads "Did Truman decide to drop the bomb, or was the use of the atomic bomb inevitable?" Students will find many interesting primary sources that include several diary entries from President Truman. There are also primary sources from Secretary of War Henry Stimson's diary regarding this issue and a news article from *U.S. News and World Report* featuring a firsthand account from General George C. Marshall. As a result, students have the opportunity to think deeply about the subject matter as they analyze the primary sources and reach their own historical conclusion.

edTPA: Student Historian Approach and the Requirements for Social Studies Teacher Candidates

Student teachers seeking licensure in social studies increasingly find themselves in teacher education programs where they need to pass the edTPA (Teacher Performance Assessment) portfolio assessment in order to attain a teaching license. Currently, thirty-four states and the District of Columbia require the edTPA portfolio for licensure (Stanford University, 2012). Each teacher candidate should check with the teacher certification officer at their college or university to learn more about the specific requirements for teacher licensure in their state.

Teacher candidates in social studies need to provide evidence that they can complete three different tasks to fulfill the requirements for the edTPA portfolio. These tasks are a major point of emphasis throughout the rubrics published by edTPA. The tasks include the following: 1) planning for instruction and assessment, 2) instructing and engaging students in learning, and 3) assessing student learning (Stanford University, 2012). Each teacher candidate is required by edTPA to submit three to five lesson plans around a single focus question that is used by the teacher candidate for one class period that he or she teaches during the student teaching semester (Stanford University, 2012). The teacher candidate is also required by edTPA to submit videotape of their actual teaching where they are able to successfully engage students in the subject matter presented in the lesson. Teacher candidates are required to obtain permission from parents/guardians of any students that appear in the videotape (Stanford University, 2012). Finally, teacher candidates are required to collect the student work, which will be used for assessment purposes. They are encouraged to analyze the student work, looking for patterns of learning (Stanford University, 2012). Teacher candidates are required to examine in depth the work from three students. One of these must be a student with a specific learning need. This can include students that fit one of the following descriptions: English language learners, gifted students, students with an IEP (Individualized Education Plan), struggling readers, or students who are underperforming in the classroom (Stanford University, 2012). Teacher candidates must demonstrate how they will use the data by identifying the next steps they will take to help these students based on the data they have collected (Stanford University, 2012).

Each teacher candidate seeking licensure in social studies who uses edTPA must demonstrate that they can successfully use the student historian approach with middle and secondary students. Teacher candidates must provide evidence that they can do this by submitting two videotapes that are no more than ten minutes each, where they have facilitated this type of teaching and learning pedagogy (Stanford University, 2012). According to the edTPA Handbook, social studies teacher candidates must submit a videotape for the portfolio where they "should be interacting with students to develop their skills and strategies by critically evaluating accounts or interpretations of historical events or social studies phenomenon" (Stanford University, 2012, p. 6). These identified expectations of edTPA encourage teacher candidates to move instruction away from drill and practice to pedagogy in the social studies classroom, where students are involved in historical inquiry and in-depth thinking about the subject matter.

Social studies teacher candidates using edTPA will find that there is a focus on using academic language to challenge students to think more deeply about the subject matter. Teacher candidates will find that the academic language is a user-friendly way to foster critical thinking about the primary and secondary sources that the middle and secondary students are viewing in the classroom. Each teacher candidate in social studies must use one language function during the lesson plan to facilitate higher-level thinking (Stanford University, 2012). Teacher candidates can pick from a list that includes the following: analyze, compare/contrast, construct, interpret, describe, evaluate, examine, identify, justify, and locate (Stanford University, 2012). For example, teacher candidates may choose to have their students develop their own historical interpretation by examining a series of primary and secondary sources online pertaining to a specific historical event.

Teacher candidates using edTPA are strongly encouraged to have their students use the vast collection of primary and secondary sources already on the Internet. These digital sources are frequently arranged around historical issues or themes and have already been mentioned in this chapter. Middle and secondary social studies students can read these sources and do the necessary historical thinking identified as the requirement for edTPA. The language functions identified by edTPA can help teacher candidates pose questions during the lesson to ensure that a deep level of analysis is taking place.

There are some additional expectations outlined by edTPA that teacher candidates should be familiar with in regard to the implementation of the student historian approach. For example, one of the rubrics suggests that each teacher candidate "provides a challenging learning environment that provides opportunities to express varied perspectives and promotes mutual respect among students" (Stanford University, 2012, p. 21). There is also a point of emphasis in the assessment for social studies teacher candidates to demonstrate that they are able to facilitate interaction among the students as they discuss their historical interpretation from the primary and secondary sources that they investigated (Stanford University, 2012). Finally, the assessment instrument identifies that they are seeking teacher candidates to demonstrate in their digital video that they are skillfully able to challenge students to defend their own historical argument or interpretation during the lesson plan (Stanford University, 2012). Most importantly, edTPA requires teacher candidates to use the student historian approach to examine whether they can facilitate a student-centered lesson where students are involved in a great deal of decision making about the subject matter.

Summary

The student historian pedagogy is increasingly being used in middle and secondary social studies classrooms. These students can do what historians do by examining primary and secondary sources. This requires a great deal of analysis and decision making as students develop their own historical interpretations in the classroom. Teacher candidates will need to demonstrate that they can incorporate this pedagogy with their students. Fortunately, teacher candidates can quickly identify prepackaged digital sources on the Internet that are ready to use with middle and secondary students. Students who have access to technology in the classroom will be well suited for lessons that incorporate the student historian pedagogy.

Middle and secondary students who participate in the student historian pedagogy in technology-rich classrooms are able to examine multiple historical perspectives, including those that have frequently been marginalized in the past by the history classroom textbook and lectures provided by teachers. Firsthand accounts from women and minorities are increasingly accessible by examining these perspectives using the Digital History site. This also moves the classroom from teacher-centered to student-centered instruction where students are involved in a great deal of decision making. Students who become historians are challenged to do more than memorize names and dates for an exam. Rather, these students are thinking more deeply. This enables them to learn the content and skill sets necessary for citizenship in our participatory democracy and the world around them.

References

Aldridge, D.A. (2006). The limits of master narratives in history textbooks. *Teachers College Record, 108*(4), 662–686.

Bolick, C.M. (2006). Digital archives: Democratizing the doing of history. *The International Journal of Social Education, 21*(1), 122–135.

Digital History. (2013). *Using new technologies to enhance teaching and research.* University of Houston. Retrieved from www.digitalhistory.uh.edu/. Accessed 1/27/14.

Doolittle, P., Hicks, D., & Ewing, T. (2005). *Historical inquiry. Scaffolding wise practices in the history classroom.* Retrieved from www.historicalinquiry.com/scim/. Accessed 1/27/14.

Drake, F.D. & Nelson, L.R. (2009). *Engagement in teaching history* (2nd ed). Columbus, OH: Pearson.

Scheuerell, S.K. (2009). The Avalon Project: Using literacy strategies with primary sources on the Internet. *Social Studies Research and Practice, 1,* 71–81.

Stanford History Education Group. (2014). *Reading like a historian.* Retrieved from http://sheg.stanford.edu/rlh. Accessed 1/27/14.

Stanford University. (2012). *Secondary education. Secondary history/social studies assessment handbook.* Stanford, CA: Pearson.

Swan, K. O. & Hofer, M. (2014). *H.S.I. Historical scene investigations.* Retrieved from http://web.wm.edu/hsi/index.html?svr=www. Accessed 1/27/14.

Yale University Law School. (2008). *The Avalon Project at Yale University Law School. Documents in law, history, and diplomacy.* Retrieved from www.yale.edu/lawweb/avalon/avalon.htm. Accessed 6/19/08.

7

AUTHENTIC ASSESSMENT

Authentic assessment involves students producing products that demonstrate what they have learned (Beal & Bolick, 2013). Middle and secondary social studies teachers who find themselves in classrooms equipped with technology are well positioned to have students participate in authentic assessment. Students can show what they have learned in the social studies curriculum by producing projects using technology. There are many possibilities. Digital videos, podcasts, blogs, portfolios, and Internet webpages are just a few examples.

Social studies teachers are likely to find that authentic assessment can transform their classroom into a student-centered learning environment where students are actively involved in producing products using technology. Students are likely to feel a great deal of accomplishment when they participate in authentic assessment (Liu, 2003). Yet, teachers need to remember that there is a great deal of research on how to successfully implement authentic assessment in the social studies classroom. Students do not magically learn by simply putting technology in front of them and assigning them technology projects. Liu (2003) suggests that project-based learning should engage students in higher-level thinking such as problem solving and decision making when they produce products using technology.

There will be a discussion in the pages that follow on the rationale for using authentic assessment in technology-rich classrooms and how to facilitate these projects successfully in the social studies classroom—in particular, how authentic assessment can be used to foster critical thinking and simultaneously help students learn the content in the middle and secondary social studies classroom. Examples will be provided to help the reader.

Benefits of Authentic Assessment

Liu (2003) discovered that authentic assessment in technology-rich classrooms can be motivating to middle and secondary students. The authentic nature of technology projects makes the learning experience quite interesting to students (Liu, 2003). For example, it is rare in the real world for students to later find themselves taking tests or quizzes at the workplace. Authentic assessment possesses real-world value by giving students the opportunity to produce products similar to the technology products they are familiar with. Students frequently listen to podcasts, watch digital videos, and surf the Internet. As a result, they find it appealing to produce podcasts, digital videos, and Internet webpages on topics in the social studies curriculum. They also benefit from the process skills that they are engaged in and simultaneously learn the social studies content.

Liu (2003) found that students who produced multimedia projects were able to connect big ideas more easily and they learned how to collaborate with others as they planned and produced the project from start to finish. Middle and secondary students also benefit greatly by using technology as a cognitive tool where they "engage in knowledge construction rather than knowledge reproduction" (Reeves, 1998, p. 21). Students can reflect on what they have learned about the subject matter from their historical research and produce a technology project on their findings rather than simply sharing what they learned from their teacher's lecture on the same subject. Authentic assessment, when designed appropriately like this, can foster in-depth thinking about the subject matter (Liu, 2003), for example, by having students analyze and interpret information as they produce a project or are involved in problem solving.

Lehrer (1993) found that students who participated in these types of teaching and learning experiences with technology increased their long-term memory on the subject matter in the social studies curriculum that they had investigated (as cited in Reeves, 1998). This does not happen by accident. Research on student-centered technology projects suggests that learners are involved in a great deal of critical thinking since they are participating in a constructivist learning paradigm where a great deal of active learning is taking place (Reeves, 1998). Students learn a great deal from technology when they participate in authentic assessment since they are challenged to think critically about the subject matter rather than using technology as a passive learner doing tutorial work (Reeves, 1998).

Authentic Assessment and Historical Understanding

Middle and secondary social studies teachers need to think strategically about the design of each authentic assessment project that they plan to introduce to their students. Frequently, students are asked to produce products using technology. Sometimes, these projects place little emphasis on higher-level thinking. This was my initial experience with technology when I began to construct lessons with 1:1 laptop computers in my high school social studies classroom. My students participated in many types of authentic assessment with their computers, but they usually did lower-level thinking and simple recall of information. I eventually recognized this and adapted as necessary to provide a more meaningful learning experience for my students using technology. Fortunately, today there are teaching and learning models that help social studies teachers with this dilemma.

Drake and Nelson (2009) have written a great deal about the need to increase historical understanding when students participate in authentic assessment. They have developed a three-tiered model that middle and secondary social studies teachers can implement when they design authentic assessment projects using technology. The model includes the following dimensions: knowledge, reasoning, and communication. Each of these dimensions can be used by teachers when they design a rubric or scoring guide for technology projects that they plan to implement with their students. The incorporation of each dimension can challenge students "to greater levels of historical sophistication" (Drake & Nelson, 2009, p. 115). Each middle and secondary social studies student can also benefit by increasing their historical literacy by participating in each of the critically important dimensions outlined in this model (Drake & Nelson, 2009). Most importantly, the model fosters critical thinking when students use technology to produce authentic assessment products in the social studies classroom.

The knowledge dimension is the first necessary component to historical understanding when middle and secondary students participate in authentic assessment. Drake and Nelson (2009) argue that students who produce authentic assessment projects should be able to develop historical knowledge by being "able to identify, define, and describe important concepts, facts, and details" (p. 115). Scoring guides and rubrics should reflect this critically important component, particularly since the knowledge dimension is the necessary prerequisite or step toward accomplishing the other two dimensions of historical understanding (Drake & Nelson, 2009).

As soon as students are able to demonstrate that they have a working knowledge of the historical issue that they are investigating, they are ready to participate in the reasoning dimension. During the reasoning dimension, students need to be able to "discover relationships among facts and generalizations, and values and opinions, so they can solve problems, make judgments, reach logical conclusions, and organize historical knowledge in their memory" (Drake & Nelson, 2009, p. 116). This involves a great deal of decision making and higher-level thinking for middle and secondary students. It is necessary to challenge students to do this critical thinking so they can have a greater level of historical understanding when they participate in technology projects in the social studies classroom. Each scoring guide should challenge students to include analysis, evaluation, and synthesis (Drake & Nelson, 2009). This enables students to be historians and do the necessary critical thinking about the subject matter.

The communication dimension is the final component to historical under-standing when students participate in authentic assessment. The communication dimension is particularly important because it requires students to organize their thoughts about the subject matter (Drake & Nelson, 2009). Students can use tech-nology to communicate their historical understanding to others, and they must be sure to communicate their thesis about the subject matter and use relevant examples to support their position (Drake & Nelson, 2009). Middle and second-ary students can use technology to communicate their historical understanding by producing a wide array of authentic assessment projects. Students can share their historical understanding with others beyond the walls of the classroom by producing blogs, digital videos, Internet webpages, web-based portfolios, podcasts, and using Web 2.0 tools. The key is for students to use all three of the aforemen-tioned components of historical understanding when they produce these projects with technology.

Each of the three dimensions of historical understanding presented in this chapter is critically important for authentic assessment and historical literacy. Drake and Nelson (2009) argue that each dimension of historical understanding enables students to move to "greater levels of historical sophistication" (p. 115). This would be difficult to replicate with traditional teacher-centered instruc-tional approaches. Technology provides the platform to more easily move to student-centered instructional approaches such as authentic assessment. In order to make this happen, middle and secondary social studies teachers can implement these three dimensions of historical understanding when they design rubrics for authentic assessment projects with technology. These dimensions for historical understanding provide the underpinnings that will help students achieve histori-cal literacy. They challenge students to think more deeply about the subject matter rather than simply having students throw together a technology project that fails to foster critical thinking. Each of the three dimensions for historical understand-ing presented in this chapter is a user-friendly way for middle and secondary social studies teachers to design student-centered projects with technology that includes the necessary rigor to challenge students.

Pivotal Decisions With Technology: Thick or Thin Questions?

There were many examples of authentic assessment produced using technology in each of the three high school social studies classrooms that I had the opportunity to observe during my research study. There was a key distinction between what would make or break a lesson when students were producing technology projects. The lessons that succeeded challenged the students to participate in thick ques-tions, or higher-level thinking, rather than thin questions, or lower-level thinking, when students produced these projects with technology. The students in each of the classrooms produced a variety of projects using technology. There was a clear consensus from each of the social studies teachers on the need to make lessons with technology authentic or relevant to the lives of students. They also believed that it was critically important for students to use technology as a catalyst for higher-level thinking. Yet, my research in these classrooms discovered that this was not always the case.

Each of the social studies teachers in the study felt strongly about the need to foster critical thinking when students produce projects with technology. They were very passionate about the need to move teaching and learning with technology in the social studies classroom from lower-level to higher-level thinking and relevancy. However, in many instances, this was not always the case when I had the opportunity to observe these classrooms. There were indeed many examples of student-centered projects with technology. Unfortunately, most of these projects tended to involve the lowest levels of Bloom's taxonomy with few examples of higher-level thinking using technology. Perhaps this can be attributed to teachers' unfamiliarity with some of the research-based frameworks that already exist to help teachers make this happen. Another possibility is that it takes a great deal of time for teachers to plan complex learning experiences involving technology that will foster in-depth thinking, or thick questions. Teachers are pressed to find time to do this. Hopefully, teachers will find the research-based frameworks presented in Chapter 1 helpful in this process.

Mr. Smith's social studies class can be used as an example to make this point on the necessity to move authentic assessment with technology from thin questions to thick questions on the subject matter. He assigned his students a topic in European history and asked the students to teach their classmates about the topic using their laptop computer to develop a Keynote presentation. There was little evidence of higher-level thinking, and the students were not asked to apply what they had learned in any fashion. Most of the students produced a Keynote presentation with their computer to use as an outline during their class presentations. Most notably, the project certainly added to the relevancy of the project since the students had an authentic audience, their peers, to teach to. However, the part that was glaringly missing was the lack of higher-level thinking in the projects produced by the students. For example, one project that I had the opportunity to view was on the Cold War. It included a series of Keynote slides that the students shared with their peers when they had the opportunity to teach the lesson. They had slides on various Cold War topics such as the Korean War, Berlin Wall, and Cuban Missile Crisis. In each slide the students simply identified answers to thin questions on what had taken place during each of these events. The review questions that the students asked their classmates at the end of their presentation included lower-level recall questions such as "When did the Cold War begin?" and "Who built the Berlin Wall?"

Although the students in Mr. Smith's class were able to participate in authentic assessment using technology, they were unable to provide any analysis whatsoever on the Cold War. Rather than analyzing how these events all fit together, the students simply listed some details relating to the Cold War. As a result, there was little in-depth learning on these important historical events. In fact, one group investigated the 1980 Olympics when the United States boycotted the summer games in Moscow in the Soviet Union. Unfortunately, the group failed to provide any meaningful analysis on why the United States boycotted the games and how it fit into the broader topic of the Cold War.

This lesson could be improved in the future by moving from lower-level thinking, with thin questions, to higher-level thinking, with thick questions, where students could be involved in problem-solving scenarios. For example, they could research these issues surrounding the Cold War and share how they would have handled the historical issue if they were president of the United States. Perhaps the students could share in their Keynote presentation how they would have handled the Korean War if they were President Truman, such as whether they would have expanded the war or not when China got involved during the conflict on the Korean peninsula.

In the Modern United States History class at Bridge High School, the students in Mr. Brown's class learned about the growing popularity of radio across the nation in the early 1900s. He had his students use Garage Band on their iPads to produce a radio jingle, much like what you would find from that historical era. Students used computers to share what they had learned about a topic in social studies, but they failed to be involved in any meaningful higher-level thinking as they produced the project. The students in Mr. Brown's class simply answered thin questions about the subject matter. Fortunately, the lesson did succeed at moving away from drill-and-practice exercises to an authentic medium in the social studies classroom. However, there was little evidence of students using technology and being challenged to think more deeply about the subject matter. In the future, perhaps the students could be challenged to think more deeply about the impact of radio on culture in the United States during the early 1900s or to compare and contrast the impact of radio to television or the Internet today. Students could also investigate issues from the early 1900s, such as immigration and civil rights, by considering how they would stand on these issues if they were a member of Congress at the time. The project produced by the students could then include a jingle outlining how they would solve these issues. This would move the project from lower-level thinking, with thin questions, to higher-order thinking, with thick questions.

During the in-depth study, the students at River High School had the opportunity to use an app called Show Me. The Apple app enabled the students to produce an interactive slideshow on African-American history in the early 1900s, and they posted it to the Internet so others beyond the walls of their classroom could have an opportunity to view their findings. Some of these topics included the Great Migration, Harlem Renaissance, Booker T. Washington, and W. E. B. Du Bois. To begin the project, Mr. Jones gave each student a rubric detailing the expectations for the project. The rubric instructed students to include the main idea of the topic in their own words and provide relevant details. The students also had to make sure the Show Me presentation that they produced was well organized and understandable to the audience that would be viewing it online. The rubric also required students to explain why their topic mattered and why it was relevant to the real world.

I had the opportunity to view many of the Show Me projects produced by the students. In my opinion, there was some in-depth analysis done by the students and some interesting findings, since they were challenged to think about thick questions rather than thin questions. Some of the projects were better than others. Yet, most of the students succeeded at developing an authentic project where they were able to share their historical findings and interpretation with others beyond the walls of the classroom. The project provides evidence that social studies students can produce technology projects that demonstrate a great deal of higher-order thinking. The frameworks presented in Chapter 1 of this book can serve as a guide on how to accomplish this by moving a lesson using computers to higher-level thinking, using thick questions rather than thin questions.

Theory and Practice: Firsthand Experience Using Technology and Authentic Assessment in Civics

The Virtual Warrensburg project enabled freshmen students to investigate local history and produce Internet webpages on their findings (Scheuerell, 2010). Each of the students was expected to conduct research on a local history topic that was assigned to them. The students went on a field trip to the Johnson County Historical Museum to investigate their topics by viewing primary and secondary sources. There was much research to investigate in the community of Warrensburg, Missouri. Some students researched the Civil War and discovered that citizens had divided loyalties between the North and South since Missouri was a border state. Students also researched famous people who were from their community, for example, Carrie Nation, who became a leading advocate for Prohibition and was known nationally as the "Hatchet Lady" since she used a hatchet to knock down beer bottles in taverns. In addition, students researched the importance of the railroad coming to Warrensburg and how it had an impact on the community. There were many other topics, including historical buildings, the origins of street names, African-American history, and a history of parks found in the community. The Internet webpages produced by the students at Warrensburg High School can be found at the following Internet link: http://warrensburg.k12.mo.us/vw/scheuerell/.

The students also had the opportunity to participate in a field trip to many of the historical sites related to their topics. The school had a block schedule, which made this much easier since there were ninety-minute class periods. Some of the field trips included visits to the downtown part of the community where many of the historical buildings were located. There were several trips to the oldest cemetery in town to find the tombstone of Martin Warren, the founder of Warrensburg, since one group produced a webpage on him. The cemetery also featured a memorial to both the Union and Confederate soldiers from Warrensburg who had fought in the Civil War. These images were featured in one of the Internet webpages produced by students. The images allowed the students to collaboratively build an Internet webpage on topics that had been long forgotten in their community.

Cooperative learning was a critical component of the project. Each student was assigned a job or role based on the P.I.E.S. (positive interdependence, individual accountability, equal participation, and simultaneous interaction) structure introduced earlier in the book. The jobs included a webpage editor who used Netscape Composer to produce the Internet webpage and a photographer who took pictures of historical sites and converted the images so they could be used on the Internet webpage that they produced. As a result, each student had an important task to perform in order to produce an Internet webpage that the class could share with others beyond the walls of the classroom. In many instances, the webpage produced by these students is the only one found on the Internet about these narrow topics. This made the project a very exciting experience to the students. Most of the students recognized that their collaborative efforts made this happen.

Technology was arguably the centerpiece that leveraged this unique learning opportunity. It enabled students to collaborate on an authentic project where each student needed to perform a task to complete the final product. There was a significant point of emphasis on higher-level thinking with the project. There is a great deal of potential for similar projects in the middle and secondary social studies classroom.

Inside Classrooms: Using Technology and Authentic Assessment in American History

The students at River High School had the unique opportunity to pilot test the Apple iPad, since the school was trying to determine which computer to purchase for its 1:1 technology program the following school year. The students were eager to try different apps. They were introduced to a user-friendly app called Show Me where they produced projects featuring their research findings on African-Americans in the early 1900s. The students soon discovered that the app allowed them to produce an interactive slideshow with images, text, and narration. Show Me enabled the students to use their fingertips to trace words or draw pictures on the screen of the iPad to enhance their story. Mr. Jones, the social studies teacher, placed the students in groups, and each group was assigned a different topic. Some of the topics included the Great Migration, the Harlem Renaissance, W. E. B. Du Bois, Booker T. Washington, Jackie Robinson, *Plessy v. Ferguson*, and the contributions of African-Americans during World War II.

Mr. Jones strategically developed a rubric that challenged students to develop their own intellectual contributions about these African-American history topics. The rubric outlined that the students needed to summarize their findings about their assigned topic in their own words and show the relevancy of the topic to the real world. Each of these expectations provided evidence that there were elements of Authentic Intellectual Work (AIW) embedded into the planning of this project since students were answering thick questions about the subject matter using technology. The students were moving beyond simply producing another technology project and were challenged to think deeply about the subject matter and share their intellectual contributions.

As soon as the students had completed their projects, they were posted on the class Edmodo site so their peers could view their finished projects and learn from them. Each group also made a presentation to their peers and played their Show Me project so their classmates could see what they had produced. The students also placed their Show Me project on the Internet so it could be viewed on the World Wide Web beyond the walls of their classroom. Many of the projects demonstrated that the students had learned a great deal about the subject matter they investigated. Some of these examples will be discussed in the pages that follow.

Show Me Project: The Great Migration

This group produced a Show Me project that included a detailed narration and historical images to share their findings about the Great Migration. Throughout the project, viewers can see how the students traced words and pictures on their iPad screen to help tell their story. During the slideshow itself, they shared in their narration how African-Americans began to migrate from the South to other regions of the country during the late 1800s. They shared how much of this migration had been to other places in the South, rather than the North. They detailed how this migratory pattern shifted during the early part of the twentieth century due to the locomotive train, which made it much easier for African-Americans to move from place to place, including destinations in the North, such as Chicago.

The group also mentioned that World War I was a pivotal event for the Great Migration because it was more difficult for foreign workers to immigrate to America. As a result, the students discussed how hundreds of thousands of African-Americans migrated from the South to industrial cities, such as Chicago, to fill the jobs in these factories. According to the group, the prospect of better wages was also appealing. The group described how the *Chicago Defender* was the most influential African-American newspaper of the era and how it was used to encourage African-Americans to migrate north. They shared that a significant number of African-Americans from the South migrated to the North. During a portion of their technology presentation, the students included a map to show these migratory patterns from 1916 to 1930. Later, the group identified how the journey north was made by train, boat, car, and bus. They also outlined the push factors that encouraged African-Americans to move away from the South, such as the cost of crops in the area, the boll weevil, and the Jim Crow laws that made life difficult for African-Americans in the region.

This Great Migration Show Me project provided evidence that these students were involved in a great deal of historical analysis about the subject matter. They explored the causes and effects of the African-American migration at the turn of the century. By doing so, the students discovered that multiple push and pull factors motivated so many African-Americans to move during this period from the southern part of the United States to the North.

Show Me Project: The Harlem Renaissance

This group of students began their slideshow by featuring artwork from the Harlem Renaissance. They also stated that the Harlem Renaissance is sometimes known as the New Negro Movement and that it began in Harlem, New York, at the end of World War I. During their narration, the students shared that the Harlem Renaissance was a movement involving a great deal of literary, artistic, cultural, and intellectual works that lasted throughout the Great Depression years. The group included a map of the United States to detail the migratory patterns of African-Americans from the South to the North, which enabled many of them to make great contributions to the Harlem Renaissance. Viewers can see how the students used their fingertips to trace on the iPad the path that many of these African-Americans took. The group also noted that Marcus Garvey was a key figure during the era and that he was well known for advocating the back to Africa movement. At this point of the technology presentation, the students included an image of Garvey and traced over his name using their iPad.

The students in the group were able to identify the key characteristics of the Harlem Renaissance. Their findings were effectively communicated through their Show Me project, and they demonstrated some in-depth analysis by developing their own intellectual contributions on this topic.

Show Me Project: W. E. B. Du Bois

The group that produced this Show Me project began their presentation with an image of Du Bois and conveyed in their narration that he was an African-American educator and social activist. They also shared that he attended an integrated high school in Massachusetts and that he later studied at Harvard University, where he was the first African-American to graduate from the school with a PhD. Later in the presentation, the group shared that Du Bois was an advocate of the pan-Africa movement and explained to viewers what the movement was about. During this segment of the presentation, the students used their fingers to trace a picture of Africa on their iPad. Toward the end of the presentation, they shared how Du Bois believed in the importance of using the courts and the law to fight against discrimination.

The students developed their own intellectual contributions on this important African-American figure since their teacher challenged them to think about some thick questions rather than thin questions, or lower-level thinking, about the subject matter. Their research enabled them to learn a great deal of information about Du Bois and why he was a pivotal leader in the Civil Rights movement at the turn of the century.

Show Me Project: Plessy v. Ferguson

This group began their presentation with images of John Ferguson and Homer Plessy. The students used their iPad to trace the names of both men next to their historical images. As soon as the viewers were able to see images of these two men, the students used their narration to explain that Ferguson was the judge in this court case and Plessy was the individual who had been arrested when he tried to board a train in New Orleans. As the presentation moves on, viewers can see a map of Louisiana, where the incident took place. The students explained that Plessy was arrested because he tried to sit in the white section of the train, but he had a mixed racial background. They detailed how he was eventually put in jail for violating Louisiana's Separate Car Act. Toward the end of the presentation, the group discussed the implications of this landmark Supreme Court ruling. The students discussed how the court ruled at the time that separate facilities for whites were constitutional as long as they were considered equal. At the very end of the presentation, the group detailed how this had a significant impact on public places in the United States, such as schools, restaurants, and restrooms.

National History Day: An Example of Authentic Assessment Using Technology

Students who participate in the National History Day event have the opportunity to produce a digital video with their computer that demonstrates their historical thinking and understanding about the subject matter (Scheuerell, 2007). Evidence suggests that students enjoy constructing knowledge using technology and they understand the information better due to their active participation in their construction of knowledge (Jonassen, 1995). Constructivism, when paired with technology, can also help students remember what they have investigated. Lehrer (1993) conducted a research study where students used computers to produce hypermedia presentations on the Civil War and compared their understanding of the Civil War with that of students in another class who used a traditional approach to learning, such as listening to lecture. Most noteworthy was the fact that there was no statistical difference in the learning between the students who produced hypermedia in one class and students who used more traditional methods to learn about the Civil War in the other class. However, when the researchers tested the students in the control and test groups a year later, there was a significant difference in their knowledge bases and conceptual understanding of the American Civil War (as cited in Reeves, 1998). The students who constructed hypermedia to demonstrate their conceptual understanding of the Civil War clearly outperformed the students who used a more traditional approach to learning. This suggests that there is a great deal of value in constructivist learning with computers.

National History Day is an organization that promotes constructivist projects since students are involved in a great deal of higher-level thinking pertaining to thick questions. The organization even sponsors a competition for middle and secondary students where they can produce technology projects on their findings around a historical theme. Digital documentaries and Internet webpages are two of the categories that students can compete in. There are many excellent examples of these projects on the National History Day Internet site. These can be helpful to readers who are designing technology projects like these for their students for the first time. These examples can be found at the following web address: www. nhd.org/StudentProjectExamples.htm.

Research suggests that the students who participate in National History Day also develop the skills used by historians (Scheuerell, 2007). According to National History Day, students benefit by developing the following skills: critical thinking, problem solving, research skills, and communication skills (National History Day, 2014). Scheuerell (2007) found that students who produced digital documentaries for the National History Day competition were very skilled at considering multiple perspectives and developing a thesis, which they were able to support with evidence. Each of the students also developed an in-depth historical understanding of the topic that they had investigated by being able to identify, describe, and define a great deal of information for their National History Day video documentary (Scheuerell, 2007).

In summary, National History Day has a long tradition of providing students with inquiry-based learning experiences using authentic assessment and technology. Students who produce video documentaries for National History Day develop skills by becoming student historians and using technology to share their findings with others. They are using technology as a tool for their mind (Mindtool). The student-centered approach and critical thinking enable these middle and secondary students to learn a great deal about the subject that they investigate for National History Day. There are many lessons that the reader can take from the National History Day initiative that can then be replicated using technology in other middle and secondary social studies classrooms.

Technology Integration Matrix: Digital Video Examples of Authentic Assessment With Technology Used in Middle and Secondary Social Studies Classrooms

The University of South Florida has designed an Internet site that includes examples of authentic assessment projects using technology in middle and secondary social studies classrooms. Most noteworthy, they have included the Technology Integration Matrix (TIM), which shows different levels of technology integration (USF, 2014). These levels are based on the five characteristics of meaningful learning environments (active, collaborative, constructive, authentic, and goal directed) discussed earlier in this book and the five levels of technology integration that can be infused into the curriculum (entry, adoption, adaptation, infusion, and transformation). These projects can be found at the following Internet link: http://fcit. usf.edu/matrix/matrix.php.

There are twenty-five examples of technology-rich projects in social studies found on this Internet site. These examples include video vignettes of middle and secondary students using technology in the classroom. In some instances, there are insights shared by the classroom teacher, which provide valuable firsthand accounts of what makes the project work. Viewers can see detailed information pertaining to the lesson plan that was designed by the teacher for the technology project. These lesson plans include information on the objectives, standards, and materials needed for the lesson. Some of the examples found on the TIM Internet site include 1) students producing an Internet podcast in a geography class, 2) students producing a PowerPoint presentation on Thomas Jefferson, and 3) students using the Inspiration software to problem-solve global issues facing our world. Each of these examples can help teacher candidates and current social studies teachers design their own technology-rich project for students. I am certain that readers will find these examples extremely helpful as they begin designing their own unit and lesson plans using technology.

Summary

Authentic assessment is well suited for middle and secondary classrooms that are equipped with technology. There are countless possibilities. Teachers need to remember to keep the focus on technology projects where students are actively engaged and challenged to think deeply about the subject matter around thick questions. The research presented in this chapter reinforces the importance of this. This can be a pivotal decision, which can make or break a lesson using technology that involves authentic assessment in social studies classrooms.

As discussed earlier in the chapter, Drake and Nelson provide readers with a user-friendly framework to help teachers design projects where students are more likely to increase their historical understanding. The framework puts a major point of emphasis on 1) identifying the main historical ideas, 2) conducting historical analysis and developing an interpretation, and 3) communicating historical findings to others. This enables students to think more deeply about the subject matter rather than memorizing information for a test or quiz. Many examples provided in this chapter capture these themes.

References

Beal, C. & Bolick, C. M. (2013). *Teaching social studies in middle and secondary schools.* Indianapolis, IN: Pearson.

Drake, F. D. & Nelson, L. R. (2009). *Engagement in teaching history. Theory and practices for middle and secondary teachers* (2nd ed.). Columbus, OH: Pearson.

Jonassen, D.H. (1995). Computers as cognitive tools: Learning with technology, not from technology. *Journal of Computing in Higher Education, 2,* 40–73.

Lehrer, R. (1993). Authors of knowledge: Patterns of hypermedia design. In S. P. Lajoie & S. J. Derry (Eds.), *Computers as cognitive tools* (pp. 197–227). Hillsdale, NJ: Lawrence Erlbaum.

Liu, M. (2003). Enhancing learners' cognitive skills through multimedia design. *Interactive Learning Environments, 1,* 23–39.

National History Day. (2014). Retrieved from www.nhd.org/. Accessed 2/25/14.

Reeves, T. C. (1998). *The impact of media and technology in schools. A research report prepared for the Bertelsmann Foundation.* Retrieved from http://treeves.coe.uga.edu/edit6900/BertelsmannReeves98.pdf. Accessed 9/4/14.

Scheuerell, S. (2007). National History Day: Developing digital native historians. *The History Teacher, 3,* 427–425.

Scheuerell, S. (2010). Virtual Warrensburg: Using cooperative learning and the Internet in the social studies classroom. *The Social Studies, 5,* 194–199.

University of South Florida. (2014). *The Technology Integration Matrix (TIM).* Retrieved from http://fcit.usf.edu/matrix/matrix.php. Accessed 2/27/14.

8

HISTORICAL IMAGES

In the early 1900s, Marcus Garvey emerged as a critical leader in the African-American community. He was leader of the United Negro Improvement Association (UNIA) and editor of the *Negro World* newspaper (Levine, 1982). Both gave him an extensive amount of influence in the African-American community. Using his gifted oratory and writing skills, Garvey encouraged African-Americans to take great pride in their culture and to take their economic future into their own hands. He also became well known for his campaign to promote African-Americans to move back to Africa. Due to these initiatives, Marcus Garvey became one of the most well-known and controversial African-Americans of his time. Yet, few high school students today have heard of him. However, there are many historical images of him and his followers on the Internet that today's students can view and analyze. This chapter highlights how I had my high school students analyze these images.

Theory and Practice: Firsthand Experience Using Technology and Historical Images in American History

The PBS American Experience webpage has an Internet link featuring Marcus Garvey. During my experience as a high school history teacher, I used the webpage to teach my students about this important figure in American history. In my opinion, the webpage provides a rich collection of primary and secondary sources on the life and times of Marcus Garvey. In particular, I found the collection of his writings and images to be the most useful segments of the webpage, especially when I used specific questioning strategies to force my students to think more deeply about the subject. Please note my students accessed the webpage at the following address: www.pbs.org/wgbh/amex/garvey/.

I found my high school students enjoyed the opportunity to view and discuss the historical images devoted to Marcus Garvey located on the PBS Internet webpage. The lesson was used in my Advanced Placement (AP) United States History course and fit extremely well into the curriculum focus on African-Americans in the early 1900s. I taught two sections of the course and had twenty to twenty-five students in each class. Approximately 15 percent of the students in the school were minorities, and about 28 percent qualified for free or reduced-price lunches. There were approximately 1,000 students in the high school, which is located in Warrensburg, Missouri, about forty-five miles southeast of Kansas City (Missouri Department of Elementary and Secondary Education, 2006).

Fortunately, I had a wireless laptop cart in my classroom. Therefore, each of my students had their own laptop computer to access the historical images of Garvey on the PBS webpage. My classroom also had a liquid crystal display (LCD) projector, which allowed my students to follow along step by step with the questioning strategies as we proceeded through the various links featured on the webpage. The high school I taught at was on the block schedule, so each class period was ninety minutes in length. This gave me a great deal of time to cover in depth some key aspects of the Internet webpage. However, I decided to limit the focus of the lesson to three major themes due to the time limitations of a single class period. The focus included Garvey's leadership in the UNIA, his emphasis on economic self-determination, and his back to Africa movement. Most importantly, I was able to find primary sources, including historical images, that enabled my students to be historians involved in higher-level thinking as they viewed the Internet webpage. It is important to note that this chapter will provide a conceptual focus on how I integrated the Marcus Garvey webpage into my AP United States History classroom and the rationale for doing so.

Rationale for Integrating Marcus Garvey into the United States History Curriculum

Alridge (2006) noted that history teachers frequently rely far too heavily on their textbook when they cover historical figures and consequently "deny students an accurate picture of the complexity and richness of American history." He added:

> At the same time, the more controversial aspects of their lives and beliefs are left out of many history textbooks. The result is that students often are exposed to simplistic, one-dimensional, and truncated portraits that deny them a realistic and multifaceted picture of American history. (Alridge, 2006, pp. 662–663)

In my opinion, Marcus Garvey is an example of this. He is someone who is given far less attention in textbooks compared to other African-American leaders. Yet, he is someone who had a profound impact on our nation, and more specifically, the African-American experience at the turn of the century. It is critical for our nation's middle and secondary students to understand the contributions of African-American leaders prior to the pivotal Civil Rights movement of the 1950s and 1960s. In particular, Alridge (2006, p. 672) noted that these African-American leaders helped to "formulate the philosophical and theoretical foundations of arguments for black economics, civil and human rights, pan-Africanism, and other pertinent issues that were the linchpins of 1950s and 1960s mass social activism."

According to surveys, the most well-known African-Americans include individuals like Martin Luther King, Rosa Parks, and Harriet Tubman (Wineburg & Monte-Sano, 2008). However, few students are able to identify Marcus Garvey and his contributions. In this chapter, I am making the case to use historical images more frequently in the curriculum, and specifically how the Internet can be leveraged to foster historical thinking about this key figure in our nation's history. This example can be easily replicated with many different subjects found in the social studies curriculum using historical images and the Internet.

Rationale for Using the Internet to Learn About Marcus Garvey

The classroom of today is dramatically different than it was even a few years ago. Today's high school students have a great deal of access to computers and the Internet. As a result, this presents a unique opportunity to integrate pivotal figures like Marcus Garvey more easily into the curriculum. Alridge (2006), himself a former high school history teacher, recommends that teachers move away from textbooks and embrace the usage of the Internet to allow students to more fully understand the contributions of many other African-Americans. The Marcus Garvey Internet webpage featured on the PBS site is one such example of this type of opportunity for classrooms today.

In the past, historical research involving primary sources had usually been exclusively done by historians and scholars (Bolick, 2006). However, today numerous primary sources are found on the Internet, including many rich resources found on the PBS webpage about Marcus Garvey. Bolick (2006) pointed out that the availability of these primary sources on the Internet has shifted the paradigm on how we think about historical research. In particular, she noted that they have "democratized historical research" (p. 122). In my opinion, this is a very exciting development for today's students. More specifically, this development allows figures like Marcus Garvey to be more easily integrated into the high school history curriculum.

Rationale and Framework for Using Historical Thinking Strategies to Investigate Garvey

Seixas (1996) wrote that it is critical to understand the past to make sense out of the present. It is important to note that students will be unable to develop meaningful historical understanding by simply viewing images of Garvey on the Internet. How can meaningful historical understanding be accomplished in today's classroom using the Internet? Strategies that integrate historical thinking offer a promising approach. History teachers can use the framework presented in this chapter to foster historical thinking about the life and times of Marcus Garvey.

Currently, middle and secondary school classrooms are using the Internet to learn about topics in the history curriculum. However, evidence suggests that use of the Internet alone does not necessarily deepen student learning in history. In fact, many teachers "have conflated technology use with instructional quality" (Burns, 2005/2006, p. 49). Instead, teachers must facilitate higher-level thinking in history when their students use the Internet in the classroom. How can history teachers accomplish this? Burns (2005/2006) asserts the need for educators to "teach critical thinking first and technology later" (p. 52). Therefore, it is necessary to teach students in the history classroom to be "student historians" where they must exercise a great deal of analytical thinking.

Drake and Nelson (2009) point out that student historians examine primary and secondary sources, consider multiple perspectives, analyze what happened, and develop an historical interpretation. During my experience with the PBS webpage, I used the student historian approach to ensure that my students were involved in a deep amount of analysis when they used the Internet sources dealing with Marcus Garvey. In particular, Drake and Nelson (2009) recommend using a Think-Pair-Share activity to help students analyze historical images and construct meaning from the past. As a result, students are given ownership in the lesson and have more confidence to contribute in a meaningful way to the class discussion (Drake & Nelson, 2009). Please note that Drake and Nelson recommend several specific questioning strategies. Each of these strategies will be presented throughout this chapter, using examples from the collection of historical images of Marcus Garvey on the PBS Internet webpage.

In summary, the lesson provided in the pages that follow encourages teachers to avoid having students engage in random web surfing as they view the webpage devoted to Marcus Garvey. Instead, I am suggesting the need to foster higher-level thinking, using historical images to help students construct meaning.

The United Negro Improvement Association

In 1918, the UNIA opened its first branch in New York City. A year later, at Madison Square Garden, the organization held its first convention, which drew 25,000 followers and sponsored a parade that stretched for ten miles. Eventually, the organization grew to 700 different branches, including millions of followers, spread out across the United States (Booker, 2000). Many of my students were wondering why so many African-Americans were attracted to this unique organization.

The PBS webpage has a number of primary sources that gave my students insights into the appeal of the UNIA. They viewed a primary source titled

"Declaration of Rights of the Negro Peoples of the World," which outlined the chief complaints and beliefs of the UNIA. My students found the source by clicking the "Primary Source" feature of the webpage. The publication informed readers how they had not been "willingly accepted as guests in the public hotels and inns of the world for no other reason than their race and color" (PBS, 2000). In addition, it described how African-Americans had been denied the right of a public trial and even lynched (PBS, 2000). Moreover, it discussed the segregation of public accommodations in the southern part of the United States and how African-American children attended inferior schools compared to white children. The source also described how they had been treated unfairly in terms of wages and civil service jobs simply because of their race (PBS, 2000).

Marcus Garvey's vision for progress also included the need for African-Americans to view themselves differently. My students read in the same publication how the UNIA wanted African-Americans to take greater pride in their heritage by developing a school curriculum, national anthem, flag, and holiday. In fact, the UNIA requested that August 31 be recognized as an international holiday to celebrate the contributions of Africans and called for red, green, and black to be used as the colors to proudly represent their African heritage (PBS, 2000).

Interestingly, Garvey also reminded African-Americans that they were no longer enslaved and questioned why many of them were still in that mind-set. He felt many still had an inferiority complex and insisted instead that they celebrate their beautiful history (Levine, 1982). Garvey used several examples to highlight his point. He told African-American men to take down their pictures of white women and questioned African-American mothers for giving their daughters white dolls (Levine, 1982).

The UNIA capitalized on Garvey's initiative to celebrate African heritage. During UNIA marches, members wore military uniforms. In 1921, a UNIA march took place in Cleveland, Ohio, where an African-American eyewitness recalled how uplifting it was for him to see thousands of African-Americans marching, recalling, "I got an emotional lift, which swept me up above the poverty and the prejudice by which my life was limited" (Levine, 1982, p. 121). My students viewed a number of photographs on the PBS webpage of UNIA marches. By clicking the "Gallery" feature of the webpage, my students saw vivid images that amplified the point of the eyewitness. Image #3 is a photograph of Marcus Garvey and other members of the UNIA, dressed in uniform, riding a vehicle in a UNIA parade. This is an opportunity to integrate some of the questioning strategies suggested by Drake and Nelson—for example, for image #3, asking the students to write five adjectives that describe the image and share why they picked these. Students will likely respond with adjectives such as proud, fancy, elegant, well groomed, or powerful to describe the images of the UNIA members dressed in uniform. This may also help students understand why UNIA members decided to wear a designated uniform in the parade.

In image #5, my students saw a marching band playing in front of a large crowd during a UNIA gathering. Using another Drake and Nelson strategy, students can view the image for thirty seconds and the teacher can then cover the image up. The students can then write down everything they observed in the image and share why each of these may be significant to what was captured in the image. Students are likely to note the precision demonstrated by those marching down the street and the curiosity shown by the people viewing the parade.

Image #6 showed UNIA members riding on horseback in a parade. Again, using a Drake and Nelson questioning strategy, students can be asked to write down a title that they would give the image and explain their justification for the title they developed. Many possibilities may emerge as answers. For example, students may note how UNIA members were marching for the equality that they had hoped for, but had not yet achieved, especially since the American flag, and the ideals it was supposed to represent, can be seen in multiple places up and down the street they were marching on.

Finally, image #8 features uniformed UNIA members marching in unison. This is one more opportunity to use a questioning strategy—for instance, asking students to describe what they think might have been the photographer's motivation to capture the image. In the discussion, students might note how the photographer was capturing a group of African-Americans who had great pride in what they were trying to accomplish. In summary, each photograph provided my students rich insights into the UNIA organization and they were forced to think critically about the historical significance of each image.

Many of my students viewed the images and wondered which specific groups of African-Americans were attracted to the UNIA. Garvey had the unique ability to appeal to many segments of the African-American community. Some of the primary groups included African-American peasants, farmers, small businessmen, teachers, journalists, and clergymen (Lewis, 1988). His followers were known as Garveyites or Garvey legionnaires. Many of them became acquainted with Garvey's ideas by reading the *Negro World* since he was the editor of the publication and wrote weekly editorials on contemporary issues facing African-Americans. The publication had a circulation of 200,000, which made him a very influential figure in the African-American community (Levine, 1982).

Garvey was also a charismatic speaker, which helped him attract many followers. There are only two known audio recordings of Garvey. My students listened to them on the PBS webpage. The speech titled "Explanation of the Objects of the Universal Negro Improvement Association" was an excellent primary source. My students got a sense of Garvey's gifted oratory skills and heard him explain the purpose of the UNIA organization. During the speech, my students listened to Garvey discuss the need for people of African descent, all 400 million worldwide, to unite to improve their lifestyle. In particular, he told the audience that the organization's goal was to improve the industrial, economic, and social conditions of their race. He also reminded listeners of the urgent need to emancipate their race and to dream big in the future (UCLA, 2000). My students found the audio recording by clicking first on the "Special Features" link and then the "In His Own Words" link. The recordings are provided by the "Sound Library" at the UCLA African Studies Center.

The Black Star Line

In 1919, Garvey launched the Black Star Line, which included a number of shipping vessels manned by African-American officers (Levine, 1982). The endeavor wouldn't have been possible without the financial support of African-American investors. In fact, Garvey raised $610,000 to purchase three ships by selling $5 stock certificates (Levine, 1982). The investment allowed African-American businessmen to send cargo from the West Indies to the United States and carried African-American passengers seeking to visit Africa (Henretta, Brownlee, Brody, Ware, & Johnson, 1997). It is important to note for students that the Black Star Line went bankrupt in three years and Garvey was convicted of mail fraud due to fundraising financial irregularities associated with the business (Henretta et al., 1997). However, the business venture provided key insights into the economic aspirations of Garvey and the UNIA.

My students viewed newspaper advertisements recruiting African-American investors for the Black Star Line. Since the webpage features more than one image dealing with the same issue (images #4 and #10), this provides an excellent opportunity to use the compare and contrast questioning strategy, which is suggested by Drake and Nelson (2009). In the "Gallery" segment of the PBS webpage, image #4 featured an advertisement appealing to investors using the slogan "Widening Horizons." According to the advertisement, investors were needed to allow African merchants to sell their products to others in distant places. The advertisement also appealed to readers by stating, "There should be no trouble about making up your mind to help your race rise to a position in the maritime world that you and every other Negro can point to with pride" (PBS, 2000).

Image #10 featured another newspaper advertisement for the Black Star Line. The advertisement appealed to investors, saying, "Now is the time for the Negro to invest in the Black Star Line so that in the near future he may exert the same influence upon the world as the white man does today" (PBS, 2000). Later, the same advertisement built on the theme, stating, "Poor men have invested small amounts in the past and became rich afterwards. What white men have done Negroes can do" (PBS, 2000). In summary, the advertisements gave my students unique insights into one of the primary objectives of the UNIA, which was to give African-Americans economic power in their lives (Cayton, Perry, Reed, & Winkler, 2000).

The images also gave my students the opportunity to compare and contrast the themes that emerged from the sources. Immediately, students were drawn to Garvey's idea that African-Americans needed to uplift their own race in terms of their economic well-being. Image #4 encourages African-Americans to purchase shares in the Black Star Line. Image #10 also encourages investors. Students also saw how both sources focused on posterity, with image #4 using the phrase "help your race rise to position in the maritime world," and image #10 reminded readers that some investors had later become rich. Finally, images #4 and #10 appeal to Garvey's notion that African-Americans should have great pride in their culture. Image #4 uses the word "pride" and image #10 states, "What white men have done Negroes can do."

It is important to note that the Black Star Line also appealed to investors by reminding them of the terror inflicted upon their lives. Image #7 was a newspaper advertisement featuring an image of a mother kneeling on the ground with her arms reached out to the sky while her two children hang onto her. In the background, there was a cross with flames emerging from it and above the mother it said, "Negroes Awake! The hour has come to save your race from the burning stake. Invest in the Black Star Line" (PBS, 2000). The primary source served to remind my students of the constant fear many African-Americans endured in the early 1900s. As a result, the advertisement motivated many African-Americans to invest in the Black Star Line to better the lives of themselves and their community.

Drake and Nelson (2009) suggest an interesting questioning strategy to analyze unique historical images like image #7 found on the PBS webpage. They suggest using what they call a quadrantal/hemispheric image analysis strategy. The strategy asks the teacher to cover up three-quarters of the image and have the students write down everything they observed in the remaining quarter of the image. The teacher can then proceed to cover up one half of the image and have students write down everything they observe at this point. If I recall, there were several items in the picture that immediately grabbed the attention of my students. They focused their attention on the flames of the fire and its symbolism, in particular, how this conveyed a fear tactic used by the Ku Klux Klan. In addition, students noticed the mother in the image and how she was very concerned about her children, with special attention given to what kind of future they may have in America. The mother's expression of reaching her arms to the heavens was also of note to the students. Many students may wonder if she was asking for some divine intervention at this moment of crisis. Finally, there was discussion centering on the phrase "Negroes Awake" found in the image. This headline was most likely used to encourage African-Americans to invest in the Black Star Line, especially since the advertisement wanted to convey the importance of African-Americans needing to help themselves amidst the chaos of the scene portrayed in the image. In summary, the students were forced to think critically about all aspects of a complex historical image, like the unique features found in image #7.

Liberia and the Back to Africa Movement

Garvey feared African-Americans would never be able to live peacefully side by side with whites in the United States, particularly since the nation was governed by whites (Henretta et al., 1997). Garvey pointed to historical examples such as Native Americans and the Australian Bushmen (Levine, 1982). Consequently, he urged many African-Americans to move back to Africa (Henretta et al., 1997). Liberia, on the western coast of Africa, became a significant focus for Garvey and the UNIA to fulfill their dream of helping African-Americans move back to Africa. However, it is important to note that Garvey didn't necessarily campaign for every African-American to move to Africa. In fact, he reminded readers of the *Negro World* that it did not take every white man from Europe to come to this country to build up the republic (Lewis, 1988).

The opportunity to transform Liberia, and potentially the rest of the continent, was very appealing to many Garveyites. They hoped to bring scientific, technical, and humanistic knowledge to Liberia, which could then possibly spread to other parts of the African continent (Levine, 1982). Image #12 of the Garvey PBS webpage provided insights into the back to Africa movement. The image contained a newspaper advertisement submitted by the UNIA in New York City. My students read the headlines, which informed African-American readers that Liberia was "A Home in Africa" and encouraged them "to help in the industrial, commercial, and cultural development of the country" (PBS, 2000). By this point in the lesson, the students will have viewed most of the historical images on the webpage. Drake and Nelson (2009) suggest asking students to pretend they are a museum curator and select their favorite image from a collection. Most importantly, have the students explain why they selected their image for their museum.

My students also viewed image #1, which featured a photograph of a UNIA delegation that traveled to Liberia in 1921, laying the groundwork for others. Interestingly, the UNIA even considered moving its headquarters from New York to Monrovia, Liberia, and planned to raise three million dollars to build up the settlement (Lewis, 1988). This is an opportunity to use one more questioning strategy offered by Drake and Nelson (2009), for example, to ask students to consider what the photograph tells us about the lives of those featured in the historical image. Students can make inferences about the individuals featured in the photograph who had recently returned from a trip to Liberia. For example, students are likely to conclude that the group of UNIA members featured in the photograph are individuals who are interested in the posterity of their race. In addition, they appear to be well-educated and successful men. Many students are also likely to remark on how they appear to be very confident in their mission and determined to accomplish its goals.

Garvey hoped to spur an independence movement in Africa since the continent had been carved up by European colonial powers (Lewis, 1988). He argued passionately that blacks needed to have their own independent Africa. Otherwise, he feared they would continue to be exploited by the white man around the world (Levine, 1982). In his "Africa for the Africans" editorial, he made this case to readers in an April 1922 edition of the *Negro World*, writing, "The Negro peoples of the world should concentrate upon the object of building up for themselves a great nation in Africa" (PBS, 2000). In the same editorial, he went a step further, describing his vision for Africa by writing, "It is only a question of a few more years when Africa will be completely colonized by Negroes, as Europe is by the white race" (PBS, 2000). By reading this primary source on the PBS webpage, my students were able to gather new insights into Garvey's vision for Liberia and the wider continent.

Arguably, Garvey's "A Place in the Sun" speech was the most interesting source for my students to read on the PBS webpage. In the speech, he made the case for the settlement of Liberia, saying, "We have no animus against the white man. All that we have as a race desired is a place in the sun" (PBS, 2000). He then continued to build momentum in his speech, saying:

> If 60,000,000 Anglo-Saxons can have a place in the sun, if 60,000,000 Germans can have a place in the sun, if 60,000,000 Japanese can have a place in the sun, if 7,000,000 Belgians can have a place in the sun, I cannot see why, under the same principles, 400,000,000 black folks cannot have a place—a big spot in the sun also. If you believe that the Negro should have a place in the sun; if you believe that Africa should be one vast empire, controlled by the Negro, then arise, and sing the National Anthem of the Universal Negro Improvement Association. (PBS, 2000)

Previously, I referenced the audio recording of Garvey's "Explanation of the Objects of the UNIA" speech featured on the PBS webpage. The same speech featured Garvey's motivational appeal for African-Americans to take an interest in Liberia. During the speech, he argued that blacks around the world should take an interest in Liberia, including the 50 million blacks in the United States, the 20 million blacks in the West Indies, the 40 million blacks in Central and South America, and the 280 million blacks in Africa. He also told the audience that it is common to hear the cry of England for the English, Germany for the Germans, Ireland for the Irish, Palestine for the Jews, and China for the Chinese. Therefore, he questioned why Africa shouldn't be for the Africans (PBS, 2000). In the same speech, Garvey outlined his plan for Liberia by discussing his vision of turning the country into a great industrial and commercial economy. Near the end of his speech, he informed listeners that African-American pioneers had already been sent to Liberia and urged them to dream of the possibilities of a settlement there (PBS, 2000). By listening to his speech, my students more fully understood Garvey's perspective on Liberia.

Overall, Garvey's vision for the movement of African-Americans to Liberia was unsuccessful. He faced many significant challenges. Following World War I, he lobbied the League of Nations to give the UNIA custody of Liberia (Franklin & Meier, 1982). Initially, he appeared to have made an arrangement whereby 500 American families could settle on the Cavalla River in southern Liberia in 1924. However, at the last minute, the Liberian government listened to the French and British and turned away American settlers. In fact, in June 1921, the Liberian government deported a team of UNIA officials and seized their equipment (Franklin & Meier, 1982). The Liberian government feared Garveyites would bring too many anticolonial feelings to the region and potentially threaten the European colonial empire on the broader continent (Levine, 1982). The US government also wanted to protect its commercial interests in Liberia. The Firestone Company had signed a ninety-nine-year lease with the Liberian government despite Garvey's warnings to Liberian government officials that they would become enslaved by American capital and business interests (Lewis, 1988).

Developing Student Historians: Using Historical Images of Marcus Garvey on the Internet

The use of computers should not necessarily make learning easier. In fact, students should be challenged to think harder about a subject when they are using technology (Jonassen, Carr, & Yueh, 1998). In this lesson, students are asked to participate in a lesson using historical images from the Internet, where they are encouraged to do higher-level thinking about the legacy of Marcus Garvey. In particular, the lesson should be designed around historical thinking skills, rather than having students participate in random web surfing and memorize an endless amount of names and dates. Instead, this lesson asked students to deepen their analysis of Marcus Garvey's legacy by doing what historians do, such as analyzing primary and secondary sources related to his life. In essence, they become student historians by using historical thinking skills, which helped them to learn a great deal more about the issues confronting African-Americans in the early 1900s. Historical images made this happen.

I am making the case that we need to rethink how the Internet is frequently being used in the history classroom. It needs to move from random web surfing and memorization of facts to higher-level thinking, such as the skills commonly used by historians. For example, Jonassen, Carr, and Yueh (1998) emphasize the need for students to be an intellectual partner with the computer. Thus, it is critical for students to conduct higher-level thinking when they are involved in a technology-rich lesson. The authors write, "Technologies should not support learning by attempting to instruct the learners, but rather should be used as knowledge construction tools that students learn with, not from" (p. 24). The Marcus Garvey Internet webpage, with its historical images, can serve as a catalyst to facilitate historical thinking when students are asked to be an intellectual partner with the computer. The strategies presented here by Drake and Nelson, such as analyzing historical images, help students do what historians do. For instance, they can explore relationships such as cause-effect, compare-contrast, and problem solving. These are some of the historical thinking skills that can arguably help to deepen students' comprehension on a variety of subjects in the history curriculum, including the contributions of Marcus Garvey.

The Internet lesson presented here is time consuming. Many teachers may question it. For example, it might be easier for students to simply fill out a worksheet on what they learned. However, this would fail to encourage students to be involved in the kind of higher-level thinking used by historians. Jonassen, Carr, and Yueh (1998) remind educators that technology is integrated most effectively when students use the computer as a tool for the mind. They write, "Learners should be responsible for recognizing and judging patterns of information and then organizing it, while the computer should perform calculations, store, and retrieve information" (p. 31). This lesson, which utilizes historical thinking skills, is based on this type of paradigm.

Summary

Marcus Garvey once said, "The world has made being black a crime. . . . I hope to make it a virtue" (as cited in Levine, 1982). In the early 1900s, African-Americans faced many significant challenges, and Garvey inspired a generation to take greater pride in their heritage. By studying his work, high school students can gather insights into the issues on the mind of African-Americans at the turn of the century and their hopes and dreams for the future.

The PBS webpage has a wealth of primary sources related to this controversial figure. Each source enabled my students to gather significant firsthand insights by viewing photographs, newspaper advertisements, and Garvey's writings and listening to his speeches. Most importantly, the webpage allowed my students to learn about Garvey by doing what historians do, viewing primary and secondary sources, examining multiple perspectives, conducting historical analysis, and developing an interpretation. In effect, they became student historians.

In the future, as more history classrooms are equipped with technology, it is important to remember to focus on facilitating higher-level thinking using the Internet, rather than the rote memorization of material. The story of Marcus Garvey, using the PBS webpage, provides one example of how to accomplish this in the classroom—specifically, by using the questioning strategies for historical images outlined by Drake and Nelson.

In summary, social studies classrooms are increasingly equipped with more technology, and social studies teachers are looking for ways to engage their students in meaningful ways. The questioning strategies suggested by Drake and Nelson provide step-by-step guidance and insights into how educators can facilitate higher-level thinking using historical images found on the Internet. Using these strategies, teachers can help their students make inferences and reach conclusions about the historical images. As a result, students in the social studies classroom will be actively engaged versus randomly surfing the web for historical information during a lesson plan. Most importantly, they will learn about a pivotal figure in African-American history.

References

Alridge, D.P. (2006). The limits of master narratives in history textbooks. *Teachers College Record, 4*, 662–686.

Bolick, C.M. (2006). Digital archives: Democratizing the doing of history. *The International Journal of Social Education, 1*, 122–135.

Booker, C.B. (2000). *"I will wear no chain!" A social history of African-American males.* Westport, CT: Praeger.

Burns, M. (2005/2006). Tools for the mind. *Educational Leadership, 4*, 48–53.

Cayton, A., Perry, E., Reed, L., & Winkler, A. (2000). *America. Pathways to the present.* Upper Saddle River, NJ: Prentice Hall.

Conklin, C. & Sorrell, C. (2010). *Applying differentiation strategies* (2nd ed.). Huntington Beach, CA: Shell Education.

Drake, F.D. & Nelson, L.R. (2009). *Engagement in teaching history.* Columbus, OH: Pearson.

Franklin, J.H. & Meier, A. (1982). *Black leaders of the twentieth century.* Chicago: University of Illinois Press.

Henretta, J.A., Brownlee, W.E., Brody, D., Ware, S., & Johnson, M. (1997). *America's history.* New York, NY: Worth Publishers.

Jonassen, D.H., Carr, C., & Yueh, H. (1998). Computers as mindtools for engaging learners in critical thinking. *Tech Trends, 43*, 24–32.

Levine, L.W. (1982). Marcus Garvey and the politics of revitilization. In J.H. Franklin & A. Meier (Eds.), *Black leaders of the twentieth century.* Champaign, IL: University of Illinois Press.

Lewis, R. (1988). *Marcus Garvey. Anti-colonial champion.* Trenton, NJ: Africa World Press, Inc.

Missouri Department of Elementary and Secondary Education. (2006). Retrieved from http://dese.mo.gov/school-data. Accessed 6/10/07.

PBS. (2000). *American experience. Marcus Garvey. Look for me in the whirlwind.* Retrieved from www.pbs.org/wgbh/amex/garvey/. Accessed 6/2/09.

Seixas, P. (1996). Conceptualizing the growth of historical understanding. In D.R. Olson & N. Torrance (Eds.), *The handbook of education and human development* (pp. 765–783). Oxford: Blackwell Publishers.

UCLA. (2000). *Marcus Garvey and Universal Negro Improvement Association papers project.* Retrieved from www.international.ucla.edu/africa/mgpp/. Accessed 6/2/09.

Wineburg, S. & Monte-Sano, C. (2008). Who is a "famous American"? Charting historical memory across the generations. *Phi Delta Kappan, 9*, 643–648.

9

DIFFERENTIATED INSTRUCTION

Middle and secondary social studies classrooms today include diverse learners. Each student varies in their readiness to learn the subject matter and their individual learning styles. Students also vary greatly in the amount of time it may take them to complete a task in the classroom. Social studies teachers need to take all of these into consideration when they plan lessons to meet the needs of all the learners found within a single classroom setting.

Social studies teachers can plan technology lessons to accommodate diverse learners by using a wide variety of differentiated instructional strategies. Some of these include tiered instruction, questioning strategies, giving students choices, self-paced strategies, and Multiple Intelligences. Teachers can also use pre-assessment instruments to determine the readiness of learners. The information from the pre-assessment can be used to design the lesson to enable each individual student in the classroom to excel at learning the curriculum in the social studies classroom. Formative assessment can also be used to determine whether the students have succeeded at learning the subject matter.

Increasingly, technology can be used to gather pre-assessment and formative assessment data. The data can then be used to follow up to help each individual learner in the classroom and make any necessary adjustments to instruction. Technology can also be used to deliver the wide array of differentiated instructional strategies. The majority of these happen to be student-centered instructional strategies.

Tiered Instruction

As discussed previously, social studies teachers today have a wide range of learners in their classroom. This presents a significant challenge to teachers. Yet, this also presents teachers with an opportunity. Teachers can use tiered instruction to help each learner based on what they already know about the objective of the lesson. This is frequently done through pre-assessment. Each student in the classroom can then be categorized into groups of learners. These include learners who are above target, on target, or below target.

The key to designing lesson plans that tier instruction is for teachers to assign different levels of complexity based on whether a student is above target, on target, or below target. Teachers also need to make sure that all students, no matter what level of tiered instruction, are learning the same objective in the social studies lesson. Many social studies teachers may question the rationale for doing this. Conklin and Sorrell (2010) write that "the entire class works toward one goal, but their paths to that goal depend on their abilities" (p. 46). These findings suggest that teachers should try to design lessons based on the abilities of each student to help them learn and to keep them motivated.

Research suggests that a zone of proximity should be used by teachers when they design tiered instructional lessons. Middle and secondary students will be motivated when they get into the learning flow. The learning flow can take place when the teacher takes into consideration the challenge of an activity and the skill sets of each student (Csikszentmihalyi, 1990, as cited in Conklin & Sorrell, 2010). Students may be anxious if they perceive an activity to be way too difficult or bored if they feel that it is too easy (Csikszentmihalyi, 1990, as cited in Conklin & Sorrell, 2010). Therefore, the goal is to use tiered instruction to appropriately challenge each student to keep them engaged in the subject matter (see Figure 9.1). Technology, when used in conjunction with tiered instruction, can help middle and secondary social studies teachers accomplish this.

Technology is well suited to individualize instruction for all students found within the middle and secondary social studies classroom. A great deal of flexibility is afforded by lessons that integrate technology. Students can investigate social studies topics online and build products using technology. Each student can learn the same lesson objective, but at varying degrees of complexity based on whether they are an above-target, on-target, or below-target learner. There is also much flexibility in terms of how long it may take each student to research their topic online and build products using technology. Most importantly, if students finish their individualized learning task early, the teacher can assign them additional tasks pertaining to the lesson objective. For example, the teacher can assign students a task that increases in complexity if they are able to demonstrate in-depth understanding of the subject matter. Tiered instruction enables students to have a greater amount of time to investigate a topic, if needed, rather than teacher-centered instructional activities where the teacher may move on, regardless of whether or not all the students have demonstrated an understanding of the subject matter.

Tiered instruction, using technology, enables the social studies teacher to be the facilitator of learning where they are able to visit with students individually

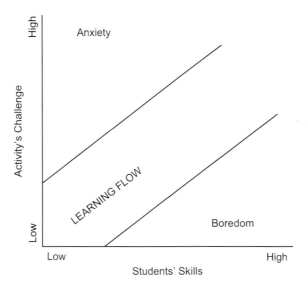

Figure 9.1 Learning flow chart.

Source: Conklin, C. & Sorrell, C. (2010). *Applying differentiation strategies: Teacher's handbook for secondary* (2nd ed.). Huntington Beach, CA: Shell Education.

or in small groups. The teacher is better suited to answer individual questions that students may have about the subject matter and to assess student understanding by asking questions that check for comprehension. This enables the social studies teacher to gather formative assessment. By using formative or informal assessment, the teacher can have students stop what they are doing and make announcements to the entire class to clarify any student misunderstandings about the subject matter. This would be more difficult to do without tiered instruction, where the teacher uses direct teaching approaches rather than being a guide on the side, as with tiered instruction. Most importantly, this student-centered instructional approach using technology enables each middle and secondary student to be actively engaged with the subject matter and to learn the subject matter based on their individual readiness.

Many teacher candidates may wonder what tiered instruction would actually look like using technology in the middle and secondary social studies classroom. Bloom's taxonomy is vitally important to designing tiered instructional lessons. Above-target students should be challenged to perform more complex levels of thinking, whereas on-target and below-target students will be involved in less rigorous thinking about the same lesson objective. Each student can explore questions pertaining to the social studies curriculum by conducting research on the Internet and producing products with technology that have varying degrees of complexity using Bloom's taxonomy. For example, above-target students can be challenged to explore questions and build products that mainly involve the evaluation and synthesis levels of Bloom's taxonomy. On-target students may be challenged to explore questions and build products using technology that involve questions from the analysis and application levels of Bloom's taxonomy. Simultaneously, the teacher can then have the below-target students involved in work that uses the knowledge and comprehension levels of Bloom's taxonomy (see Figure 9.2). As mentioned previously, each student is learning the same objective, regardless of whether they are identified as an above-target, on-target, or below-target student.

Middle and secondary social studies teachers can use the Bloom's taxonomy verbs, which are associated with each of the six levels, to design Internet investigations and authentic assessment projects with technology. For instance, above-target students may be asked to critique or evaluate how President Obama has dealt with the war on terrorism, whereas on-target students may be asked to compare and contrast how President Obama handled the war on terrorism compared to President George W. Bush. Below-target students can also investigate the war on terrorism, but may be asked to describe how President Obama has handled it by identifying some of the main events or turning points that demonstrate his initiatives to combat terrorism and protect our homeland. This is one example that can be replicated for just about any lesson in social studies using tiered instruction.

Questioning Strategies

Social studies teachers can use a wide array of questioning strategies to differentiate their instruction. Kaplan's framework for depth and complexity provides teachers a user-friendly way to develop questions that foster critical thinking about the subject matter (Conklin & Sorrell, 2010). These questions can also be incorporated into lessons when students are using technology in the middle and secondary social studies classroom. The questions are well suited to challenge

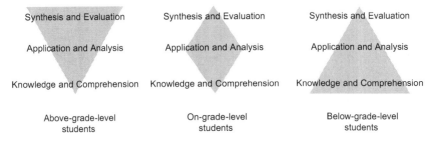

Figure 9.2 Bloom's taxonomy and differentiated instruction.

Source: Conklin, C. & Sorrell, C. (2010). *Applying differentiation strategies: Teacher's handbook for secondary* (2nd ed.). Huntington Beach, CA: Shell Education.

students to analyze what they have found on the Internet or to produce products with technology where they share their analysis.

According to Kaplan's framework, there are eight categories of questions that challenge students to think about the depth of the subject matter. These include patterns, trends, language of the discipline, details, unanswered questions, rules, ethics, and big ideas (Conklin & Sorrell, 2010). Questions that involve patterns challenge students to identify recurring events by searching for repetition and then making predictions (Conklin & Sorrell, 2010). For example, students can examine economic data on the Internet and identify how the American economy has a business cycle of ups and downs. Questions that involve trends challenge students to examine the underlying causes or influences of an event (Conklin & Sorrell, 2010). For example, students can examine polling data on the Internet to identify which constituencies supported the winning and losing candidate in a presidential or congressional election.

Questions that involve the language of the discipline challenge students to learn the specialized vocabulary used by those in the discipline (Conklin & Sorrell, 2010). For example, middle and secondary students may be asked to learn the terminology used by professional historians so they can access primary sources on the Internet and analyze these in the social studies classroom. Questions that involve details challenge students to describe the parts and attributes of a theory, fact, or principle (Conklin & Sorrell, 2010). For example, students can use the Internet to research historical concepts, such as imperialism or nationalism, and use technology to produce a product that demonstrates their own conceptual understanding of these terms in their own words.

Questions that involve ethics challenge students to think deeply about a dilemma or controversial issue (Conklin & Sorrell, 2010). Perhaps students in an American Government class can use the Internet to examine multiple viewpoints on global warming or immigration. Questions that involve big ideas encourage students to identify generalizations about the concept that they are investigating (Conklin & Sorrell, 2010). Students might be able to use the Internet to research different theories about a subject matter, such as theories on how to stimulate the economy.

According to Conklin and Sorrell (2010), questions that involve unanswered questions challenge students to consider the gap that exists in the literature in a particular field of study. Middle and secondary students might be able to investigate local history topics to contribute to the field of knowledge. These may be topics that have been long forgotten or never even researched in a community. Questions that involve rules challenge students to consider the hierarchy or structures that explain a phenomenon (Conklin & Sorrell, 2010). Students may be able to use databases found on the Internet to investigate this and perhaps even produce a graphic organizer with their computer to capture or demonstrate what they have learned about the subject matter—for example, identifying how the US government is organized or showing all of the steps involved for a bill to become law in our nation.

Kaplan's framework for questioning also involves three categories for thinking about complexity. These include over time, points of view, and interdisciplinary connections (Conklin & Sorrell, 2010). Questions that challenge students to think about time encourage them to compare and contrast the past to the present. For example, students can use the Internet to investigate how civil liberties have been curtailed when America has been at war in the past and today during the war on terror. Questions that involve points of view encourage students to examine a topic from the perspective of opposing viewpoints (Conklin & Sorrell, 2010). For instance, students can use the Internet to see differing viewpoints on whether to allow the Keystone Pipeline to be built across the United States. Questions that involve interdisciplinary connections encourage students to think about cross-disciplinary connections. For instance, students in middle and secondary social studies may use online databases to examine mathematical data on pollution in urban areas in the United States to think more deeply about environmental issues facing our nation.

In summary, Kaplan's framework for depth and complexity can be used by middle and secondary social studies teachers to foster a great deal of critical thinking about the subject matter. Teachers increasingly find it difficult to design teaching and learning activities that differentiate instruction. The Kaplan questioning framework is a user-friendly way for teachers to design lessons that differentiate instruction when students use technology in the middle and secondary social studies classroom. Each questioning strategy enables students to analyze what they find on the Internet or share their findings with others beyond the walls of the classroom by producing products with technology. Most importantly, above-target, on-target, and below-target students are challenged individually to think critically when they use technology in the social studies classroom rather than passively learning with technology.

Using Choices

As mentioned previously, students in the same classroom have many different learning styles. Social studies teachers can utilize this by giving each student a choice on how they will provide evidence of what they have learned. It is critically important that all students learn the same objective in the social studies curriculum even when given a choice on how they might demonstrate what they have learned. Students can use technology to accomplish this.

Tic-Tac-Toe Chart

Social studies teachers can develop a lesson plan where they produce a tic-tac-toe chart to show students the choices they have for learning the lesson objective. These choices can be based on Multiple Intelligences since they enable all learning styles and students can pick something that interests them. For example, students might be learning about the causes of World War I. The teacher can then give them several choices to show what they have learned about this. Some of these may include the following: 1) compose lyrics to a song using Audacity, 2) write a poem, 3) develop a script for an Internet podcast, 4) record a digital video documentary, 5) perform a skit, 6) construct an Internet site, 7) create a blog, 8) produce a newscast, or 9) conduct an interview based on diverse historical perspectives. These choices enable students to have some ownership and autonomy in the project but still keep the focus on the lesson's objective. In this case, each student must learn about the causes of World War I and teach others about these events by producing a product that provides evidence that they comprehend this pivotal moment in history.

Learning Stations

Learning stations are another way to differentiate instruction for students (Conklin & Sorrell, 2010). Middle and secondary teachers can set up several learning stations in the classroom where each focuses on the lesson's objective. Each learning station may have a different focus about the objective or enable students to comprehend the objective through a different learning style. Sometimes, the teacher may give students a choice of what learning station they want to go to.

Technology can be embedded into these learning stations. For example, students can learn about the causes of the Civil War by participating in learning stations organized by their teacher. There may be one learning station where students use technology to read primary sources on the Internet that provide firsthand accounts of slavery. Perhaps the students can use a graphic organizer to identify the main ideas in the text. The second learning station may have a digital video where students learn about the issue of states' rights and economic factors that were some of the underlying causes of the war. In order to keep students on task, the teacher can have students use their computers to share what they learned from the video by posting comments to the class Edmodo site.

Students can then go to the third learning station, which can be located at the classroom Smartboard where there is a famous image of John Brown. The students can use the Smartboard pen to analyze the image and circle what they find interesting in the painting. For example, there is a lot of symbolism in the image. The students can then move to another corner of the classroom where learning station number four is set up. Students can read online several primary sources pertaining to the events leading up to the Civil War. These include the Missouri Compromise, the Compromise of 1850, the Fugitive Slave Act of 1850, and the Kansas-Nebraska Act. The students can then use what they have learned from at least one of these sources to write a letter to the editor from the perspective of a Northern abolitionist or Southern plantation owner by blogging online about it.

In summary, there is much merit to giving students choices in the classroom. Many students find it appealing to have a voice and respond favorably to this.

Learning stations and tic-tac-toe boards enable teachers to accomplish this in the classroom by using a student-centered instructional approach. Most importantly, each of these strategies differentiates instruction to meet the individual needs of each learner in the middle and secondary social studies classroom.

Self-Paced Strategies

Self-paced strategies are an important type of differentiated instruction. They enable middle and secondary students to work at a comfortable pace (Conklin & Sorrell, 2010). Frequently, social studies teachers will find that not all students work at the same pace (Conklin & Sorrell, 2010). Some students will finish their work early, and other students in the same classroom need a greater length of time since they may be slow workers or perfectionists (Conklin & Sorrell, 2010).

Conklin and Sorrell (2010) argue that some students will thrive when they have the opportunity to work independently. Social studies teachers can design assignments that meet the appropriate challenge level and learning style for each student in the same middle or secondary classroom. Many students find these self-paced strategies to be very motivating and they learn how to manage their time more efficiently (Conklin & Sorrell, 2010).

Personal Agendas

Several different types of self-paced strategies can be used in the social studies classroom. Personal agendas are one example. They typically include a list of activities that the student will complete over a few weeks. The teacher develops the list of activities for each student to complete based on their readiness and interests (Conklin & Sorrell, 2010). Each personal agenda will vary. The key is to develop a list of activities that will help each student learn the same objective in the social studies curriculum. As soon as the students complete each activity, there is a place on the personal agenda for the teacher to sign off on it. These activities can involve technology where students participate in Internet investigations and produce products using technology.

Learning Contracts

Learning contracts are another form of self-paced strategy. Teachers use them most frequently with research topics (Conklin & Sorrell, 2010). They include a list of student-driven goals and the teacher's expectations. The student and teacher typically have a brief conference and both sign off on the student's learning contract prior to the investigation. The learning contract enables each student to explore topics that interest them and meet their readiness level. This enables students to get into the learning flow (Conklin & Sorrell, 2010, as cited in Csikszentmihalyi, 1990). Each learning contract may involve different tasks, but they are each designed to help students learn the same objective in the social studies curriculum. These tasks can also involve technology.

Independent Investigation Contracts

Independent investigation contracts are another important type of self-paced strategy. They enable students to determine how they might provide evidence of what they have learned about the subject matter in the social studies curriculum. For example, students might show others what they have learned from their research by producing a public service announcement by composing a digital video or performing a skit that they can videotape. This can be based on the learning style that is preferred by each student in the classroom. However, the teacher and student will sign the learning contract, which outlines these expectations for the student and helps to make sure that the student will learn the specified objective (Conklin & Sorrell, 2010). Most importantly, each student in the classroom is learning the same objective in the curriculum, but is able to have some ownership in how they would like to show what they have learned about it. Many students will want to use technology to accomplish this.

Self-paced strategies give teachers some flexibility to work individually and in small groups with students when they are using technology. Frequently, these are the students who need the extra attention and support (Conklin & Sorrell, 2010). There may be students who are English language learners or students with a disability who can receive some individualized attention when all of the students in the social studies classroom are working on self-paced strategies. Self-paced strategies enable the teacher to move around the classroom to meet individually with students, whereas this may be impossible with direct instruction. Self-paced strategies also enable students to have some ownership by giving them some choice in their activities as long as they align with the learning objective. This is quite empowering for students.

As noted earlier, self-paced strategies differentiate instruction for each individual learner found within the social studies classroom by taking into consideration their readiness and interests. Technology is well suited for self-paced strategies. Students can easily use technology to investigate topics on the Internet to produce products that demonstrate to others what they have learned. There are countless possibilities to integrate technology in self-paced learning activities since they enable above-target, on-target, and below-target students to learn at their own pace or readiness, and the technology can cater to their interests. Additional examples are provided later in this chapter.

Pre-assessment

Differentiated instruction often begins by determining the readiness of each student for the objective that will be covered in the curriculum. There are many ways to capture the readiness of each learner in the social studies classroom. The information gathered in pre-assessment enables the social studies teacher to design tasks appropriate for the above-target, on-target, and below-target student. Students can become bored if they are taught something that they already know. Pre-assessment data can help to prevent this from happening. The pre-assessment data can also help teachers design lessons that challenge each student at the appropriate level with tasks designed to help them learn the objective in the social studies curriculum. Students can use technology to investigate the objective in depth using the Internet and to build products. Above-target, on-target, and below-target students can take part in investigations that vary in complexity based on the data from the pre-assessment, which reveals the readiness of each student in the classroom.

Pre-assessment can take many different forms. "Boxing" is one example. Students begin by drawing a box on a sheet of paper and then drawing another box inside their first box. The students are then asked to write any questions that they have about the lesson's objective in the inside box at the beginning of class. They can write what they already know about the lesson's objective in the outside box. This gives the teacher a great deal of information in a relatively short amount of time. As a result, the social studies teacher can then quickly differentiate instruction based on each student's readiness for the subject matter.

KWL Charts are another user-friendly way to gather pre-assessment information. Students are asked to write down what they already know about the subject matter in the K (Know) portion of the graphic organizer. Later, students can write down what questions they have about the subject matter in the W (What they want to learn) portion of the graphic organizer. Finally, students can write down what they learned about the subject matter in the L (What they learned) portion of the graphic organizer. This works well with inquiry-based lessons using the Internet since the teacher is able to gather a great deal of pre-assessment information before the students begin investigating the subject matter on the Internet, and students are able to organize their findings with the graphic organizer.

The graffiti wall is another way to capture pre-assessment information from students. In this activity, students find poster paper placed on the classroom walls at the beginning of class. Each poster may have different questions about the subject matter. The students are encouraged to write their answers on the poster paper. This enables the teacher to quickly determine the readiness of each student for the subject matter presented that day.

Yes/No cards are frequently used by social studies teachers as another type of pre-assessment. At the beginning of class, each student has a notecard with "Yes" on one side and "No" on the other side. The teacher can ask a series of questions and have each student show their "Yes" or "No" side of the notecard and quickly gather a great deal of information about the readiness of each student for the subject matter that will be presented that day.

Many social studies teachers also like to ask students five difficult questions about the subject matter that will be presented in class that day. This can quickly differentiate the readiness of each student and can be done with a paper-and-pencil quiz or electronically using clickers or through a course web-based management system such as Edmodo.

Several other pre-assessment techniques can be used to determine student readiness. Social studies teachers can ask students to complete an entrance slip by submitting a notecard where they write down everything they know about the subject matter. The teacher can then use the data to differentiate the instruction for each student based on their prior knowledge. Teachers can also ask students to participate in journaling by considering a particular prompt from the teacher. For example, the teacher might ask students to consider what it may have been like to live during the Great Depression by composing a diary entry. This gives the social studies teacher a great deal of information and can be done through a web-based course management tool such as Edmodo or Google Docs.

Many social studies teachers also like to use a pre-assessment activity called "How Sure Are You?" The graphic organizer is categorized into three areas. These include "In-Pencil Facts," "In-Ink Facts," and "In-Stone Facts." "In-Pencil Facts" are things that students are not too sure about pertaining to the subject matter. "In-Ink Facts" are things that the students are pretty certain are true. "In-Stone Facts" are things that the students are absolutely certain are true about the subject matter to be presented in class that day. The teacher can quickly use this information to tier instruction based on the readiness of each student found within a single social studies classroom.

Middle and secondary social studies teachers can also use historical images to determine the readiness of each student. Historical portraits, images, and political cartoons all serve as interesting and effective pre-assessment instruments. The students who have prior knowledge about the subject matter are much more likely to make sense out of the image.

Pivotal Decisions With Technology: Tiered Instruction or "One Size Fits All"

In the qualitative study that I conducted, there were many examples of students using technology to reflect on the subject matter they were investigating. Yet, it was common for many of the students to not feel comfortable with the task they were given, whether it was an Internet investigation or building a product with technology. Some students found the subject matter too challenging, and for others, the activity was too easy. Therefore, a pivotal decision that sometimes was a make-or-break decision for each social studies lesson with technology was whether there was any consideration of using differentiated instruction to challenge each student where he or she was at with the subject matter. As mentioned previously, differentiated instruction is a great fit for the 1:1 computer classroom in social studies since it allows students to explore topics online based on their readiness for the subject matter. In order to accomplish this, social studies teachers must use some type of pre-assessment or informal assessment to determine what their students know about a subject matter, and hence, their readiness for the material.

As discussed previously, students who are above target are able to consider more in-depth questions with their Internet investigations. This was rarely taken into consideration in each of the three social studies classrooms that participated in the study. Each classroom would have been better served using questions that originated from various levels of Bloom's taxonomy such as the synthesis and evaluation categories of Bloom's taxonomy to challenge the above-target students. The below-target students would have been better served answering questions that involved the knowledge and comprehension categories—levels one and two of Bloom's taxonomy—for example, to explain and summarize what they have learned about the subject matter. Finally, the remaining students, characterized by being on-target learners, would have been better suited and ready to participate in investigations that involved more analysis and application of information in terms of where they were on the Bloom's taxonomy spectrum. As noted earlier, it is important for teachers to identify a "happy medium" where each learner feels challenged, but not overwhelmed, by the investigation online, depending on the student's readiness.

In Mr. Jones' United States History class at River High School, he used formative assessment almost daily at the beginning of class, sometimes informally through questions, and at the end of class with various closure activities. This information greatly helped him determine the readiness of each learner in his classroom. For example, during Mr. Jones' unit on the Civil Rights movement, each student had to examine how the events unfolded in the struggle for equality. There were many things for the students to consider, such as the important figures and events that were turning points in the Civil Rights movement. Each of these was pivotal in the cause for freedom. In one class, the students read two different perspectives on the Civil Rights movement. The authors were Steven Larson and Charles Payne. Each offered different opinions on whether the federal government or ordinary people should be credited with winning the Civil Rights movement. The students then had the opportunity to debate the issue in the class. Perhaps in the future, Mr. Jones could take the lesson to another level by using the information he had obtained from the pre-assessment and put the students in tiers based on their readiness for the subject matter. For example, students in a lower tier might be asked to simply identify some of the main points found in the Larson and Payne articles, whereas students in the on-target and above-target tiers could be asked to compare and contrast the arguments, and others may be asked to evaluate or defend the arguments. The depth of the articles that the students were asked to read could also vary based on the readiness of each student.

At Bluff High School, Mr. Smith frequently used "thick" questions, or big picture questions, to challenge his students to think more deeply about topics in world geography and world history, and they used their computers to investigate these topics more deeply on the Internet. In one lesson, he used the following question: "Why do you think it is important to understand the beliefs of other religions around the world?" In another class, he asked, "Why do you think colonization took place?" and "What are some of the positives and negatives of colonization?" The students were very engaged in the lesson and succeeded at identifying some of the big ideas around these focus questions. For example, they had the opportunity to think about the possessions that a colony sometimes brings to another country and, adversely, how diseases are sometimes spread from one culture to another during colonization.

However, one way that Mr. Smith could improve the lesson in the future would be to determine the readiness for each learner and use tiered instruction based on this information. The students could be asked to investigate different focal points about the issues involving colonization. For example, the below-target students could simply identify some of the key points about colonization, such as where it has occurred. In order to challenge on-target and above-target students, they could be asked to compare and contrast different colonies and evaluate how colonists have been treated by the nation that is occupying them. Most importantly, these are examples of taking the lesson to the next level, based on the readiness of each learner, to maximize their experience with technology in the middle and secondary social studies classroom.

In another example in Mr. Smith's class, the students were asked to research various Cold War topics and produce a Keynote presentation on their findings. The topics ranged from the Berlin Wall to the Korean War. It was evident to me that several students had difficulty knowing even the basic differences between democracy and communism. These students would have benefited greatly from tiered instruction based on whether they had prior knowledge that was above target, on target, or below target on the core ideological differences between these two governmental systems.

Finally, at Bridge High School, there were many examples of students using their iPad computer to conduct inquiry or reflection on various topics and issues in the social studies curriculum. In the Modern US History class, students were in the middle of a World War II unit. Mr. Brown asked them to research various leaders during World War II. These included Franklin D. Roosevelt, Harry S. Truman, and Winston Churchill. The students had to answer questions such as "What were their political beliefs?" and "How did they try to help their citizens?" The students used technology to investigate these questions online. Most of the students were able to identify significant insights pertaining to these questions posed by their teacher. However, as noted in the other classroom examples from this study, one way to move the lesson forward would be to determine the readiness of each student for the subject matter based on a pre-assessment instrument. Then, based on the data from the pre-assessment instrument, students could be placed into the below-target, on-target, or above-target tier. The students would then be able to investigate the topic with different focal points based on their readiness. For example, students identified as below target might be able to identify simple recall information about the leaders, whereas students at the on-target and above-target levels could be asked to compare and contrast the leaders or evaluate their leadership qualities. This would have helped to cognitively challenge each student appropriately and motivate each student in the classroom.

In summary, there is a great deal of merit to using tiered instruction. During the study, there was some evidence of this taking place in each of the classrooms. Yet, there were many missed opportunities to use pre-assessment to determine the readiness of each learner. In fact, this was a pivotal decision that sometimes was a make-or-break moment for the lesson, in particular, since some students were better suited or well positioned for critical thinking questions and would have benefited from more rigorous expectations in terms of Bloom's taxonomy involving the subject matter that they were investigating. Adversely, some of the students in the classrooms that I observed struggled with the course topic because of their lack of readiness. These students would have also benefited from tiered instruction. In conclusion, differentiated instruction has a great deal of potential in addressing this issue when students are using technology in the social studies classroom.

Summary

Differentiated instruction is well suited for social studies classrooms that are equipped with technology. The teacher can adjust instruction to meet the individualized learning needs of each student in the classroom. Pre-assessment can be used to determine the readiness of each student, and surveys can be used to identify the preferred learning style. Depending on each student's readiness and learning style, there are many strategies that the social studies teacher can use to differentiate instruction. Teachers can use tiered instruction, questioning strategies, and self-paced strategies to help the learning needs of each student in the social studies classroom.

Technology can be leveraged to facilitate differentiated instruction more easily. Pre-assessment can be easily gathered and used immediately. Technology also allows students to explore topics of interest more easily using the Internet. Students can work at a pace that fits their learning needs. In addition, teachers can have students explore other topics on the Internet pertaining to the same curriculum objective if they finish their assigned task early. Students can also produce products using technology based on their findings. Finally, students can have a choice in the type of product they produce to show their findings.

Increasingly, differentiated instruction is becoming an expectation in middle and secondary social studies classrooms. Teachers are trying to identify ways to integrate differentiated instruction into their lesson and unit plans. Fortunately, technology opens the door for many possibilities. The student-centered strategies that have been covered in this chapter enable the social studies teacher to move around the classroom from student to student and group to group while students are engaged in working at their appropriate pace to match their readiness and learning style. As a result, the social studies teacher can more easily check for student understanding and clarify any misunderstandings that students may have. As a result, the teacher can act as the facilitator of learning, or the guide on the side. Meanwhile, the teacher is able to conduct informal assessment and adjust the lesson as needed. In addition, there is an opportunity for students to help each other. Frequently, students can be peer helpers, and in some instances, even explain the subject matter more effectively to their peers than can the classroom teacher.

In summary, differentiated instruction encourages social studies teachers to rethink how they are doing things. Technology can foster differentiated instruction by enabling students with varied learning styles to identify learning tasks that meet their interests, as suggested by Multiple Intelligences. The differentiated classroom offers a student-centered approach where there is a great deal of collaboration taking place. I encourage middle and secondary social studies teachers to start out by using one or two differentiated instructional lessons per unit with technology over the course of an academic year. As soon as they become more comfortable with differentiated instruction, they can build off of these experiences and try more approaches over time. In particular, keep in mind that technology is a wonderful marriage with differentiated instruction due to the aforementioned arguments presented in this chapter.

References

Conklin, C. & Sorrell, C. (2010). *Applying differentiation strategies: Teacher's handbook for secondary* (2nd ed.). Huntington Beach, CA: Shell Education.

Csikszentmihalyi, M. (1990). *Flow: The psychology of optimal experience*. New York: Harper & Row Publishers.

10

READING STRATEGIES

Increasingly, middle and secondary students are using technology to conduct research in the social studies classroom. Many students have difficulty comprehending what they have read online. Teachers can use reading strategies to help students make sense of what they are reading. Pre-reading, during-reading, and post-reading strategies can greatly help middle and secondary students when they are reading a complex text on the Internet. Some of the primary sources that students can access on the Internet were written hundreds of years ago. These sources often include vocabulary that is not used by students today. As a result, there is a need for reading strategies to help students when they encounter challenging text on the Internet.

Graphic organizers can be used as a reading strategy when middle and secondary students use technology to view primary and secondary sources. They are increasingly found on the Internet and can be easily accessed by social studies teachers. There are many different types of graphic organizers. Some of these include Venn diagrams, cause-effect charts, and problem-solution charts. These visual aids help students make sense out of the text that they are reading on the Internet and organize their findings from online databases.

In the pages to follow, there will be a greater discussion on reading strategies that can be used by middle and secondary students to interpret text when they are using technology in the social studies classroom. Examples will be provided to give the reader a more comprehensive view of what this looks like in the classroom. Readers will also learn where they can find some of these reading strategies so they can replicate many of the ideas presented in this chapter. The ultimate goal of the reading strategies is to help the middle and secondary student more easily understand what they are reading when they encounter text on the Internet. This can increase the confidence of each student in the classroom and reduce their level of frustration. This is often an overwhelming experience for the middle and secondary student in social studies classrooms. The pre-reading, during-reading, and post-reading strategies, used in conjunction with the graphic organizers, can help the reader solve this dilemma.

Pre-reading Strategies

Middle and secondary social studies teachers can use pre-reading strategies to help students comprehend the primary and secondary sources that they will be reading on the Internet. Teachers can use pre-reading strategies before students investigate topics online. To begin with, the social studies teacher can discuss what type of text structure the student will be reading online (Readence, Bean, & Baldwin, 1998), for example, whether the text is a primary or secondary source, such as a diary entry or newspaper editorial. This enables students to more fully understand the text structure that they will be reading in class and make sense of what they are reading. The teacher can also take some time beforehand to motivate the students to read the text (Readence et al., 1998). There may be some interesting facts or stories to share that are related to the text that the students will be viewing online.

The Whiskey Rebellion: Pre-reading Strategies

In my American History class, I had students read on the Internet President Washington's 1794 Proclamation about the Whiskey Rebellion (Scheuerell, 2009). I shared with the students some interesting facts about the Whiskey Rebellion before they began to read the primary source to spur some interest in the text. The students were surprised to learn that President Washington actually led a force of 12,900 volunteer troops to confront the farmers in western Pennsylvania (Woods & Gatewood, 1998).

It is important to have students make predictions on what they think the text is going to be about. Perhaps the students can base this on the title or the structure of the text. The teacher can also determine how much prior knowledge the students may already have about the subject matter. This enables the students to connect their prior knowledge about the subject to any new information that they will encounter in the text that they read on the Internet. The social studies teacher can also review the vocabulary in the text that may be difficult for students or impede their ability to comprehend the big ideas conveyed in the primary or secondary source. For example, if students were using the Internet to read President Washington's proclamation on the Whiskey Rebellion in 1794, the teacher can review terms such as treason and militia before the students begin reading the text.

Thesis-Proof Chart: The Great Migration Website

During my experience as a high school social studies teacher, I had students use the Thesis-Proof Chart when they were involved in problem-based learning. For example, I had my students use problem-based learning when we covered the Great Migration of African-Americans from the southern part of the United States to the northern part at the turn of the century. The question that I posed to them was the following: Why do you think 1,000,000 African-Americans migrated from the southern part of the United States to the northern part of the United States from 1916 to 1930? Each student had to develop their own hypothesis on the Great Migration (Scheuerell, 2008c).

I had my students use several Internet sites to investigate the topic online as soon as they had completed their hypothesis. One of the Internet sites is titled "The Great Migration: A Story in Paintings by Jacob Lawrence." The site includes a series of interesting paintings with captions that inform viewers about this significant migration event. During the reading of the text, students can write down details pertaining to the actual proof or answer to the question posed by the teacher prior to the reading phase of the lesson. The site is hosted by Columbia University and can be viewed by students at the following Internet link: www.columbia.edu/itc/history/odonnell/w1010/edit/migration/migration.html.

During-Reading Strategies

Social studies teachers can use several strategies when students are actually reading text on the Internet. During-reading strategies are aimed at helping students with vocabulary and comprehending difficult text (Readence, Bean, & Baldwin, 1998). One example of a during-reading strategy is the Question Answer Relationship (QAR) strategy. In QAR, the teacher can design questions where the students have to find the answer right in the text (see Figure 10.1). This can help students more easily identify the important details and big ideas from a text on the Internet. The teacher can also write questions where students have to think more globally about the text and answer some higher-level thinking questions. Additional questions ask students their opinion on the subject matter in the text. This is much like the decision-making model of social studies. For example, if the students read President Washington's Proclamation about the Whiskey Rebellion on the Internet, the students can be asked why they think President Washington took the issue so seriously or why it is sometimes considered a turning point in American history. Finally, the QAR strategy frequently will include questions where students pretend they are an individual experiencing the situation identified in the text. Students might pretend they are a Whiskey Boy in western Pennsylvania who read President Washington's proclamation and are asked to consider how they might have reacted to the proclamation if they had read it in the local newspaper in 1794. Some students may be quite nervous to learn that nearly

13,000 troops opposed them, whereas other students might be itching for a fight. Countless graphic organizers can also be used for during-reading strategies. These will be discussed in greater detail later in the chapter.

Concept maps are another example of a during-reading strategy that has a great deal of merit in the middle and secondary social studies classroom. The during-reading strategy can be used by students when they examine primary and secondary sources on the Internet. Students can use concept maps to help organize their findings into categories and identify the types of relationships that exist among them (Beal & Bolick, 2013). For example, students can use a concept map to identify the major themes from President Washington's proclamation, including the allegation that some of the Whiskey Boys had attacked federal tax collectors in western Pennsylvania.

The concept map begins by having students identify the main idea in a circle on the middle of the page and then identify the connections to the main idea (Beal & Bolick, 2013). Students can show these connections by drawing a line between the main circle and the other circles that connect to it. By using

---

Right There Questions: The Whiskey Rebellion

1. What had the Whiskey Boys done to the public officers on the highways?
2. What happened to John Neville, a tax collector?
3. What happened to David Lenox, a marshal in Pennsylvania who had tried to enforce the tax?

Think & Search Questions: The Whiskey Rebellion

1. How did President Washington demonstrate leadership during the Whiskey Rebellion? Include examples in the document to support your position.

On My Own Questions: The Whiskey Rebellion

1. Why do you think President Washington took this issue so seriously?
2. Why do you think this was a turning point in American history?

Author & Me Question: The Whiskey Rebellion

1. Pretend you are a Whiskey Boy in western Pennsylvania who just read President Washington's declaration on the issue. How would you react to this? What are you thinking? How are you feeling?

Figure 10.1 QAR Example: Whiskey Rebellion

during-reading strategies such as the concept map, students organize their find-ings from the primary source on the Internet as they read the text word by word. This can help students make sense of the text that they are reading rather than completing the usual fill-in-the-blank worksheet from the Internet investigation.

The Common Core State Standards (CCSS) also place an emphasis on the integration of knowledge and ideas when students read primary and secondary sources. This includes information from multiple sources, including written text, visual images, and quantitative data (CCSS, 2014). Frequently, students in middle and secondary social studies classrooms can examine these sources on the Internet. For example, teachers can utilize many historical images and political cartoons in the social studies classroom. In addition, many Internet sites have data, includ-ing the Gallup Poll, Open Secrets, and the US Census Bureau. During-reading strategies, used in conjunction with graphic organizers, can help students analyze the data found online and capture the big ideas. Many students have difficulty interpreting these types of sources. Teachers can implement reading strategies to help students more fully understand the information and data that can be har-nessed from these sites. Graphic organizers work exceptionally well. For example, students can use a Venn diagram to compare and contrast findings from a United States Census Report from the past to today or they can identify the origins of campaign contributions to finance the elections of politicians across the country.

Open Secrets Internet Site: Using a During-Reading Strategy

The Open Secrets Internet webpage, sponsored by the Center for Responsive Politics, has a great deal of data that tracks the origins of campaign contributions to finance the elections of politicians across the country (Scheuerell, 2008a). Stu-dents can use a cause/effect graphic organizer to examine the sources of these contributions and the impact they may have on the politician. There is much to examine from the data, and the graphic organizer can help students read the infor-mation online and can be used as a during-reading strategy to analyze the themes from the Internet site. Students can put campaign contributions in the main circle with causes in a circle above the main box and effects in the box below it. The majority of campaign contributions come from individuals and political action committees (PACs). The PACs include labor unions, businesses, and ideological interest groups. Teachers can ask students to examine whether there is a cor-relation between the committees that members of Congress serve on and those whom they receive campaign contributions from.

There is also a great deal of data that enables students to explore how Demo-crats and Republicans differ in regard to whom they are receiving campaign con-tributions from. These differences include labor unions versus major corporations. Students will also find it interesting to examine data related to the advantages that incumbents have in terms of raising money for elections. These are just a few examples of how students can analyze the data when they read the database online and use the cause/effect chart to identify some of the major themes. The Internet site can be found at the following link: www.opensecrets.org/.

Opinion-Proof Chart: United States Supreme Court Website

During my experience as a high school social studies teacher, I had my students examine judicial decisions from the United States Supreme Court (Scheuerell, 2011). There were many opportunities to have my students analyze the decisions made by the nation's highest court. The Opinion-Proof Chart is an example of a graphic organizer that can help students capture the main ideas from the text found on the Internet site. The Opinion-Proof Chart that is featured on the site encourages students to write down their opinion about the subject matter in the left column of the graphic organizer prior to reading the text on the Internet. The students then complete the proof portion of the graphic organizer during the reading of the text or following the reading of the text. This enables students to assess whether their opinion was correct or not while they are reading the text.

Students can participate in a great deal of critical thinking when they analyze the text from these federal court decisions. Students can write their opinions on each of the Supreme Court decisions that the teacher wants them to analyze. As soon as students have put their opinion down, they can look for proof to support their stance on the judicial decision. I asked several questions to foster critical thinking about three Supreme Court decisions that we examined in class. These questions included the following: 1) Explain which constitutional issue applies in this particular case and provide evidence to support your position; 2) Pretend you were on the Supreme Court. How would you have ruled on the issue? and 3) Do you agree or disagree with the majority opinion? Why or why not? The three Supreme Court decisions that we analyzed in class were *Panetti v. Quarterman, Morse v. Frederick*, and *Brendlin v. California*. The United States Supreme Court site can be found at the following link: www.supremecourt.gov/.

Post-reading Strategies

It is very important for middle and secondary social studies teachers to help students comprehend the text as soon as they have finished reading primary and secondary sources on the Internet. Readence, Bean, and Baldwin (1998) emphasize the need to debrief students since they "need reinforcement to retain the material learned" (p. 8). Students can work in small groups, or the teacher can facilitate a large group discussion to help students identify some of the major themes that emerged from the text. Students can complete a graphic organizer during the post-reading phase of the lesson to identify these major themes. Teachers can use a liquid crystal display (LCD) projector to put the graphic organizer on the whiteboard. This can be used to facilitate a discussion on the major themes from the text. For example, a Venn diagram can help students compare and contrast two ideas. There are many possibilities for post-reading strategies, and many of these involve graphic organizers, which will be discussed in greater detail in the forthcoming pages.

Discussion webs are another example of a post-reading strategy. Middle and secondary social studies teachers will find them suitable when students are examining questions that have not been resolved yet (Beal & Bolick, 2013), in particular, when students are presented balanced arguments for the pros and cons of a debate from text on the Internet. There are many examples of these in the social studies classroom, such as whether guns should be regulated more in the United States, or whether the death penalty should exist in our nation.

Gallup Poll Internet Site: Post-reading Strategy

The CCSS also emphasize the need for middle and secondary students to consider differing points of view when they read text (CCSS, 2014). This is vitally important when students are reading primary sources that convey different perspectives on historical events or issues. The Gallup Poll Internet site provides one example of how a post-reading strategy can be used to help students examine different perspectives online. Students can use a Venn diagram to capture the main ideas or themes that emerge from the large amount of data on the site. They can capture similarities where two circles intersect in the middle and put the differences on the outside areas of the two circles. For example, students can examine how Democrats and Republicans differ on domestic affairs and foreign policy according to the online polling data (Scheuerell, 2008b). There is much to examine. Students can explore how the demographics of Democratic and Republican voters are statistically different according to the data. In addition, students can view data on how both constituencies have different opinions on a wide array of domestic issues, including immigration, health care, the economy, and the environment. Students will also find it interesting to examine how the viewpoints of Democrats and Republicans are quite different in regard to foreign policy, including polling data on the war on terrorism and the war in Iraq. Post-reading strategies such as the Venn diagram can help middle and secondary students analyze the online data and identify the key points from it.

Discussion Webs: President Truman's Decision to Drop the Atomic Bomb

The discussion web requires students to write down their findings from the text after they have read both sides of the argument on the Internet. As a result, students are challenged to consider both sides of the issue and eventually put together their argument after they have weighed the evidence. The discussion web helps students accomplish this. For example, students might read primary and secondary sources on the decision by President Harry S. Truman to use the atomic bomb on Japan.

Students can use the discussion web to write down the "Yes" arguments on the left side of the page and the "No" arguments on the right side of the page. In the middle of the page, it might simply ask students whether the United States should have dropped the atomic bomb (Beal & Bolick, 2013). The middle and secondary social studies curriculum is filled with these types of scenarios and fits with the decision-making model of social studies instruction where students are encouraged to participate in higher-order thinking and student-centered learning.

Graphic Organizers: Reading Quest.org

Social studies teachers can find graphic organizers on the Internet by using a site called Reading Quest. The Internet site is hosted by Dr. Raymond Jones at the University of Virginia. The website includes many user-friendly graphic organizers that both teachers and middle and secondary social studies students can use when they read text on the Internet. The slogan for the website is "Making Sense in Social Studies," which speaks to the importance of these reading strategies. The graphic organizers can be found at the following Internet link: www.reading quest.org/.

Teachers will find several graphic organizers that encourage students to compare and contrast different concepts or ideas. This challenges students to participate in higher-level thinking as they read text. This type of graphic organizer works well as a post-reading strategy when students have finished reading the text. For example, a compare-and-contrast diagram is featured on the site that encourages students to consider how two concepts are alike and different. The other Venn diagram featured on the site enables students to compare and contrast three concepts.

KWL Chart

KWL is another strategy featured on the Reading Quest website. Several types of KWL graphic organizers can be used by middle and secondary social studies students when they read text on the Internet. Teachers can use the KWL graphic organizers to encourage students to participate in the pre-reading, during-reading, and post-reading segments of the reading strategies. Students are encouraged to consider what they already know about the subject matter that they are about to read on the Internet (K). They are challenged to consider what they think they might learn from the reading or think about what they hope to learn from the reading online (W). Finally, students can write down what they have learned from the reading on the Internet (L). There are some variations to the KWL graphic organizers, and social studies teachers can consider which strategy would work best with the objective that students are going to learn for the lesson they are teaching. For example, students can use the KWL chart to examine the debate on whether the United States should use some forms of coercive interrogation techniques to gather intelligence information from terrorists to protect the homeland. They can begin by writing down what they already know about both sides of the debate before they begin to investigate the issue on the Internet.

History Frames and Story Maps

The Reading Quest site also features several graphic organizers that are categorized as history frames or story frames. Each of these graphic organizers can be used as a during-reading strategy to help middle and secondary students analyze the text they are reading on the Internet. Students can search for step-by-step items while they are reading the text. For example, the History Frame graphic organizer asks students to identify the key participants, important events, and the resolution or outcome of the event that they are reading about on the Internet. The site also features the Story Map graphic organizer. This challenges students to identify the big ideas as they are reading the text. The graphic organizer features a portion or segment where students need to list two major themes from the text and identify the problem or goal facing the individuals in the text. The students are also challenged to consider the key events and outcome of the historical period described in the text. One more graphic organizer is featured on the site: the Story Pyramid. This graphic organizer challenges students to synthesize what they have learned from the text by writing down four words describing the event that they read; on another line, students are asked to write down five words describing the main idea or importance of the event.

In summary, the Reading Quest website is a robust site since it enables middle and secondary social studies teachers to quickly identify graphic organizers that work. This is vitally important since teachers have a limited amount of time to find these resources. Most importantly, each graphic organizer featured in this chapter enables students to more easily comprehend what they have read when using technology in the social studies classroom.

Theory and Practice: Firsthand Experience Using Technology and Reading Strategies in United States History

In November 2000, I was teaching American government and United States history at Warrensburg High School in Missouri. The election featuring Governor George W. Bush and Vice President Al Gore became a teachable moment. I recognized that there was an opportunity to have the students compare and contrast the 2000 election to the election of 1876. Both were disputed elections where the individual who won the popular vote lost the presidency in the Electoral College. In 1876, Democrat Samuel J. Tilden won the popular vote by a narrow margin, but Republican Rutherford B. Hayes had more electoral votes, which gave him the presidency. The students found some other interesting parallels between these elections using a Venn diagram.

The students quickly discovered that there was a great deal of controversy surrounding the results in the election of 1876. Four states had disputed election results. These included Louisiana, South Carolina, Oregon, and Florida (Cayton, Perry, Reed, & Winkler, 2000). The students were amazed to learn that Florida was also the focus of a disputed election back in 1876. At this time, Florida was still under the control of the federal government and the Republican Party due to Reconstruction following the Civil War (Cayton et al., 2000). The Republicans and Democrats submitted different election results in Florida, which put the state's 1876 presidential election results in disarray (Cayton et al., 2000). However, the outcome of the 1876 presidential election was reached quite differently than the 2000 election that my students were more familiar with.

My students learned from their Internet research that a compromise was reached between the Republicans and Democrats to resolve the disputed election of 1876. The Democrats agreed to give the presidency to Rutherford B. Hayes. In return, the Republicans agreed to remove the federal troops from the South, which ended Reconstruction (Cayton et al., 2000). Each of the students noted this on their Venn diagram by identifying how it was different from the approach to resolving the 2000 presidential election. In 2000, the election went all the way to the Supreme Court, and George W. Bush was determined the winner.

I also had the students analyze the electoral maps of 1876 and 2000. These can be easily found on the Internet. I asked the students to compare and contrast the electoral results of these two elections based on what they saw. The students saw that there were deep regional divides both in 1876 and 2000, and they noted this in the similarity part of their Venn diagram. In 1876, Rutherford B. Hayes won the majority of the states in the Midwest and Northeast, while Samuel J. Tilden won the majority of the states in the Mid-Atlantic and South. My students realized that the electoral map was flip-flopped in terms of its political strongholds. In 2000, Democrat Al Gore had strength in the Midwest and Northeast. However, this was strikingly different from Democrat Samuel J. Tilden in 1876, who had his strength in the Mid-Atlantic and South (Cayton et al., 2000). The students noted these differences on their Venn diagrams as well.

Finally, the students considered the impact of both elections. The Compromise of 1877 had a profound effect on civil rights in the South. The removal of federal troops led to many new restrictions on freedoms for African-Americans in the South (Cayton et al., 2000). Many of the gains for African-Americans in the South following the Civil War were lost due to the Compromise of 1877. The students noted this and considered the impact of the election of 2000—more specifically, how the pivotal decision by the Supreme Court had a profound impact on the country. My students wondered how our nation may have been the same or different in terms of domestic or foreign policy if Vice President Gore had won the election.

In summary, the Venn diagram served as an excellent way for my students to more fully comprehend the subject matter that they were reading online. This reading strategy helped the students make greater sense out of what they were reading. I highly suggest using graphic organizers such as a Venn diagram when students are reading primary and secondary sources on the Internet.

Summary

There is a great need for reading strategies in the middle and secondary social studies classroom. Reading strategies can help students make sense out of what they are reading, in particular, if students are reading primary and secondary sources pertaining to the subject matter in the social studies curriculum. These same reading strategies can also be implemented when students use the Internet to conduct investigations both during class and outside of class time.

As mentioned previously, students can be involved in pre-reading, during-reading, and post-reading strategies. The social studies teacher can determine which of these strategies will be best suited for the reading that the students will participate in when they are using the Internet, in particular, the strategy that helps students comprehend the main ideas from the text that they are engaged with.

This chapter provided several examples of how these reading strategies can be leveraged with specific objectives in the social studies curriculum. There are countless ways that teachers can implement similar teaching and learning strategies with their students. The key is to identify the strategy that will sincerely help students understand more deeply the main ideas featured in the text. Graphic organizers can help students greatly. However, in other instances, a pre-reading strategy, such as activating prior knowledge and making predictions about the text, may be better suited for the text that the students will read on the Internet. Most teacher candidates will find that it becomes easier to identify the appropriate reading strategy as they become more experienced at lesson planning and forecasting what will work best for their students. They will also have a quicker learning curve as they become more familiar with the individualized learning needs of each student in their classroom.

Increasingly, middle and secondary social studies classrooms are being equipped with technology. Fortunately, this gives students access to primary and secondary sources unlike any classroom experience in the past. Yet, this also presents a challenge. Students need to be able to make sense out of the text that they are reading on the Internet and the electronic textbooks that they are using. Reading strategies can help students more easily comprehend text that is accessed using technology.

References

Beal, C. & Bolick, C. M. (2013). *Teaching social studies in middle and secondary schools* (6th ed.). Indianapolis, IN: Pearson.

Cayton, A., Perry, E., Reed, L., & Winkler, A. (2000). *America: Pathways to the present*. Upper Saddle River, NJ: Prentice Hall.

CCSS. (2014). *Common Core State Standards initiative*. Retrieved from www.corestandards. org/ELA-Literacy/RH/11-12/#CCSS.ELA-Literacy.RH.11-12.9. Accessed 3/10/14.

Readence, J. E., Bean, T. W., & Baldwin, R. S. (1998). *Content area literacy: An integrated approach*. Dubuque, IA: Kendall/Hunt.

Scheuerell, S. (2008a). Open secrets: Using the Internet to learn about the influence of money in politics. *Social Education, 3*, 152–155.

Scheuerell, S. (2008b). Gallup Poll: Using the Internet to learn about the influence of public opinion in politics. *The Social Studies, 4*, 181–186.

Scheuerell, S. (2008c). The Great Migration: Using a problem-based learning approach and the Internet. *Social Studies Research and Practice, 1*, 68–79.

Scheuerell, S. (2009). The Avalon Project: Using literacy strategies with primary sources on the Internet. *Social Studies Research and Practice, 1*, 71–81.

Scheuerell, S. (2011). Authentic Intellectual Work: Using the Internet to learn about the Supreme Court. *Social Studies Research and Practice, 3*, 81–90.

Woods, R. & Gatewood, W. (1998). *America interpreted: A concise history with readings*. New York: Harcourt Brace.

11

WEB 2.0 TOOLS

Web 2.0 tools are becoming more accessible to social studies students due to the increasing amount of technology found in middle and secondary classrooms. Countless Web 2.0 tools can be leveraged in the social studies classroom. Each tool enables students to actively participate in learning and demonstrate to others what they have learned. Teachers can also use these tools for formative or summative assessment purposes covering almost any segment of the curriculum found in the social studies classroom.

Many students find Web 2.0 tools to be quite appealing since they move the classroom to a student-centered instructional approach using the Internet. They tend to facilitate active learning and engage the student more deeply about the subject matter. A wide variety of Web 2.0 tools are available to students. Students can use these interactive web-based tools to produce avatars, cartoons, video documentaries, and graphic organizers.

Teachers need to challenge students to participate in a great deal of critical thinking about the subject matter when they produce Web 2.0 tools. Bloom's taxonomy should be a point of emphasis to move Web 2.0–enhanced lessons from lower-level thinking to higher-order thinking. Social studies teachers can foster higher-order thinking when students use Web 2.0 tools by using the decision-making model of social studies instruction. For example, students can identify their opinion on a constitutional issue or take a stand on a historical issue. The point of emphasis is to have the students share their in-depth thinking on the issue by developing a persuasive argument, via the Web 2.0 tool, to communicate their analysis to others.

In the pages to follow, readers will learn about specific Web 2.0 tools that can be used in the middle and secondary social studies classroom. Readers will also learn more detailed information on how these tools can be used by students.

Readers should keep in mind that new Web 2.0 tools are being developed frequently and no matter which tool students use, they should continue to be challenged to participate in critical thinking about the subject matter.

Rationale for Using Web 2.0 Tools

According to Solomon and Schrum (2007), "Web 2.0 tool" is a term used to describe online tools that are interactive and collaborative for users. Examples of Web 2.0 tools include blogs, wikis, and digital media. These types of tools enable students to easily generate content in real time (as cited in Wilson, Wright, Inman, & Matherson, 2011). Students can use Web 2.0 tools to produce products using technology. Wilson, Wright, Inman, and Matherson (2011) reported that students who used Web 2.0 tools found them to be quite engaging and that they foster higher-level thinking about the subject matter in social studies. Rather than focusing a lesson on drill-and-practice exercises and lower-level thinking, a lesson with Web 2.0 tools should challenge students to use technology as a cognitive tool. In the literature, Jonassen (1995) argued this point, suggesting that technology should be used in the classroom to do what computers are good at—storing information—and this should free students up to participate in critical thinking about the subject matter. He wrote:

> When students work with computer technology, instead of being controlled by it, they enhance the capabilities of the computer, and the computer enhances their thinking and learning. The results of an intellectual partnership with the computer is that the whole of learning becomes greater than the sum of its parts. (p. 44)

As a result, students are able to focus their mental energy on higher-level thinking about the subject matter using the computer. Students can participate in deep reflection, problem solving, and discussion about a subject in social studies and produce products with Web 2.0 tools where they share their intellectual contributions with others (Jonassen, 1995).

Many social studies teachers find it difficult to think about how they might design a lesson that incorporates an intellectual partnership between their students and Web 2.0 tools. There are many possibilities. Students can view electronic databases on topics related to the social studies curriculum and analyze the data. The United States Census Report is one such example. Students can analyze immigration patterns and produce a Web 2.0 tool, such as Popplet, where they show the causes and effects of immigration patterns in the United States. They can also compare and contrast immigration patterns in the United States today to immigration patterns from the past. Perhaps they could write a blog about this. In this example, the computer stores the information in the database in regard to the immigration patterns, but the student is challenged to conduct the necessary analysis. The students can share their findings using a Web 2.0 tool, since the intellectual partnership enables the student to be freed up to conduct the analysis while the computer memorizes, or stores, the information.

Benefits of Web 2.0 Tools

Web 2.0 tools have many benefits for teaching and learning in social studies. VoiceThread is one example of a Web 2.0 tool that is beneficial to middle and secondary students. This is a user-friendly, interactive, multimedia slideshow tool that enables students to produce web-based documentaries. Students can use VoiceThread to share their findings on the subject matter that they are learning in the middle and secondary social studies curriculum. According to Brunvand and Byrd (2011), students benefit greatly from VoiceThread because it can "be used to promote student engagement, motivation, and ultimately enhance the quality of the learning experience for all students" (p. 28).

Blogging is another Web 2.0 tool that can enhance the teaching and learning experience in the social studies classroom. Blogging can encourage students to participate in higher-level thinking about the subject matter when they are asked to reflect and write about in-depth topics related to the social studies curriculum. Wilson, Wright, Inman, and Matherson (2012) detailed how blogging challenged students to do a great deal of critical thinking in an Advancement Placement United States History course. Students can provide their analysis on just about any topic in the curriculum for the course by blogging about it. Blogging provides a web-based platform or medium for students to share their intellectual contributions with their classmates and potentially with others beyond the walls of their classroom.

Google Maps, another Web 2.0 tool, is being used increasingly in middle and secondary social studies classrooms. The key is for teachers to develop lesson plans where students use Google Maps to think more deeply about the subject matter rather than passively using the web-based tool. Doering, Scharber, and Miller (2009) detailed how social studies teachers can use Google Maps to foster critical thinking by challenging students to think more deeply about geographic concepts. For example, students can use Google Maps to participate in problem-solving scenarios. These scenarios can involve issues such as climate change and migratory patterns. Some questions that the teacher could pose include "What do you think are the top five places in the world being impacted by climate change?" or "What is the location in North Dakota that is most impacted by emigration?" (Doering, Scharber, & Miller, 2009, p. 327). The teacher can ask additional questions that challenge students to analyze data that may be retrieved from Google Maps. The key is for the teacher to consider how Google Maps might be used for a specific learning objective in the middle and secondary social studies curriculum and design the rest of the lesson by harnessing data from the site.

Wikis can also be used by students to learn the subject matter in the social studies curriculum. Students can investigate issues pertaining to the content that they are learning in social studies and share their findings with others by working collaboratively to produce a wiki. Students may even have the opportunity to produce the first-of-its-kind wiki on the subject matter that they are investigating. For example, perhaps they could have the opportunity to write a wiki about a local history topic or share their own intellectual contributions on an issue that they are learning about in class. Most importantly, wikis enable students to participate in active learning and critical thinking using web-based technology in the social studies classroom. Wilson, Wright, Inman, and Matherson (2011) argued that students can benefit from these types of wiki experiences since they have the opportunity to work collaboratively and participate in peer reviews.

Pivotal Decisions With Technology: Background Knowledge or "Blank Slate"?

A great deal of active learning with technology took place in each of the social studies classrooms that participated in the research study. The active learning was almost daily, but what seemed to make or break a lesson with technology was whether enough background information was shared with the students prior to an investigation using the Internet or before they used Web 2.0 tools in the classroom. Previous literature has underscored the need for this. Students are more likely to fully comprehend what they are investigating if they are able to connect what they have previously learned about the topic or issue to new information that they are presented with (Lawless & Brown, 1997). This highlights the need for students to have some background knowledge about a subject matter rather than going into a lesson with a blank slate when they are using technology in social studies.

Lawless and Brown (1997) have suggested that knowledge is organized by learners into abstract mental structures. These are known as schemata. Lawless and Brown (1997) detailed how this works by writing:

> As an individual acquires information, there are attempts to match existing schemata with the information represented by the material being examined. As the learner does this, he or she builds a mental concept of their interpretation of the meaning of the content. This concept is constructed partially out of information previously known and partially by the new information presented. (p. 118)

This assertion about how students learn applies to the research investigation that I conducted. Each social studies teacher in the study had to decide how much information to share with students prior to their investigation using the computer. This was a pivotal decision in these classrooms. The teacher had to decide whether to give the students any background knowledge before they gave the students an opportunity to explore a topic on the Internet. If the teacher did decide to give the students some background information, they also had to decide how much information to give to the students and how to deliver the information to the students before their Internet investigation or Web 2.0 technology project began.

At River High School, Mr. Jones spent a great deal of time and effort providing background information so his students would have some prior knowledge before they investigated topics pertaining to the Civil Rights movement. Mr. Jones used the "flipped classroom" approach to build up the background information for his students. By doing so, his students were more easily able to comprehend the subject matter that they were investigating online. He regularly posted readings on the Edmodo class webpage, and the students were assigned these readings for homework on a daily basis. The following day in class, Mr. Jones reviewed the material with the students at the beginning of the class period to check their understanding of the material and their readiness to apply what they were learning during the remainder of the class period. This happens to be a defining feature of a "flipped classroom."

The "flipped classroom" approach used by Mr. Jones utilizes the majority of class time for the application of the course material instead of using it for lecture purposes. Mr. Jones' students spent the beginning of one class period reviewing a reading that he had posted on Edmodo. The reading came from the Digital History Internet collection and compared the beliefs of Martin Luther King Jr. to Malcolm X. In another lesson, Mr. Jones began class by reviewing the reading he had posted on Edmodo involving the Civil Rights Act of 1964 and the Voting Rights Act of 1965 from the iCivics Internet webpage. In each case, it was extremely effective at preparing his students for their Internet investigations later on during class, and for the students to produce products with their computers since they had become much more familiar with the subject matter that they were asked to investigate rather than diving in without any background information given to them.

Lawless and Brown (1997) wrote about the importance of building background knowledge for students and creating interest in the subject matter before students actually investigate topics on the Internet by suggesting that it helps students use the navigation tools to find the appropriate information they are looking for and helps them make better sense of what they have read. In the example from Mr. Jones' classroom, he skillfully was able to use the "flipped classroom" approach to build up the knowledge base of his students before they began their online investigation of significant issues pertaining to the Civil Rights era.

During the semester, Mr. Jones' students worked collaboratively to produce a Weebly Internet webpage featuring pivotal events from the Civil Rights movement. Each group focused on one of the following topics: Jim Crow, contributions of African-Americans during World War II, landmark Supreme Court cases, Freedom Riders, Freedom Summer, and sit-ins. The students had to identify five artifacts that pertained to their assigned topic and include them on their Internet webpage. The students used a free, user-friendly, online webpage program called

Weebly to compose their projects. During the project, students were actively involved as they made decisions on what to include and what to leave off of their Internet webpage on the Civil Rights movement. It was also evident that the students were able to connect what they had previously learned about the Civil Rights era to the topics they were investigating. In fact, Bob, a student at River High School, spoke about how much he appreciated the review each day in Mr. Jones' class, stating, "The review that happens the next class helps you refresh your memory or if you didn't understand it, it helps you understand it more." The sentiment shared by Bob fits with the research already discussed in this chapter emphasizing how students learn by taking information they have previously learned about a topic or giving them background information and combining it with the new information that they are presented with (Lawless & Brown, 1997). This is what happened successfully in Mr. Jones' unit on the Civil Rights movement where his students produced Internet webpages on a variety of topics pertaining to this pivotal event in our nation's history.

At Bluff High School, students spent about one week actively engaged in producing a Keynote presentation on European history topics. Each group picked from one of the following topics: feudalism, the Reformation, the Enlightenment, the Industrial Revolution, Communism, the Cold War, and the European Union. During the project, students collaborated in groups and were required to teach the information to their classmates using a visual aid, such as a Keynote or PowerPoint presentation. Mr. Smith also required the students to develop an outline for their lesson and to include an introductory activity for it. He emphasized the need for students to get their classmates involved when they taught the lesson and to include a review activity for assessment purposes. During class time, students did most of their research online using Google to identify Internet webpages that would help them to research their topic in depth.

During each class period, students were actively engaged researching their topic and collaborating with their peers rather than being passive learners. However, many of the students failed to capture the big ideas pertaining to each of the topics that they were researching. I noted this as I walked around the classroom, since it was evident that many of the students had failed to identify several of the main ideas involving the topic that they were assigned. This also manifested itself in the Keynote presentations that I had the opportunity to observe since the students barely conveyed any higher-level thinking or analysis in these presentations. Unfortunately, this was likely due to the lack of background knowledge or information that the students had about their topics prior to their research online. Lawless and Brown (1997) argued this point, suggesting that teachers must remember that many students in their classroom will not have the necessary cognitive ability, knowledge base, or motivation to explore a topic with computers, so it is imperative for teachers to build some level of background knowledge before students begin to explore a topic or build a project using technology.

In Mr. Brown's class at Bridge High School, he usually began class with a short lecture to build up some background knowledge for his students before they began an active learning lesson with the computers. He spoke about the importance of building prior knowledge before his students researched topics online by stating, "Some things obviously are not easy to comprehend in history without giving a little background or knowing a little bit about the subject." The thoughts shared by Mr. Brown are aligned with the large body of already-established research on this issue. According to Dillon (1991), prior knowledge is necessary for student online investigations because "results revealed that individuals with higher topic familiarity struggled less with navigation through the content and thus were able to focus more on areas of interest" (as cited in Lawless & Brown, 1997, p. 125). Mr. Brown also noted in detail how important background knowledge was when his students used their iPad computers to explore topics in his social studies classroom. He said:

> I think it's important to have that background information. One example I use with my kids a lot is, I'm going off topic here, political cartoons. If I show them a political cartoon at the beginning of the unit, on something we haven't talked about yet, they usually have no idea what it is, or what it should stand for, but as we talk about things and we come back to it, oh this is the answer for this, so if they don't have the background information on whatever topic you might have them researching or doing a project on the iPad, they spend a lot of time looking up information that might not be helpful to them.

During my experience in his classroom, the students were actively engaged in producing a Keynote presentation on the Allied leaders during World War II. In order to establish background knowledge for his students, Mr. Brown lectured on many of these leaders before they began to research and produce their products using their iPads. Gary, a student in Mr. Brown's class, spoke about the helpfulness of having some background knowledge before he investigated a topic with his iPad computer, saying, "I think it helps before you start searching because then you can know what you're looking for. You're not like completely blind going into it."

The students in Mr. Brown's class worked collaboratively in groups to research and produce a Keynote presentation on one of the following Allied leaders: President Roosevelt, President Truman, Winston Churchill, or Joseph Stalin. Mr. Brown instructed each group to include the following in their Keynote presentation: background information on the leader, how the leader rose to power, the political beliefs of the leader, examples of how the leader helped the citizens of his country, and the leadership style exhibited by this person during World War II. Mr. Brown's students spent the majority of the class period actively engaged in researching their topics and identifying images that could be used as a part of their Keynote presentation. The rubric for the project also required the students to include at least five slides, and this is where the students spent most of their energy on the project.

There may be some exceptions to the need for background knowledge or information in technology-rich lessons. For example, during problem-based learning, a teacher may ask students to develop a hypothesis about a subject in social studies and then have students test their hypothesis by researching the topic online. A student in this scenario may have a very limited amount of background information, but even then, they have an opportunity to at least begin to brainstorm about the topic and possibly trigger any prior knowledge they have about it. In addition, if the teacher asks all of the students to share their hypothesis before they investigate online, the students are then likely to activate a greater knowledge base beforehand, even if it doesn't involve class readings or a lecture by the teacher to build background knowledge. However, in most instances, and in most lessons, a social studies teacher should build background knowledge for their students before they investigate topics online or build products such as Web 2.0 tools by delivering a short lecture, showing a brief video, or reviewing a class reading. In summary, there are many possibilities on how to build background knowledge, but it certainly is a must to help students more fully comprehend what they are investigating online.

Examples of Web 2.0 Tools

In the pages to follow, there are examples of Web 2.0 tools that can be used in the middle and secondary social studies classroom. Each can be used by students to produce products that demonstrate what they have learned about the subject matter they are investigating. As the findings presented in this chapter show, students should be exposed to some background knowledge before they begin to investigate the subject matter and produce a Web 2.0 tool.

Voki: An Online Avatar

Voki is a Web 2.0 tool that is becoming increasingly popular. Middle and secondary social studies teachers can have their students use Voki to produce a web-based avatar. Students can use the avatar to share what they have learned about the subject matter that they are investigating in class. They can pick from a wide variety of figures for their avatar. Some include cartoon figures and famous politicians. There are several politicians that students can pick from. President Obama, President George W. Bush, President Clinton, and President Reagan are some that are featured on the site.

There are many interactive features that students can use with Voki, but it is critically important for teachers to have students participate in critical thinking when they are using this Web 2.0 tool. Students can share their analysis about the subject matter by typing text into the web-based site. The text the students type is then used to activate the avatar to speak what was written by the student. For example, the students could be asked to compare and contrast the war on terrorism to the Cold War. The students could research the topic and offer their analysis by pretending they were the president of the United States, using their avatar to make a speech on national television about the subject. In summary, there are many countless ways that students can use Voki in the classroom. This Web 2.0 tool can be found at the following Internet link: www.voki.com/.

Popplet: An Online Graphic Organizer

Popplet is an interactive Web 2.0 tool that enables students to easily produce a concept map or graphic organizer on the Internet. Students can produce a graphic organizer by using different colors, inserting images, drawing items, and displaying their conceptual understanding of the subject matter. Popplet also enables students to collaborate virtually on the site in real time. Popplet, when used appropriately, can challenge students to think deeply about the subject matter. Students can use it to show their conceptual understanding by exploring the following types of higher-level thinking: cause-effect, compare-contrast, problem-solution, experiential, and reflection. Most importantly, Popplet enables students to make sense out of what they are reading or learning by organizing information conceptually using technology.

Popplet can also be used by students to consider the pros and cons of the subject they are investigating in social studies. For example, students can research the pros and cons of the United States becoming an imperialist nation in the late 1800s/early 1900s. The activity may be a part of a wider unit where students are learning about Manifest Destiny and the Spanish-American War. Popplet can be found at the following Internet link: http://popplet.com/.

Prezi: An Online Presentation Tool

Prezi is a Web 2.0 tool that enables students to easily produce an interactive presentation for viewers. There are some similarities between Prezi and PowerPoint. However, Prezi is web-based and much more interactive than PowerPoint. Students can use Prezi to display their findings on the subject matter from their middle or secondary social studies classroom. There is a tutorial on the Prezi Internet site for beginners on how to use the tool. I have seen firsthand that students quickly learn how to use Prezi with very little trouble.

Prezi can be used in the social studies classroom to enable students to share their findings with others by using technology. Students can even use Prezi to potentially share their findings with others beyond the walls of the classroom by posting their presentation to the Internet. For example, students can investigate the debate on whether the US government should negotiate with terrorist organizations to save prisoners of war and journalists who are held as hostages—in particular, whether the United States should swap prisoners or pay a ransom to free them. The Prezi Web 2.0 tool can be found at the following Internet link: http://prezi.com/.

PowToon: An Online Tool to Produce Animated Videos

PowToon is a Web 2.0 tool that enables middle and secondary students to produce animated video presentations. Students can incorporate text, visuals, cartoon figures, and music to teach others what they have learned about the subject matter they are investigating. The website features many examples that can help students get started with their very own PowToon.

As mentioned, students can produce a PowToon to present what they have learned or their interpretation of the subject matter. Students can also produce a PowToon to develop their argument for or against something they have been researching. For example, students can develop a PowToon to argue for or against the use of force in Syria and Iraq to combat ISIS (Islamic State in Iraq and Syria). The PowToon Web 2.0 tool can be found at the following Internet link: www. powtoon.com/.

Bubbl: A User-Friendly Online Tool to Produce Graphic Organizers

Bubbl is a Web 2.0 tool that functions as an online, interactive graphic organizer. The website allows students to create a bubble graphic organizer. Students can also import images to the site to produce the graphic organizer. In addition, students can change the colors of the graphic organizer to present material conceptually by themes. There is also a tab that enables students to make the graphic organizer bigger or smaller by zooming in or out, depending on what works best to convey the main ideas of the subject matter.

There are many ways students can use this site to present information. For example, students can pretend that they are a member of the city council and need to make a presentation on whether their city should host some of the children who have recently immigrated to the United States from Central America. Bubbl can be found at the following Internet link: https://bubbl.us/.

VoiceThread: An Online Tool to Produce Videos

VoiceThread is a Web 2.0 tool that enables students to produce a web-based visual presentation. Middle and secondary students can integrate text, audio, images, and narration to tell a story or present findings from an investigation to share what they have learned about the subject matter with their classmates and potentially others beyond the walls of the classroom by posting it to the World Wide Web.

A video is posted on the site to help students get started, and there are several examples of VoiceThread projects.

In an American Government class, students can research the debate on whether to legalize marijuana for medical purposes. Students could produce a VoiceThread presentation where they argue for or against this issue. Perhaps they can also research and discuss how it has already been legalized for medical purposes in many different parts of the country. VoiceThread can be found at the following Internet link: https://voicethread.com/.

Theory and Practice: Firsthand Experience Using Web 2.0 Tools and the Decision-Making Model in United States History

Middle and secondary social studies teachers are increasingly incorporating lessons about the war on terrorism. Many of these lessons focus on issues pertaining to the balance between civil liberties and national security. For example, students can be asked to investigate whether surveillance cameras should be used more frequently. Students can develop a hypothesis on the argument for and against the increased use of surveillance cameras. As soon as they have finished their hypotheses, students can test them by using the Internet to see what the evidence suggests. Finally, students can analyze the themes that emerge from the research by comparing and contrasting their findings. The students can also share aloud what they have learned from their research. These are the steps found in problem-based learning and the inquiry arc associated with the College, Career, and Civil Life (C3) Framework for Social Studies.

There are many other possibilities for investigating problems associated with our nation's war on terrorism. For example, students can investigate a problem such as whether our nation's airports should increase their security by limiting some of our civil liberties. Many Americans are debating whether more detailed security checks should take place even though this may mean longer lines at the airport. There are countless Internet webpages that include arguments on both sides of this issue that middle and secondary students can investigate in the classroom. In addition, teachers can pose a question about racial and ethnic profiling. Students can develop a hypothesis on what they think some of the arguments are for and against the use of racial and ethnic profiling in relation to the broader issue of civil liberties versus national security. Interestingly, students can also compare and contrast the issue to other events in our national history. This also fits with the C3 Framework, which encourages students to examine issues in social studies through a multidisciplinary lens. For instance, students can research the Japanese-American internment camps during World War II.

Students can examine other periods in our nation's history when there was a conflict between civil liberties and national security. During World War I, President Wilson used the Sedition Act to prosecute those who said malicious things about the war effort. President Lincoln suspended the writ of habeas corpus during the

Civil War, and President Adams enforced the Alien and Sedition Acts during a time of conflict with France during the early years of our young democracy.

There are many other potential issues or problems for middle and secondary students to investigate related to the war on terrorism. Gun control, the use of drones, immigration, wiretapping, and cyber surveillance are issues that our democracy is currently debating within the larger issue of civil liberties versus national security. Each of these issues has a great deal of potential for planning investigations using the problem-based learning framework and simultaneously enhances the twenty-first-century skills necessary for middle and secondary students. There are additional issues to explore, such as "Should the United States close the prison at Guantanamo Bay?" or "Should the United States use military force in Syria?" Each of these is a complex question with no easy answer. This is why there is a great deal of merit in using problem-based learning to facilitate higher-level thinking for each of these investigations. A great deal of decision making is involved in each of these inquiries. I had students share their views on these issues using Web 2.0 tools such as Voki and Popplet.

Is Edward Snowden a hero or villain? This is another example of a problem or question that middle and secondary students can investigate in the social studies classroom. A great deal has been written about Edward Snowden, and students will easily find arguments supporting the actions taken by Snowden and many articles arguing that he has betrayed his nation. This inquiry enables middle and secondary students to weigh the evidence and to share where they stand on this issue by producing a Prezi and supporting it with evidence. The question on whether to perceive Snowden as a hero or villain is no easy problem to solve. Yet, this is what makes this question an excellent example of how middle and secondary students should be challenged to think for themselves in the social studies classroom rather than spending their entire classroom experience being a passive learner. Our democracy needs students who can think for themselves, analyze evidence, weigh differing opinions, and reach their own conclusion. This is what participatory citizenship should look like in our democracy, and it is critically important for middle and secondary students to develop these skill sets in the social studies classroom. Problem-based learning with technology can help to build up these skills in our students, the future leaders of our democracy.

Summary

Web 2.0 tools can actively engage students with technology in the middle and secondary social studies classroom. There are many Web 2.0 tools to pick from, and there are increasingly more available to students. Yet, it is critically important to remember to have students involved in higher-level thinking about the social studies subject matter when they produce Web 2.0 tools. These tools can be the catalyst to foster critical thinking in a technology-rich classroom.

In this chapter, several Web 2.0 tools were featured in depth. Readers can use these tools in their own social studies classroom in conjunction with the research-based frameworks presented earlier in the book. The Technological, Pedagogical, and Content Knowledge (TPACK) framework and the constructivist model of technology integration are two examples of such frameworks. Each of these encourages the teacher to consider the content, pedagogy, and technology to foster higher-level thinking about the subject matter.

In summary, Web 2.0 tools are growing in popularity. Social studies teachers won't have trouble identifying tools that can be used in their classroom. Yet, the key is to design a lesson that will keep the emphasis on encouraging students to participate in rigorous thinking and produce authentic products using the web-based technology tool. In addition, students can share their findings and intellectual contributions with their classmates and beyond.

References

Brunvand, S. & Byrd, S. (2011). Using VoiceThread to promote learning engagement and success for all students. *Teaching Exceptional Children, 4*, 28–37.

Dillon, A. (1991). Readers' models of text structure: The case of academic materials. *International Journal of Man-Machine Studies 35*: 913–925.

Doering, A., Scharber, C., Miller, C., & Veletsianos, G. (2009). GeoThentic: Designing and assessing with technology, pedagogy, and content knowledge. *Contemporary Issues in Technology and Teacher Education, 3*, 316–336.

Jonassen, D.H. (1995). Computers as cognitive tools: Learning with technology, not from technology. *Journal of Computing in Higher Education, 2*, 40–73.

Lawless, K.A. & Brown, S.W. (1997). Multimedia learning environments: Issues of learner control and navigation. *Instructional Science, 25*, 117–131.

Wilson, E. K., Wright, V. H., Inman, C. T., & Matherson, L. H. (2011). Retooling the social studies classroom for the current generation. *The Social Studies, 1*, 65–72.

12

LOCAL HISTORY

During my experience as a high school teacher, I looked for ways to make connections between local history and the subject matter in the social studies curriculum. In my opinion, local history is an excellent opportunity to capture the interest of middle and secondary students. There are so many interesting examples of history that can be found in any community. This makes history come alive for students. Frequently, topics are covered in the typical American history textbook that seem too distant or remote to the typical middle or secondary student. These same students are often amazed to learn that many of these same issues happened in their very own community. I frequently saw this firsthand with my high school students.

Local history also gives students the opportunity to examine primary and secondary sources in their own community. Students can go to a local history museum and search the archives to investigate topics that have been long forgotten in their community. I remember seeing my students enjoying looking at old newspapers and taking notes on what they had learned from them. This also allows students to do what historians do. The students can examine these primary sources, analyze them, and develop their own historical interpretation.

Students enjoy the opportunity to share what they have learned from their local history investigations. Frequently, students discover something new about their community or something that has been long forgotten. This presents an opportunity. Middle and secondary students can produce the first-ever Internet webpage, podcast, wiki, or digital video on the topic that they investigated. As a result, students can teach others in their community about local history by posting their technology product via the World Wide Web. This is also an excellent example of Authentic Intellectual Work (AIW) since the students are developing their own intellectual contributions that have value beyond school.

Rationale for Local History

Local history investigations can transform the classroom from a teacher-centered to a student-centered classroom. These inquiry-based lessons are also characterized by an emphasis on higher-level thinking, as students analyze primary and secondary sources related to local history topics. Middle and secondary students benefit from inquiry-based lessons, such as local history investigations, where they are challenged to think deeply about the subject matter rather than participate in drill-and-practice activities memorizing names and dates.

The newly adopted College, Career, and Civic Life (C3) Framework for Social Studies State Standards encourages inquiry-based lessons, such as the lessons that can be facilitated with local history. The C3 Framework encourages social studies teachers to develop lesson plans that foster higher-level thinking by having students explore answers to questions by performing their very own investigations. Local history is a prime opportunity for this. Students can use primary sources such as newspapers, census reports, plat maps, tax records, letters, and diaries to investigate local history topics. This enables students to explore history as if it were a mystery and they were detectives seeking answers to their questions. Many students are motivated when they are challenged to participate in this type of lesson. This also presents a paradigm shift to the social studies classroom. Rather than relying on lecture and the classroom textbook, students participate in active learning, investigating sources beyond the singular classroom text.

In the typical social studies classroom, there is a heavy reliance on the classroom textbook. Many voices are left out of these textbooks, so students do not have the opportunity to read in depth about the contributions of minorities and women to our nation's history. Local history presents an opportunity to accomplish this. Teachers can help students identify primary sources that capture insights and perspectives from minorities and women in their very own community. These firsthand insights can be quite meaningful to students. Bonney (1995) wrote that "learning about a community and its people brings a reality to history often missing in the general textbook" (p. 11). This can also make history come alive to students who feel disconnected from the subject matter year after year.

Many students find history to be boring. Many of these same students respond favorably to local history because it comes alive for them when they are able to find connections between the subject matter in their classroom textbook and their very own community. For example, when I taught social studies in Kansas, I had students research the Census Reports from Pawnee County, Kansas, in the 1870s and 1880s to learn about the impact of the Homestead Act on the immigration patterns to the Great Plains. This was a topic in their comprehensive classroom textbook, but it came alive for them when they could analyze the data from their very own community and county. Rather than listening to me lecture on the Homestead Act in general terms and reading about it in their classroom textbook, the students were able to see firsthand how the legislation had a direct impact on their community of Larned, Kansas. This was transformative for many of the students and sparked some interest in history.

I encourage social studies teaches to consider using local history as a catalyst to foster interest in the subject matter. Many students enjoy local history because they can access primary sources firsthand. Teachers can take students on a field trip to a local museum or archive to view these primary sources. These primary sources help local history come alive for students since there is potential for students to develop "a deeper understanding of course content and relating it to real life, primary source readings can also help students become excited about the content" (Dutt, 1995, p. 3). Countless primary sources on local history topics are often accessible to students at libraries, museums, and archives found in communities across the nation. Some of these include diaries, letters, newspaper articles, account books, business records, probate records, court dockets, scrapbooks, photo albums, wills, property records, birth certificates, death records, marriage records, city ordinances, immigrant guides, gazetteers, speeches, and cemetery inscriptions (Bonney, 1995). Each of these sources would be impossible to replicate in any textbook. They can provide the necessary clues into a community's forgotten past and frequently connect to larger issues facing the nation at the same time.

Local history enables students to be historians. Middle and secondary students can view these primary sources, conduct their own analysis, and share their findings with others. The inquiry-based process of discovering the past of their very own community can be quite appealing to many students. Bonney (1995) wrote, "Local history provides a positive learning experience for students, guided carefully, students will feel the excitement of working with a variety of historical sources, gathering and organizing the information, and drawing conclusions" (p. 11). Students are then in a position to share their findings from their local history research.

Technology and Local History

Students can share their historical findings using technology. Frequently, they can even produce the first Internet webpage, digital video, or podcast on the local history topic that they have researched. This can be quite motivating to many middle and secondary students since their historical findings can teach others about their own community.

Technology is making it increasingly possible for students to share their findings with others via the World Wide Web. In the past, students could research local history topics and write a paper or make a speech about their findings. These students had a limited audience for their work since their classmates and teacher were the only individuals to learn about the findings. Fortunately today, the Internet enables students to share their findings with a much wider audience.

There is a great deal of merit when students share their local history findings using technology. The student benefits from the process of interpreting what they have learned about the subject matter and thinking about how they want to organize it for their technology project (Jonassen, Carr, & Yueh, 1998). There are many ways that students can use technology to share their local history findings. Regardless of the technology format chosen, students do benefit from the process of having to produce their very own instructional materials using technology rather than viewing what others have produced about the same subject matter (Jonassen et al., 1998).

There are countless local history topics for students to pick from. Marino and Crucco (2012) suggest that students construct a timeline of a city's history, analyze a city's census data, conduct a neighborhood quest, use the "it happened here" approach, or conduct a "then and now" analysis of a city street. The students can then share their findings by producing a product using technology. This can help students remember what they have learned about their community. In fact, Jonassen, Carr, and Yueh (1998) assert that "students are more likely to learn more by constructing instructional materials than by studying them" (p. 34). The local history topics described here present an opportunity for students to produce technology products that have never been featured before.

Many social studies teachers may question the validity of focusing on local history and technology in the classroom. It can be a time-consuming project, but much value can be gained from it. In my opinion, local history and technology are a perfect marriage to actively engage students in the social studies classroom. There are sound arguments to integrate these together. Fabbri (2013) argued that local history is an example of the type of teaching and learning pedagogy that social studies classrooms should be moving to since it is inquiry based and student centered. The same can be said for the integration of technology when it is used meaningfully by students to investigate topics and produce products using technology. Technology can challenge students to analyze what they have learned from their local history research and how to organize this for an audience to view.

There are many opportunities for teachers to foster higher-level thinking when students investigate local history topics. Students can be challenged to explore the relationship behind the local history phenomena that they are investigating by examining cause/effect, compare/contrast, or problem/solution questions. There are many themes that students can examine when they are researching the history of their very own community. Some of these themes include urbanization, entrepreneurship, innovation, industrialization, and a city's demographics (Marino & Crucco, 2012). The reader may wonder what this might look like in the classroom. There frequently is a great amount of data on demographic trends, such as immigration patterns to and from a city, over a period of time. Census reports can provide this data to students. More of this data can be found on the Internet. Marino and Crucco (2012) described a local history investigation in New Brunswick, New Jersey, where students analyzed the city's most significant population trends, including Hungarian immigrants who migrated there in the early 1900s, the Great Migration of African-Americans following World War I, and the recent growth of the city's Hispanic population. This is a prime example of how students can be challenged to analyze data or trends involving local history. Students can then share their analysis by producing a product using technology. Most importantly, students are then using technology meaningfully as a tool for their mind, or Mindtool, where the technology itself is an unintelligent tool, "relying on the learner to provide the intelligence, not the computer" (Jonassen, Carr, & Yueh, 1998, p. 37). The combination of local history and technology provides many opportunities for students to analyze data, just like this example, and to share the findings about their very own community.

There is a great need to bring history alive for students. Local history, used in conjunction with technology, can arguably make this happen in the middle and secondary social studies classroom. Many students find it appealing to learn about the historic contributions of people from their own community rather than the distant historical events that are chronicled in the traditional textbook (Marino & Crucco, 2012). Students can then investigate these individuals and see how they relate to the broader themes of a specific time period or movement in history. For example, when I taught high school social studies, I had students investigate those who fought in the Civil War in their own community. In my opinion, this brought the topic alive for many of my students. They learned how their city in western Missouri was divided during the Civil War. There were some who fought for the Union and others for the Confederacy. There was a great deal of guerilla warfare throughout the region since Missouri was a border state during the conflict. The students then used technology to produce Internet webpages on their findings.

In summary, technology can help to foster in-depth thinking about local history. There are fewer examples of webpages, digital videos, or podcasts currently on the Internet pertaining to local history topics. As a result, local history, used in conjunction with technology, presents a rich and dynamic opportunity for the middle and secondary social studies classrooms to fill this gap.

Local History Projects

In the pages to follow, readers will see examples of how students can use technology to explore the history of their very own community. The list includes oral history, historical buildings, and historical images. These are just a few examples that highlight the potential of harnessing local history and technology in the middle and secondary social studies classroom.

Oral History Projects

Students will likely find people in their community who would be happy to be interviewed about their lifelong experiences. The insights gathered from these interviews can provide valuable firsthand insights into the past. These are priceless insights that are typically left out of the traditional classroom textbook. Fabbri (2013) pointed this out, writing, "By limiting sources of information, social studies classrooms are leaving out enriching and valuable resources such as family or oral histories that can be easily accessible and relevant to students" (p. 4). For example, if students are learning about the Great Depression, there will be a great deal of information about it in their classroom textbook, but they will be unlikely to find any details on what it was like in their own community during the 1930s. There is an opportunity for students to interview people in their community who remember life during the Great Depression. They can provide interesting insights that would be difficult to match in their textbook. Most importantly, they provide insights on the challenges that people in their own community faced during the Great Depression and not some distant place that is mentioned in the students' textbook.

The Veterans History Project, sponsored by the Library of Congress, is an excellent example of how middle and secondary students can interview people in their own community to gain insights into the experiences of veterans in foreign wars. Students can use their computer to interview veterans. Interviews can be submitted to the Library of Congress Internet webpage. The interviews can be captured using a digital video camera and editing the film with Windows Movie Maker or Apple iMovies. However, students do not necessarily have to capture film to submit the firsthand accounts of the veterans. Students can also submit an audio file of the interview. This can be submitted using free software from the Internet called Audacity. This is a user-friendly way for students to produce an MP3 audio file. Transcripts of the interview can also be submitted to the Library of Congress. The webpage can be found at the following link: www. loc.gov/vets/.

Local history also enables students to capture multicultural perspectives from their own community. These are the perspectives that are frequently not covered in depth in the classroom textbook. These firsthand insights can be captured by middle and secondary students to provide them with diverse perspectives on a wide variety of issues. According to Marino and Crucco (2012), it is important for students to learn about the experiences of the diverse groups who have arrived in a community and those who have left. Middle and secondary students can utilize oral history to learn about the perceptions of others from multicultural backgrounds in their very own community. This enables students to see the relevancy of what they are learning by making connections to these personal experiences in their community (Fabbri, 2013). Students can then use technology to share their findings from the oral history interviews they have conducted.

During my experience as a high school social studies teacher, I had my students research local history topics and produce Internet webpages on their findings. The project was called Virtual Warrensburg (Scheuerell, 2010). Some of these webpages focused on diversity topics, and one of them included the perspective of an African-American who was interviewed by one group of students. The students captured insights from the individual, who reflected on some instances of discrimination that he faced many years ago. Despite these struggles, the students learned from the individual that he became the first African-American to be elected to the city council in the community. My students produced additional webpages featuring topics such as the history of Native Americans in Johnson County, Missouri; slavery prior to the Civil War; and the unique history of an African-American school that was located in Warrensburg, Missouri. The webpages can be found at the following Internet link: http://warrensburg.k12.mo.us/vw/scheuerell/.

Historical Buildings

Marino and Crucco (2012) suggest that social studies teachers encourage students to look at the historical buildings in their community and have students analyze them to determine clues to the past. Students can capture images of these buildings. During my Virtual Warrensburg project, we typically had at least one day of the unit where we would go on a school-sponsored field trip to enable the students to capture images of the historical sites. These images were frequently used on the websites that they created for the Virtual Warrensburg project. The same can be done with historical buildings in any community.

Students can analyze historical buildings from the past to compare and contrast how the community has developed (Marino & Crucco, 2012). Historical images can often show how a community was profoundly affected by the Industrial Revolution by viewing historical images of factories from a city's past. This was the case in New Brunswick, New Jersey (Marino & Crucco, 2012). This exercise can be replicated in most communities that middle and secondary students will find themselves in across the country. Images of communities around the nation can even be accessed on the Internet at the Library of Congress webpage featured at the following link: www.loc.gov/pictures/.

Google Maps and Local History

Google Maps can be utilized to identify where many of the businesses from the past were located. Students can create mashups where they capture an image of a historical site in their community and then write details about the site on the Google Map that they are creating. Students can then analyze what it would have been like to have lived in the community during a specific historical era by examining what types of jobs, housing, restaurants, and entertainment would have been available in the downtown area of their community fifty years ago or one hundred years ago.

Google Maps enables students to produce interactive maps where they can share their findings with others beyond the walls of the classroom. Frequently, it will be the first-of-its-kind Google Map produced on such a topic, which can be motivating to many students. This is what makes local history quite exciting to many students. I have included a rubric from a Google Map mashups activity that I developed for an investigation designed for high school students who participated in a lesson about the history of the downtown corridor in Dubuque, Iowa (see Figure 12.1).

Google Maps Mashups: Dubuque in 1912

Area	Met (10 Points)	Emerging (5 Points)	Not Met (0 Points)
The student used Google Maps to identify the location of each business featured on the *A City at Work* online collection.	The student identified the location of at least ten of the businesses from the *A City at Work* online collection using Google Maps.	The student identified at least five of the businesses from the *A City at Work* online collection using Google Maps.	The student identified fewer than five of the businesses from the *A City at Work* online collection using Google Maps.
The student used Google Maps to identify the location of each business featured in the *Telegraph Herald* advertisements from the 1912 newspapers.	The student used Google Maps to identify at least ten of the businesses featured in the *Telegraph Herald* advertisements from the 1912 newspapers.	The student used Google Maps to identify at least five of the businesses featured in the *Telegraph Herald* advertisements from the 1912 newspapers.	The student used Google Maps to identify fewer than five of the businesses featured in the *Telegraph Herald* advertisements from the 1912 newspapers.
The student will analyze the Google Map that they produced and the mashups that they created. The student will share their interpretation on what it would have been like for someone living and working in downtown Dubuque in 1912 based on the space and place of the city by posting to the class online discussion board.	The student analyzed the Google Maps that they produced and the mashups they created. They provided a great deal of analysis on what it was like to live and work in downtown Dubuque in 1912 and provided at least five supporting details to strengthen their argument about space and place using the class online discussion board.	The student analyzed the Google Maps that they produced and the mashups they created. They produced some analysis on what it was like to live and work in downtown Dubuque in 1912, providing at least three details to support their argument about space and place using the online discussion board.	The student analyzed the Google Maps that they produced and the mashups they created. They failed to provide analysis on what it was like to live and work in downtown Dubuque in 1912.

(Continued)

Google Maps Mashups: Dubuque in 1912 (Continued)

Area	Met (10 Points)	Emerging (5 Points)	Not Met (0 Points)
The student will compare and contrast what it would have been like to live and work in Dubuque in 1912 to what it is like today using the class online discussion board.	The student compared and contrasted what it would have been like to live and work in Dubuque in 1912 versus what it is like today using the class online discussion board. They provided good analysis and three supporting details to make their argument.	The student somewhat compared and contrasted what it was like to live and work in downtown Dubuque in 192 versus today. They provided at least two supporting details to make their argument using the class online discussion board.	The student failed to provide the necessary analysis to compare and contrast living and working in downtown Dubuque versus today. They provided fewer than two supporting details using the class online discussion board.
The student will consider the geographic imagination of Dubuque in 1912 based on the photographs, advertisements, an oral history interview, and Google Maps using the online discussion board.	The student provided solid analysis on the geographic imagination of Dubuque in 1912 based on photographs, advertisements, an oral history interview, and Google Maps using the online discussion board.	The student provided some analysis on the geographic imagination of Dubuque in 1912 based on photographs, advertisements, an oral history interview, and Google Maps using the online discussion board.	The student failed to provide any analysis on the geographic imagination of Dubuque in 1912 based on photographs, advertisements, an oral history interview, and Google Maps using the online discussion board.

Score: _____/50 Points

Figure 12.1 Rubric: Google mashups.

Source: *A City at Work: 1912 and 2012* (http://acityatwork.com/).

Theory and Practice: Firsthand Experience Using Technology and Local History in American History

A City at Work: 1912 and 2012 is an excellent example of how historical images can be used in the classroom to help students learn about their community's past. Organizations across Dubuque, Iowa, came together to develop a collection of photographs where students can compare and contrast the past and the present to learn about their community. Students can learn a great deal about work in factories at the turn of the century. Some of the images include women and children working in 1912. Many valuable insights can be gained by having students view the images and captions found underneath each photograph. There are many collections of images to pick from on the Internet site. These can be found by clicking the Gallery tab. Some of the images include collections pertaining to women at work, orphanages, factories, cafes, small businesses, medical offices, grocers, bars, and pool halls. The photographs from the William Klauer, Sr. Collection, Center for Dubuque History, Loras College, can be found at the following Internet link: http://acityatwork.com/. Also see Figures 12.2 to 12.6.

According to Marino and Crucco (2012), local history enables students to understand important themes in American history by sparking their interest and generating empathy toward the subject matter. Progressivism was one important theme in American history. The photographs from the *A City at Work* collection are from the Progressive Era. Every American history textbook covers the Progressive Era, yet students find it difficult to connect with the themes from this time since they seem distant or remote. Marino and Crucco (2012) noted that local history can solve this dilemma by enabling students to see connections to their own community. The *A City at Work* photographic collection presents an example of how this can be done. Students have the unique opportunity to see connections from the Progressive Era that might seem quite distant or remote in their textbook by examining images from their own community. The students can analyze these images and be presented with questions such as "What was life like for ordinary citizens working in Dubuque during the Progressive Era?" Many communities across the country will have photographs of people working during the Progressive Era, and teachers can develop their own series of questions for students to investigate on their own.

Students can participate in a Think-Pair-Share activity to analyze a photograph of the men working at a factory in 1912. The students can pretend that they are one of the workers in the photograph and describe what they are thinking or feeling. Since it is a Think-Pair-Share activity, students can begin by writing down their own thoughts pertaining to the question posed by the teacher. The students can then share their thoughts with a partner and participate in a large group discussion on the subject matter. A photograph of the Milwaukee Railroad Shop can be found at the following Internet link: http://acityatwork.com/2012/09/12/factories/.

There are two images in the collection from the Forge Company dated 1912. The students can be asked to give a title to one of the images and explain why they chose that title. In the second image, the teacher can ask the students to pick five words that they would use to describe what they see in the historical image and summarize why they picked these. As a result, these historical images enable students to see firsthand what it would have been like for a factory worker in Dubuque living in 1912. As Marino and Crucco (2012) pointed out, primary sources do not need to always be documents. Rather, teachers should consider having students see images of buildings to learn about the past. These images provide one example of how to accomplish this.

Marino and Crucco (2012) suggest that students compare and contrast historical images from the past and present to comprehend more deeply why communities change and how they change. There are many examples of this in the

A City at Work collection. There are seven photographs of the Adams Company taken in 1912 and 2012. Students can compare and contrast these images, and the teacher can facilitate a discussion on what the students discover from the images. The teacher can also connect themes from the Progressive Era to the images, in particular, how working conditions have improved greatly over the last one hundred years in terms of the eight-hour work day, minimum-wage laws, and better working conditions due to federal regulations. The images of the Adams Company can be viewed at the following Internet link: http://acityat work.com/2012/09/17/adams-company/.

The *A City at Work* Internet site also includes a vast collection of photographs of women at work in 1912. There are twenty-eight images. The images include women at work in Dubuque at jobs such as factory workers, clerks at businesses, and nurses at hospitals. There are interesting captions under each photograph in the collection, which give facts and details about women in the workforce in 1912. The teacher can have the students participate in a Jigsaw cooperative learning activity where one student in the pair examines one half of the images and the other student examines the other half of the images. Following this, the two students can teach each other what they have learned from the images about women

Figure 12.2 Milwaukee Railroad Shop.

Source: A City at Work: 1912 and 2012 (http://acityatwork.com/). William Klauer, Sr. Collection, Center for Dubuque History, Loras College.

Figure 12.3 Forge Company #1.

Source: A City at Work: 1912 and 2012 (http://acityatwork.com/). William Klauer, Sr. Collection, Center for Dubuque History, Loras College.

Figure 12.4 Forge Company #2.

Source: A City at Work: 1912 and 2012 (http://acityatwork.com/). William Klauer, Sr. Collection, Center for Dubuque History, Loras College.

Figure 12.5 Adams Company #1.

Source: A City at Work: 1912 and 2012 (http://acityatwork.com/). William Klauer, Sr. Collection, Center for Dubuque History, Loras College.

in the workforce and how it connects to the broader themes from the Progressive Era. These images can be found at the following Internet link: http://acityatwork. com/2013/03/07/iowa-women-in-the-workplace-3/.

Child labor was another interesting issue that the Progressive Era confronted. Students can find a few images of children working in the *A City at Work* collection. The teacher can show these images on the classroom Smartboard and ask students to circle items that they find interesting in the image. The students can then share why they circled these images. For another image, the teacher can ask the students to go to the Smartboard and stand next to one of the children in the image. The students can then explain how they might feel if they were one of the children in the image who spent their day working in a factory or business. The teacher can use this local history example to point out the themes of the Progressive Era related to child labor, including how it became much more regulated to protect children from dangerous working conditions and to encourage children to attend school to receive an education to better their lives. These images can be seen at the following Internet link: http://acityatwork.com/2013/02/07/ faces-dubuque-iowa-1912-2/.

According to Marino and Crucco (2012), local history can be used to help students practice historical inquiry by thinking deeply about their own community. Problem-based learning is one example of this. As mentioned earlier, the

Figure 12.6 Adams Company #2.

Source: A City at Work: 1912 and 2012 (http://acityatwork.com/).William Klauer, Sr. Collection, Center for Dubuque History, Loras College. Photographer Tim Olson.

A City at Work collection has many images of women at work. In order to connect this to another Progressive Era theme, the issue of women's suffrage can be explored. In particular, the teacher can pose a question such as "Why do you think Dubuque County voters were less supportive of women's suffrage than voters in western Iowa counties?" The students can then write their hypothesis and test it

Internet Website #1: Northern Iowa Women Suffrage Association. www.encyclopediadubuque.org/index.php?title=NORTHERN_IOWA_WOMAN_SUFFRAGE_ASSOCIATION

Internet Website #2: Dr. Nancy Hill. www.encyclopediadubuque.org/index.php?title=HILL,_Nancy

Internet Website #3: Anna Lawther. www.encyclopediadubuque.org/index.php?title=LAWTHER,_Anna

Internet Website #4: Mary Newbury Adams. www.encyclopediadubuque.org/index.php?title=ADAMS,_Mary_Newbury

Figure 12.7 Women's Suffrage Internet Links – Dubuque County, Iowa.

by investigating several websites on the Internet. These websites include information on Catholicism, the Daughters of the American Revolution, and education of women. Each of these topics had an impact on the issue in Dubuque County, Iowa.

Marino and Crucco (2012) argue that local history gives students the opportunity to learn how everyday people in their community lived. The *A City at Work* collection provides an example of how students can do this in the classroom by encouraging students to write a diary entry from the perspective of an ordinary person living in Dubuque in 1912. This can include one of the following: 1) children working in a factory, 2) women working in a factory, 3) a male working in a factory, or 4) the factory owner. The students can base this exercise on the images and research they have done on these issues and connect it to the themes from the Progressive Era in their textbook and lecture notes from the teacher.

Summary

Local history has a great deal of merit. Social studies teachers can use local history to enable students to see connections between themes in history and their community. Many students will respond favorably when they see the relevancy of what they are studying. Technology can help students engage in local history and be a vehicle to produce products where they share what they have learned about their local history with others beyond their classroom. As discussed previously, students can produce the first-of-its kind webpage or podcast on the local history topic that they have investigated, which can be motivating.

Middle and secondary students can do what historians do when they investigate local history topics. Most communities have a wealth of primary sources, many of which have been long forgotten, and middle and secondary students can use these primary sources to participate in their own historical inquiry about their own community.

Technology, when used in conjunction with local history, can provide powerful social studies instruction. Students are able to participate in a student-centered instructional approach where they are involved in higher-level thinking. Technology enables students to share their historical findings and increasingly access historical information about their community. In summary, teachers should consider how they can utilize local history in their technology-rich classroom.

References

Bonney, M.A. (1995). Iowa local history: A teacher's guide. In L. Wessel & J. Florman (Eds.), *Prairie voices: An Iowa heritage curriculum* (pp. 14–73). Iowa City, IA: State Historical Society of Iowa.

Dutt, K.M. (1995). *Using primary sources in teacher education: Linking research and practice.* San Francisco, CA: American Education Research Association.

Fabbri, H. (2013). Making history relevant: Bringing local history into the social studies classroom. *The Rising Tide, 10,* 1–21.

Jonassen, D.H., Carr, C., & Yueh, H. (1998). Computers as Mindtools for engaging learners in critical thinking. *Tech Trends, 43,* 24–32.

Marino, M.P. & Crucco, M.S. (2012). Doing local history: A case study of New Brunswick, New Jersey. *Social Studies, 6,* 233–240.

Scheuerell, S. (2010). Virtual Warrensburg: Using cooperative learning and the Internet in the social studies classroom. *The Social Studies, 5,* 194–199.

13
EMERGING TECHNOLOGIES

Many new technologies are being introduced and can be utilized in the classroom. Gaming, geospatial tools, social media, Smartboards, and Edmodo are just a few examples. Social studies teachers are trying to identify how these items can be used in the classroom. The College, Career, and Civic Life (C3) Framework for Social Studies State Standards and the Framework for 21st Century Learning provide teachers with the necessary structures to develop meaningful lessons using emerging technologies in the social studies classroom. Each of these has a significant emphasis on problem-based learning and higher-level thinking.

Emerging technologies have already altered teaching and learning in the social studies classroom. Teachers are beginning to rethink how they present materials to students and how these technologies can be leveraged to ultimately benefit students. The flipped classroom is one example of this. Teachers can pick from a growing list of new technologies to deliver a lecture to students and then post it to a classroom website, such as Edmodo, where students can view the materials prior to class. This frees up classroom time to move instruction from a teacher-centered to a student-centered focus. Students can use this class time to participate in higher-level thinking and application of the subject matter rather than passively listening to lecture. Social studies teachers today must be ready to embrace these technologies. Most of their students already have.

Students can also use emerging technologies to investigate topics related to the social studies curriculum and to show what they have learned about the subject matter. In the past, teachers frequently had to sacrifice a considerable amount of instructional time to show students how to use many of the new technologies when they emerged on the market. I remember spending a class period or two showing my students how to use Netscape Composer so they could produce their own Internet webpage. The vast majority of these emerging technologies require very little, if any, time to help students get started. Students learn these new technologies quickly, and they present little distraction from learning the content that is necessary in the social studies classroom.

Emerging Technologies and the College, Career, and Civic Life Framework for Social Studies State Standards

The C3 Framework encourages a student-centered approach to teaching and learning in the middle and secondary social studies classroom. Inquiry-based or problem-based learning is at the heart of the C3 Framework. According to Swan and Griffin (2013), it is important to "support your students as they begin to ask questions and conduct academic inquiries" (p. 321). There are many ways students can use emerging technologies to participate. Geospatial tools enable students to test their hypothesis by analyzing data from geographic information system (GIS) software. In the C3 Framework, there is an emphasis on a "push for more rigorous and authentic assessment that measure inquiry and not just names, dates, and places" (Swan & Griffin, 2013, p. 321).

The C3 Framework encourages teachers to develop compelling questions. These are questions that challenge middle and secondary students to analyze or debate an enduring issue or concern (Grant, 2013). It is vitally important for the problem or question to be student friendly by being developmentally appropriate (Grant, 2013). Some examples of compelling questions include 1) Who won the Cold War? 2) Was the American Revolution revolutionary? and 3) What path should a new transcontinental oil pipeline take? (Grant, 2013). Gaming is one example of an emerging technology that is used increasingly in social studies classrooms to challenge students to problem-solve environmental, economic, political, and historical issues.

The C3 Framework moves students from being receivers of information to producers of information. Long (2013) wrote, "Gone are the days of students passively reading the standard textbook passage with the end goal of preparing a summary or performing well on a culminating chapter test" (p. 343). Today's students must be challenged to simultaneously learn the content in the social studies curriculum and demonstrate the skill sets needed for their future. Emerging technologies, such as iPads, enable students to share their findings from inquiry investigations by producing products with technology. For example, students can use the Show Me app to share their own intellectual contributions.

Social studies teachers must be willing to adapt their instruction to use the C3 Framework and emerging technologies. Long (2013) pointed out that this type of teaching and learning can be "loud, messy, unscripted, and not always predetermined" (p. 343). In order to accomplish this, middle and secondary social studies teachers must be willing to embrace a student-centered instructional approach where the teacher is the facilitator of learning, or the guide on the side. Social studies teachers today need to be able to assess students' learning interests and needs, and enable students to produce Authentic Intellectual Work (Long, 2013). Joe O'Brien, at the University of Kansas, has put forth a proposal for a virtual laboratory for democracy where students can participate in an online democratic commons (O'Brien, 2008). For example, students can participate in a virtual Town Hall Meeting Place to dialogue about current events facing our nation and world (O'Brien, 2008).

Partnership for 21st Century Skills: A Catalyst for the C3 Framework and Emerging Technologies

The Partnership for 21st Century Skills has developed the Framework for 21st Century Learning, which is well suited for emerging technologies in the social studies classroom. Lesson plans in social studies that integrate problem-based learning and emerging technologies can leverage many of the skill sets identified in the framework. Students can simultaneously develop the necessary skills for the twenty-first century and learn the content in the middle and secondary social studies curriculum.

Learning to think creatively is a key skill identified by the Framework for 21st Century Learning. The document states that it is necessary for students to "use a wide range of idea creation techniques (such as brainstorming)" (p. 3). Problem-based learning begins with the students developing a hypothesis where they spend a great deal of time brainstorming what they think the answer might be to the question posed to them. Social studies teachers can use Smartboards to feature historical images. Students can develop a hypothesis on what the image is about and make predictions on what they might find out about the individuals featured in the portrait or photograph.

Critical thinking is another key skill identified by the Framework for 21st Century Learning. The framework states that students should be able to "use various types of reasoning (inductive, deductive, etc.) as appropriate to the situation" (p. 4). Problem-based learning gives middle and secondary students the opportunity to participate in deductive reasoning rather than the traditional teaching and learning structures that involve inductive reasoning. The framework also states that students should be able to "effectively analyze and evaluate evidence, arguments, claims and beliefs" (p. 4). Due to the increasing amount of information found on the Internet, middle and secondary students can access a great deal of data online, where they can evaluate the information for themselves. This also moves the classroom from a teacher-centered to a student-centered model. Edmodo is an example of an emerging technology that enables teachers to easily post a series of resources that students can access electronically. Students can then reach their own conclusion about a contemporary or historical issue by analyzing and evaluating the sources for themselves.

Examples of Emerging Technologies

There are many emerging technologies for social studies teachers to pick from. In the remaining pages of this chapter, the reader will see examples that can be leveraged in the middle and secondary social studies classroom. Each technology has unique features that can foster learning in the social sciences when they are used in combination with the pedagogical frameworks outlined in Chapter 1 of the text. The International Society for Technology in Education (ISTE) standards for teachers also encourage the use of technology in classrooms to "promote, support, and model creative and innovative thinking and inventiveness" (ISTE, 2014, p. 1). The examples featured in this chapter arguably capture the intent of this ISTE standard.

Virtual Laboratory of Democracy

As discussed previously, Joe O'Brien (2008) has proposed that students participate in a virtual laboratory of democracy. Middle and secondary students can use emerging technologies to participate. The C3 Framework and Framework for 21st Century Learning can be used as the underpinnings that drive the virtual laboratory. Students who participate will be challenged to think deeply about the subject matter in the social sciences. Engle and Ochoa argued that social studies instruction should challenge students to be decision makers where they are involved in "intellectual analysis, decision making, and social action" (qtd. in Evans, Newman, & Saxe, 1996, p. 13).

The virtual laboratory of democracy can feature the intellectual contributions of middle and secondary students by featuring their discourse and the products that they produce with technology. O'Brien (2008) has envisioned several parts that would compose the virtual laboratory. These include a Town Hall Meeting Place where students can participate in discourse on current events. Perhaps students can use problem-based learning to investigate issues confronting our nation and world. The students can then share their proposals to solve these problems in the Town Hall Meeting Place. According to O'Brien (2008), the Research Center could be another key component of the virtual laboratory by providing an online democratic commons for students. Students can use emerging technologies to produce products that they can share in the online forum. The Research Center could potentially feature content-rich material that is age appropriate and enables students to share their work by posting products such as wikis or digital video via YouTube (O'Brien, 2008).

The virtual laboratory of democracy can feature a Public Issues Information Center where students learn firsthand about issues facing the world (O'Brien, 2008). Students can use the virtual space to collaboratively problem-solve issues. In addition, students may have the opportunity to gather firsthand insights from individuals who can offer testimonials. O'Brien (2008) uses the example of former child soldiers who could participate in the virtual laboratory by blogging or podcasting about their experiences in Africa. Students can also use the virtual laboratory to participate in an Editorial and Student-Centered Discourse Center where they have the opportunity to participate in electronic voting on a wide array of issues (O'Brien, 2008). This would allow students to participate actively in our democracy and think critically about issues related to the social studies curriculum. Evans wrote that this type of teaching and learning is a "facilitative process that helps students define problems and resolve issues" (qtd. in Evans, Newman, & Saxe, 1996, p. 13). Accordingly, the C3 Framework and Framework for 21st Century Learning can work in conjunction to provide the building blocks for this type of innovative learning experience in the virtual laboratory of democracy.

O'Brien (2008) also proposed a Bill of Digital Learning Rights that can be included as a part of the virtual laboratory of democracy and other similar online experiences for students. Some of these rights include 1) freedom of expression online, 2) right to assemble online, 3) freedom of access to appropriate resources, and 4) equitable access to digital tools needed for learning (O'Brien, 2008). In the future, as emerging technologies continue to be introduced in the social studies classroom, the Bill of Digital Learning Rights can be used to guide the online learning experiences for students.

Gaming

Gaming and online simulations are being used more frequently in middle and secondary social studies classrooms. There is a growing list of online games and simulations to pick from. Some of these enable students to role-play historical scenarios, to be involved in urban planning, or to pretend that they are a politician who has to make difficult decisions for their constituents. Each of these online games and simulations can be effective since they challenge students to think more deeply about the subject matter rather than using technology for drill-and-practice exercises.

Prensky (2001) argues that gaming works because students perceive it as a fun way to learn by engaging them in the subject matter and challenging them to reflect more deeply on what they have learned from the online game or simulation. Debriefing after a game or simulation can help students to reflect on the main ideas that they learned and to see the connections to the lesson objective.

GeoThentic is one example of an online simulation that can be used in the middle and secondary social studies classroom. The online simulation is sponsored by the University of Minnesota. GeoThentic is designed to help students learn about the environment through an online gaming experience. The site enables students to learn about the complexity of environmental issues. Some of the simulations cover topics such as global warming, population changes, avian flu, and where to build a hospital in San Francisco. According to the site, the purpose is to expose students to authentic problems facing our world and to challenge students to problem-solve these complex issues (LT Media Lab, 2011). Students who participate in the web-based simulation will certainly recognize that these are not simple issues to solve. As a result, GeoThentic challenges students to use technology to think more deeply about the subject matter. For example, students could simply view an Internet video posted on YouTube about the same issues, but this would fail to replicate the in-depth thinking that is fostered by this online game. The GeoThentic simulation can be found at the following web address: http://lt.umn.edu/geothentic/.

iCivics is an Internet site that hosts a wide array of games and simulations that actively engage middle and secondary students in decision-making scenarios about the three branches of government. These simulations deal with domestic and foreign policy issues. Each of these issues pertains to the United States Constitution. For example, students can write their own legislation as a member of Congress and then try to get the bill passed through both houses of Congress. Students can also pretend that they are the president of the United States and participate in the difficult decision making that he or she faces as leader of our nation each day. There are also a wide variety of Supreme Court decisions that students can weigh in on as a justice of our nation's highest court. In addition, students can participate in simulations where they are a member of a jury during a trial, pretend that they are running for president of the United States, or participate as a campaign manager for a national candidate running for office. The iCivics simulation can be found at the following web address: https://www.icivics.org/.

Each of these web-based games or simulations enables students to participate in higher-level thinking with technology since they are challenged to be a decision maker and solve problems. These are key skills identified in the C3 Framework and Framework for 21st Century Learning. In the iCivics example, it gives middle and secondary students an appreciation for the difficult decisions that each person in an elected office faces each day when they try to determine what is best for our country. The amount of in-depth decision making involved in gaming can help students comprehend detailed information. The Oregon Trail game is one example of this, and many teachers may recall playing it themselves (Prensky, 2011). Games such as the Oregon Trail help students remember detailed information since the simulation involves a lot of decision making about something in the social studies curriculum (Prensky, 2011). In the future, it will be interesting to see new web-based games emerge as researchers explore the best ways to utilize them and software engineers continue to develop them to meet the growing demand in classrooms.

Geospatial Tools

GIS software can be used in the middle and secondary social studies classroom to engage students in critical thinking about the subject matter that they are investigating. Hammond (2014) predicts geospatial tools will transform the history curriculum by enabling teachers to introduce historical topics in more depth, foster historical thinking, and facilitate the inclusion of local history. Teachers can also use the technology to design lessons that engage students in a great deal of analysis, data interpretation, and inquiry-based learning (Hammond & Bodzin, 2009).

Hammond and Bodzin (2009) highlight an example of how GIS can be used to explore the impact of the 1862 Homestead Act on the bison population in the Great Plains region of the United States between 1862 and 1900. The lesson is also designed to help students transfer what they learned about the environmental consequences to contemporary environmental issues (Hammond & Bodzin, 2009). This type of teaching and learning fosters higher-order thinking that would be difficult to replicate without this unique technology. In another example, Hammond and Bodzin (2009) posed a question to middle school students where they had to identify the best place to put storm drains in a specific neighborhood in a community. Inquiry-based lessons like this one enable students to use GIS software to solve problems that deal with contemporary and authentic real-world issues.

Milson and Curtis (2009) developed a lesson where students used the GIS software to determine the best geographic location for a store. The students had to use a great deal of demographic information from the software to make an informed decision. GIS provided statistical information on the population of American cities, median home values, and the proximity to physical geographic features such as rivers (Milson & Curtis, 2009). Each student had to analyze the data that they found using GIS, determine the best location for their business, and be ready to defend their decision using the data from the software (Milson & Curtis, 2009). Geospatial tools can also serve as an interdisciplinary tool (Hammond, 2014). Students can use geospatial tools to see connections between each of the social sciences (history, government, economics, geography) and between the social sciences and other subject areas (math and science).

Edmodo

Teachers are increasingly looking for ways to host their classroom materials in a virtual fashion. Edmodo can help social studies teachers accomplish this. Many middle and secondary students find the site to be user friendly and attractive since it looks much like Facebook. The free online site enables teachers to communicate announcements to students, post course assignments, and attach reading materials, and is a place for students to submit their work virtually. Students can log in to the secured site by using an access code created by the teacher for each class that they teach. This enables the students to access these materials electronically and saves the school a great deal of money in terms of printing costs normally associated with any social studies class.

Many social studies teachers like to use Edmodo to copy links to Internet sites that pertain to the individual objective for the lesson. This can enable students to more quickly access sites on the Internet rather than having the teacher verbally tell all the students the exact URL address. I can recall how frustrating this was for me as a teacher and the students when they might mistype one character in the URL address, and they were then unable to access the Internet link. Edmodo can solve this classroom dilemma by enabling students to simply click on the hot link for the Internet site that has already been copied and pasted for them on the Edmodo class webpage. Many social studies teachers like to include links to primary sources that can be accessed on the Internet. Students can use Edmodo to find a collection of primary sources pertaining to a specific historical subject or issue that the students will investigate for the remainder of the class period. In particular, this is helpful when students participate in a lesson where they are student historians. Edmodo can be found at the following Internet link: https://www.edmodo.com/.

Flipped Classroom

Edmodo is also being used increasingly for the flipped classroom. The flipped classroom is a relatively new teaching and learning pedagogy that is being used in social studies classrooms that are equipped with technology. In social studies, the flipped classroom encourages students to access pre-recorded lectures from their classroom teacher, or from some other expert, typically using the Internet, prior to the beginning of class. Most teachers will require students to view the pre-recorded lecture as a part of their homework assignment. These lectures can be easily placed on Edmodo for students to access from home, school, or anywhere else with Internet access.

In the flipped classroom, the teacher will typically begin the class period by reviewing the lecture material that was posted on the Edmodo site. The teacher can give students a pre-assessment or call on students to determine their readiness. If necessary, the teacher can clarify any misunderstanding or confusion that students may have about the subject matter. Since the flipped classroom requires students to view lectures electronically, the teacher can devote a greater amount of instructional time during the actual lesson for hands-on and inquiry-based learning. In fact, the flipped classroom is designed to move instruction from a teacher-centered to a student-centered instructional model and put a greater point of emphasis on critical thinking and application of the content. Social studies teachers can also use the newly found instructional time to have students participate in simulations, in-depth discussions, analyzing sources like a historian, and producing products with technology. Most importantly, the flipped classroom provides the necessary time to rigorously challenge middle and secondary students in social studies to participate in critical thinking and apply what they have learned from lecture.

Smartboards

Smartboards are another example of a technology that is increasingly finding its way into social studies classrooms. They are interactive whiteboards that enable students to actively engage in the subject matter by going up to the front of the classroom and touching the electronic board. There are countless ways for teachers to utilize them in the classroom. Maps are frequently used by students to trace immigration routes or the trails blazed by pioneers. Many social studies teachers also like to use Smartboards to facilitate a classroom discussion by utilizing the board to capture student ideas. They prefer to have the students use the interactive board to actively engage in the lesson rather than using it as a teacher-centered activity. For example, students can go to the board to produce concept maps or graphic organizers where they capture higher-level thinking relationships pertaining to the subject matter that they are investigating. Some examples include cause-effect, compare-contrast, and problem-solution.

Students can also use the Smartboard to analyze a primary source that is posted on the Internet. The teacher can have students go to the board and circle words or phrases from the source that help them develop a conceptual understanding of the subject matter. Teachers can also post historical images, portraits, or political cartoons on the Smartboard. Students can circle or highlight items from the image and provide a rationale on why they chose it. Specific items from an image can provide the necessary clues to help students understand the past. Social studies teachers can also use Smartboards to show data from online sites, such as polling data or demographic information from the Census Report. Students can then circle, highlight, or underline what they find important or interesting about the data. This can foster critical thinking by having students search for themes that may emerge from the data.

iPads

iPads are an emerging technology that has a great deal of merit. Many social studies classrooms across the country are equipped with iPads. Students can use them to perform investigations related to the subject matter they are investigating. There are many apps that teachers can utilize in the classroom. Some of these enable students to more easily capture lecture notes so that students can follow along slide by slide on their own iPad. In addition, students can use the iPad to take a photograph of notes on the whiteboard or homework reminders that are posted there. This can be especially helpful to students who have trouble keeping up with taking notes during lecture. Students can also use the iPad to access electronic worksheets and write their answers. They can then submit these electronically to their social studies teacher. More apps are becoming increasingly available in the social studies curriculum, but it is important for teachers to remember to find apps that will facilitate active learning and critical thinking about the subject matter rather than drill-and-practice apps where students are passively learning lower-level facts or dates from history.

Show Me is an app that helps students to actively construct knowledge with technology and, if used appropriately, foster critical thinking about the subject matter in the social studies curriculum. The app enables students to use the interactive screen of an iPad to produce mini-documentaries on what they have learned. Students can import images, record a narration, and use their fingertips to draw things on the iPad to convey what they have learned. For example, the app allows students to draw arrows to show migratory patterns on a map or trace stick figures to tell the story about a historical figure. There are many additional apps located on the Internet that have a great deal of potential and can be utilized in the classroom to engage middle and secondary students in the social studies subject matter.

Electronic Clickers

Clickers are another interesting type of technology being used in social studies classrooms. Each clicker looks like a remote control that would be used for a television. The teacher can assign each student in the classroom their own clicker. This allows the teacher to then collect individual data on the progress of each student in the classroom. The clickers can be used to gather formative or summative assessment data. They can be used at the beginning of class for pre-assessment purposes, during the middle of a class lecture to assess whether students understand the material, or for closure purposes at the end of class to assess whether the students learned the necessary content from the lesson.

Due to the increasing focus on differentiated instruction, electronic clickers have gained popularity, in particular, since the clickers allow the teacher to determine the readiness of each student in his or her classroom. The data can then be used to plan lessons involving tiered instruction where students are assigned tasks based on their readiness for above-target, on-target, or below-target work. For example, a series of five questions on the subject matter can quickly give the social studies teacher a great deal of data about their students within a single classroom setting. These students can vary greatly in their readiness, and the data will enhance the teacher's ability to challenge each student as needed. Most importantly, he or she can design a lesson plan where all of the students are learning the same lesson objective in social studies, but tiered to meet their cognitive learning needs using Bloom's taxonomy and considering the learning style of each student in the classroom, rather than having all the students learn in the exact same way.

Hippo Campus

There are many places where students can access mini-lectures or digital videos to learn about social studies–related topics. Hippo Campus is one example. The site was produced with middle and secondary students in mind. It enables students to find a great deal of information in a short amount of time. The site is especially effective at providing introductory materials to students to help them make sense of the topic before they investigate it more deeply. Many teachers are posting introductory materials to Edmodo for flipped classroom instructional purposes. This enables students to quickly learn information about the topic so they are ready for the review at the beginning of class the next day. These students are then ready to apply what they have learned in the flipped classroom. These types of instructional materials will continue to grow on the Internet, and social studies teachers can think about how they will use them strategically in their classroom setting.

The Hippo Campus Internet site includes introductory text and videos on a wide array of social studies topics. There are topics involving American history, world history, and American government. Most readers will be surprised to see the depth and breadth of the topics to pick from. The introductory videos can also be used for an anticipatory set activity to "hook" students into the subject and provide them with the necessary background information so they can activate their prior knowledge about the subject later in the lesson when they have a chance to apply what they have learned. The Internet site also has some interactive features that enable students to learn more deeply about various subjects in the social studies curriculum. These can be found by clicking the Simulations tab of the webpage. The Hippo Campus site can be found at the following web address: www.hippocampus.org/.

Google Drive

Google Drive is a web-based site that includes several features that middle and secondary social studies teachers will find useful. Google Docs is one of its most popular features that enable students to work together virtually in real time. It is a user-friendly way for students to work collaboratively on a project or assignment in class or at home. Google Docs enable students to work simultaneously by using a word processing document where they can work on a paper or project together.

Some students may also find it to be a nice way to brainstorm ideas together in a virtual environment.

There is also a feature on Google Drive that enables students to produce presentations that look much like a PowerPoint presentation. However, many students will find it more appealing to produce the presentation in a virtual online environment, and it offers most of the same features as PowerPoint. Google Drive also enables students to produce spreadsheets. Spreadsheets enable students to use technology as a Mindtool where they can participate in a rigorous intellectual activity by entering data from a social studies investigation and examine how the data may provide answers to an inquiry or problem. Students can conduct many investigations with the aid of a spreadsheet such as the one provided through Google Docs.

Finally, teachers can use Google Drive to produce forms. These forms enable teachers to produce tests or quizzes in a virtual environment for students to access. Some teachers may prefer to use the forms to collect data from students for pre-assessment purposes or for closure. Teachers can also use Google Drive to distribute information to students in regard to homework worksheets, graphic organizers to be used with reading primary and secondary sources, or to share project rubrics with students. Please note it is necessary for students to have a Gmail account to access any of the aforementioned features on Google Drive.

Skype

Skype has a great deal of potential in the middle and secondary social studies classroom. Currently, teachers are using Skype to have their students engage virtually and dialogue with other students around the country, or even around the world. This enables students to learn about cultures that are different from their own and engage with students from diverse perspectives. For example, students who participate in an ePals or keypals project frequently use Skype to discuss global events as they unfold and share what they are learning in their social studies classroom to create a community of learners.

Social studies teachers are also using Skype to bring guest speakers to the classroom virtually. Students can learn from experts on various history topics. There is also the opportunity to take students on a virtual field trip to a museum or historical site to learn from someone who works there. In addition, students can interview people who may have a great deal of expertise on a social studies topic or gain from their firsthand experience with an historical event. Social studies teachers have used Skype to talk to American soldiers serving in Afghanistan. As technology continues to improve, Skype will likely grow in popularity and social studies teachers will find new and unique ways to use it in the classroom.

Theory and Theory Practice: Firsthand Experience Using Emerging Technologies in United States History

Keypals, or ePals, is a teaching strategy that originated from the tradition of pen pals. Due to the increasing access to the Internet, pen pal programs can now use e-mail to deliver messages to other students around the world. Keypals can help students appreciate other cultures around the world. According to Cotton (1998), the goal of keypals is "to broaden the horizons of your students while encouraging reading and writing skills, higher level thinking skills, and civilized discourse with other members of the human community" (p. 135).

There are many Internet websites designed to connect classrooms around the world. For example, one can be found at www.epals.com. The Internet webpage has a number of features for students in middle and secondary social studies. Among them are an electronic translator, online learning projects, and discussion boards. A teacher can also get started through a personal contact. I was introduced to Mr. Ralph Grandberg, a social studies teacher in Sweden, when he was visiting Warrensburg, Missouri, where I taught high school social studies. This led to a keypals project between students in our classes over five school years.

Mr. Grandberg and I decided that we would have our students teach each other what they were learning in their social studies classes. In my American History course, students taught their Swedish e-mail partners about topics such as the American Civil War and the Civil Rights movement. Meanwhile, my students learned from their e-mail partners about the politics and history of Sweden. The students were required to e-mail their partners every other week. However, it is interesting to note that much of the learning happened when the students communicated with their e-mail partners on their own about what they were doing in their ordinary day-to-day lives. This enabled the students to capture a glimpse into the cultural landscape of their partners on another continent. In most instances, the students quickly realized that they had much more in common than any differences.

There is a great deal that students can learn about culture when they are encouraged to dialogue with other students in foreign countries. Cotton (1998, p. 3) wrote, "You and your class can exchange cross-cultural communication, explore others' points of view, learn about distant countries, and expand your minds and hearts to awareness of other people's holidays, celebrations, clothing styles, food, hobbies, hopes, and loves."

In my social studies classes, students learned about some of the differences between Sweden and the United States. For example, students learned that Sweden had a different drinking age than the United States. In Sweden, eighteen years old is the drinking age, so this was occasionally a topic of conversation for the students. The students also dialogued about issues ranging from gun control to the death penalty, in particular how Sweden is much more restrictive in terms of gun regulation compared to the United States, and the death penalty is outlawed by its government. These were prime opportunities for my students to be involved in discourse with their e-mail partners on issues such as these to identify similarities and differences between our two nations.

Interestingly, the Framework for 21st Century Learning emphasizes the need for students to develop social and cross-cultural skills. As mentioned earlier, students in this initiative had plenty of meaningful opportunities to converse about cultural issues. These were teachable moments for the students as they collaborated and dialogued about issues in the middle and secondary social studies curriculum, including history, government, economics, and geography. In some instances, students also used technology to dialogue about current events. The aftermath of 9/11 was one of the topics frequently mentioned in their e-mail exchanges.

Cooperative learning activities, such as keypals, can empower middle and secondary students to learn from one another. Johnson (1998) wrote, "Through the Internet, school children around the globe are learning from each other" (p. 3). Each student involved in this partnership enjoyed learning about the major holidays that were celebrated in Sweden and the United States. For example, the Swedish students were very curious to learn about the Super Bowl in the United States. Most of them had heard something about it and wondered if it was an official national holiday. The students also learned that there were similarities and differences pertaining to how Christmas was celebrated in each country. These exchanges were memorable and taught the students a great deal about each other's culture. Technology, used in conjunction with cooperative learning, made these exchanges possible, and a great deal of learning took place on subjects related to the social studies curriculum.

Summary

There are countless ways that teachers can use these emerging technologies. There will certainly be more and more of these technologies in the future. It will be exciting to see what they look like, and I encourage teachers to identify ways to embrace them when appropriate to motivate students and especially to help students learn in the social studies classroom. However, always keep in mind the aforementioned research-based frameworks to utilize these technologies in the most effective fashion possible. By doing so, middle and secondary students can participate in technology-rich classrooms that challenge them intellectually as they prepare for readiness for college, careers, and citizenship in our participatory democracy.

It is also important for the reader to remember the research on pivotal decisions with technology that have been presented in the text when using these emerging technologies. Students need to have some background knowledge before they investigate topics and build products using technology. Differentiated instruction can greatly enhance the technology experience for students in the middle and secondary social studies classroom based on their readiness to challenge them appropriately and to make sure they are not bored with the activity. In addition, social studies teachers should consider using cooperative learning structures with jobs or roles when students are working in groups on technology-related investigations or projects. There is also much merit for the need to focus technology-rich lessons in social studies on higher-level thinking rather than lower-level thinking such as drill-and-practice exercises. The use of focus questions that foster critical thinking and challenge students to think more deeply about big ideas can help with this greatly when students are using technology in the social studies classroom. In the future, as new technologies emerge on the market, these are pivotal decisions that teachers can use as predictors of success.

References

21st Century Skills Framework. (2004). *Twenty-first century skills framework*. Retrieved from www.21stcenturyskills.org. Accessed 10/15/14.

Cotton, E. (1998). *The online classroom*. Bloomington, IN: EdInfo Press.

Evans, R. W., Newman, F. M., & Saxe, D. W. (1996). *Handbook on teaching social issues. NCSS Bulletin 93* (pp. 2–4). Washington, D.C.: National Council for the Social Studies.

Grant, S. G. (2013). From inquiry arc to instructional practice: The potential of the C3 framework. *Social Education, 6*, 322–326, 351.

Hammond, T.C. (2014). Transforming the history curriculum with geospatial tools. *Contemporary Issues in Technology and Teacher Education, 3*, 266–287.

Hammond, T. C. & Bodzin, A. M. (2009). Teaching with rather than about geographic information systems. *Social Education, 3*, 119–123.

ISTE. (2014). *ISTE standards teachers*. Retrieved from www.iste.org/docs/pdfs/20-14_ISTE_Standards-T_PDF.pdf. Accessed 9/14/14.

Johnson, M. (1998). Trends in peace education. ERIC Digest. www.ericdigests.org/1998-3/peace.html

Long, M. (2013). From receivers to producers: A principal's perspective on using the C3 framework to prepare young learners for college, career, and civic life. *Social Education, 6*, 342–344, 350.

LT Media Lab. (2011). *GeoThentic*. University of Minnesota. Retrieved from http://lt.umn.edu/geothentic/. Accessed 9/14/14.

Milson, A.J. & Curtis, M.D. (2009). Where and why there? Spatial thinking with geographic information systems. *Social Education, 3*, 113–118.

O'Brien, J. (2008). Are we preparing young people for 21st-century citizenship with 20th-century thinking? A case study for a virtual laboratory of democracy. *Contemporary Issues in Technology and Teacher Education, 2*, 125–147.

Prensky, M. (2011). *From digital natives to digital immigrants. An introduction*. Retrieved from http://marcprensky.com/writing/Prensky-Intro_to_From_DN_to_DW.pdf. Accessed 9/5/14.

Swan, K. & Griffin, S. (2013). Beating the odds: The College, Career, and Civic Life (C3) Framework for Social Studies State Standards. *Social Education, 6*, 317–321.

INDEX

Note: Page numbers in italic indicate figures.